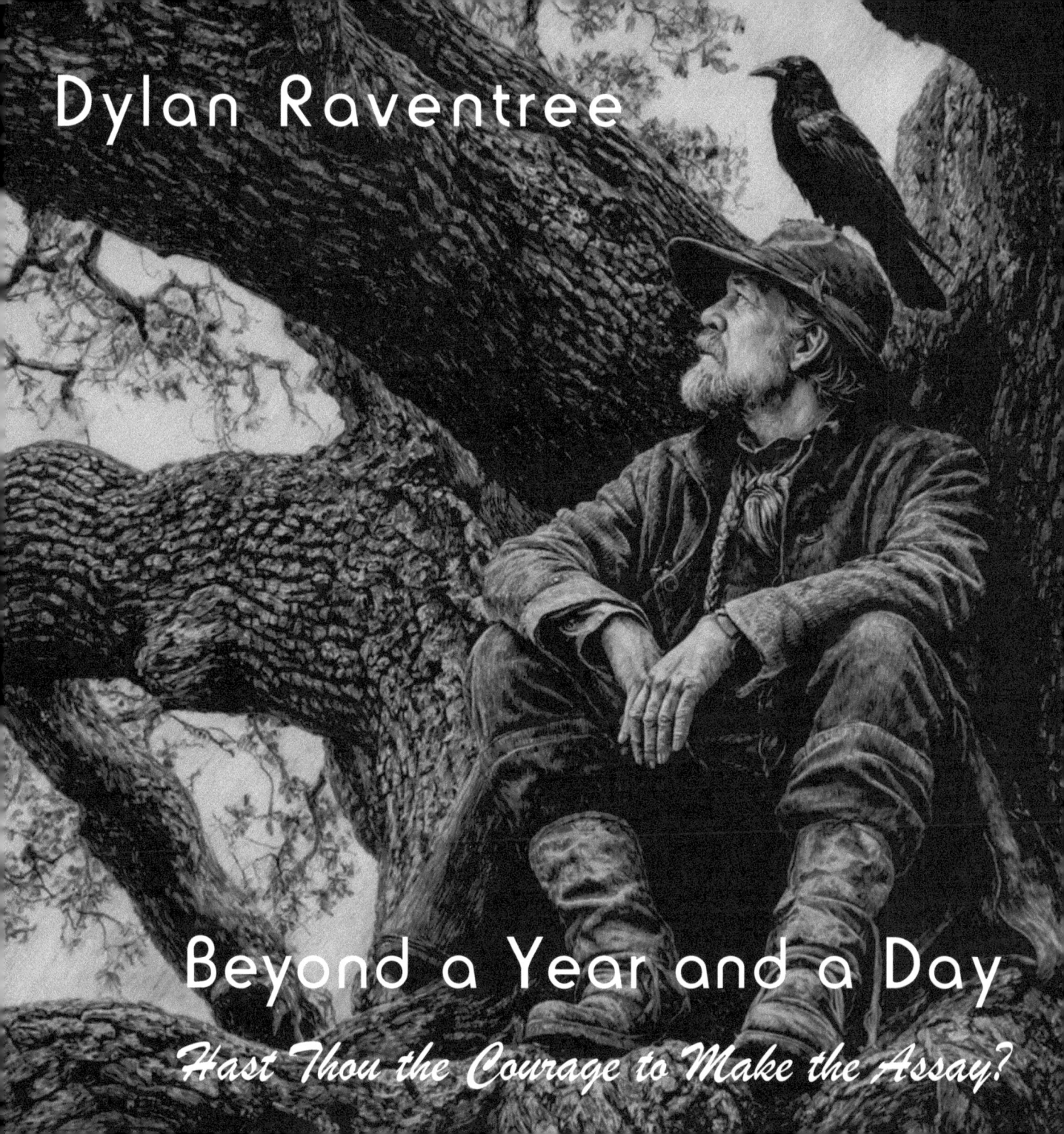

FOREWORD

I have known the author for over 30 years and this book has been that long in the making. During that time Dylan has been my student, my High Priest on occasion and a great supporter of the Traditional Witchcraft path. He became a patient teacher of many, a respected researcher and practitioner of Wicca but above all, a friend.

One of the most important things in magic and in life, is achieving balance and this book walks a tightrope of teaching the art to any who reads it but without revealing all the mysteries.

After all, mysteries can't be taught, only experienced. This book, which is long overdue, will inspire any heart that is seeking the Old Ways and explains how to find them.

While Wicca was once a very secret and jealously guarded path, the recent explosion of pagan groups and books have made paganism and a love of the Old Gods much more open and available to all. This is a great thing.

However, the pagan movement, while sharing old secrets, has not been able to teach what lies behind the secrets.

People who have published Books of Shadows, and the rituals they have experienced, do not show the layers of knowledge and understanding those books and rituals have within them.

This book does.

The Lady Nicole

Copyright 2025 Dylan Raventree
All rights reserved

Published under the BERNE CONVENTION

ISBN 978-1-7640447-1-4
Contact for permission to use images or text:
Email: dylanraventree777@gmail.com

Magic is the brush that paints the unseen, the instrument that plays the silent chords of amazement. — Jon Finch

Dedicated to the memory
of Simon Goodman

For the Lady Evelyn,
Witch Queen

He was born, where shadows lie,
By haunted shores, and slate-grey sky.
A silver wheel, turns stone and flame,
Then whispers low, his calling name.

He took the vow, in a midnight storm,
Raven and oak, his totem form.
He chased the wind, broke bread with fate,
Through mist and myth, beyond the gate.

City smoke, and altar dust,
Ink-stained lies, and broken trust.
But faery dreams, and elder lore
Called him back, to the hidden door.

The wheel still turns, the stars still burn,
Through ash and blood, the old return.

Contents

A Note to the Reader...7
Acknowledgements..8
About the Author..9
Introduction..11

Part 1 - Our Beginnings......................................13
Chapter 1 – The Ordeal..14
Chapter 2 – The Source..19
Chapter 3 – The Beginning.......................................23
Chapter 4 – Coffee?...26
Chapter 5 – A Course in the Old Religion.................30
Chapter 6 – The Supergroup.....................................37
Chapter 7 – Coven Dedication..................................43
Chapter 8 – The First Esbat......................................44
Chapter 9 – Our Sacred Space..................................51
Chapter 10 – The Wheel of the Year........................57
Chapter 11 – Our Sabbats..59
Chapter 12 – The Priesthood....................................73
Chapter 13 – Our Coven...75

Part 2 – Our Wiccan Ways..................................77
Chapter 14 – The Craft...78
Chapter 15 – The Laws...83
Chapter 16 – The Magic Circle..................................85
Chapter 17 – The Tools...90
Chapter 18 - Ritual...97
Chapter 19 – The Goddess......................................100
Chapter 20 – The God...105
Chapter 21 - Initiation..108
Chapter 22 – The Ordeal Revisited.........................115
Chapter 23 – The Book of Shadows........................117

Part 3 – Working the Craft................................121
Chapter 24 - Morthwork...122
Chapter 25 – Laws of Magic....................................127
Chapter 26 – Pentagrams and Watchtowers..........131
Chapter 27 – Altered States of Consciousness.......137
Chapter 28 – Magical Scripts..................................144
Chapter 29 – Practical Magic..................................147
Chapter 30 – Herbcraft...161
Chapter 31 – Energy in Healing..............................167
Chapter 32 - Runecraft...172

Part 4 – Various Rituals....................................178
Chapter 33 – Ritual Etiquette.................................179
Chapter 34 – The Sussex Round.............................182
Chapter 35 – Wiccaning..192
Chapter 36 – Handfasting.......................................193
Chapter 37 – Funeral Rite.......................................197
Chapter 38 – Dark Moon Esbat...............................200
Chapter 39 – The Fire of Azrael..............................205
Chapter 40 – Pathworking......................................208
Chapter 41 – The 29th Path....................................210
Chapter 42 – Pathway to the Sun...........................212
Chapter 43 – Elemental Pathworking.....................216
Chapter 44 – Lesser Banishing Ritual of the Pentagram.....219
Chapter 45 – Elemental Balancing..........................222

Part 5 – The Future..225
Chapter 46 – Beyond a Year and a Day..................226
Final Reflection – Beyond the Veil, Into the Flame............229
Appendix 1 – Suggested Reading List....................230

A Note to the Reader

This book is for you, the seeker who has felt that quiet tug beneath the surface, the one that whispers, *'There's more to this world than what you've been told'*. Maybe you've raised a family, built a career, lost and begun again. Maybe you've always sensed something else moving just beyond the veil, a rhythm, a calling, a mystery.

If you're new to the Craft, or simply circling the edges with curiosity, I want you to know: you are not alone. I've stood where you're standing now, uncertain, excited, maybe a little sceptical. And let's be honest, the beginning is rarely graceful. It's messy, magical, and sometimes daunting.

I've written this not as an expert perched above, but as a companion beside you. My hope is simple: to teach, to share, and to offer you the kind of welcome I once longed for. This isn't a textbook; it's a hand extended, a laugh shared over candlelight, a space where questions are sacred and intuition reigns.

When I began my journey into the Craft, I often wondered if I truly belonged. I second-guessed myself constantly: Was I doing it right? Was I imagining things? That's why this book exists: to be the voice I needed back then, whispering, *'Yes, you belong. Yes, you are enough'*.

I owe much to the pioneering work of Janet and Stewart Farrar, particularly *'What Witches Do'*, which illuminated so many shadows in my early days. This is, in many ways, a thank-you to them. But it's also my own offering, told from the perspective of someone still very much on the path.

Inside, you will find stories, real ones. Rituals and reflections shaped by experience, rooted in both the Alexandrian tradition and the evocative beauty of the Sussex variant. It's a memoir, yes, but it's also a map and mirror.

I have tried to keep the sacred things sacred and the words honest. If you are seeking connection, meaning, or simply wondering where your spirit fits within the great tapestry of the Craft, welcome. This book won't hand you all the answers, but it might help you trust your own.

Take what stirs your soul. Leave what doesn't. Most importantly, walk in a way that feels true. This path is yours. And if my words kindle even a small flame in your heart, I'll count that as magic.

The Brightest of Blessings to all who read my words

Dylan Raventree

Beyond a Year and a Day

Acknowledgements

To all my Initiates and students, this is for you.

To those born of Simon's lineage, stretching back through Alex, through Gerald, and further still into the mists of time, you are held in these words as well.

To Janet and Stewart Farrar, whose writing has guided and inspired so many: thank you for your companionship on our shared pilgrimage, your encouragement toward the Third, and your unwavering support. And to William Le Kat - witness and way-shower - you are not forgotten.

I extend heartfelt thanks to our Pagan friends in Tasmania, especially Jo, for her generous proofreading and encouragement throughout this journey.

To the members of my Covens, and especially the original Super Group, you have given me the space to explore and embrace the mysteries. I am grateful beyond measure.

To Lady Michelin, may the Goddess always hold you close to Her heart. There is none greater.

I fondly remember the late Lady Olivia Robertson and the sacred time Evelyn and I spent with her in the Temple at Clonegal Castle during our ordination. Her presence, grace, and wisdom remain etched in memory.

To James, Nicole, and Ian, teachers, guides, and kindred spirits, my love and gratitude are always with you.

And finally, to all who dance with the Goddess and run with the God in this time, in this realm, this book is dedicated to you.

About the Author

My Craft name is Dylan Raventree. I was born in a small country village on the northwest coast of Wales, directly opposite the mythical Isle of Arianrhod. She is the primal figure of female power and authority in Celtic lore - the ancestral Goddess of the Celts and, as the myth goes, the mother of a son named Dylan.

Her name means Silver Wheel. Goddess of the Moon, of justice, of initiation and the ever-turning seasons - the Wheel of the Year - Arianrhod governs the destinies of mortals and walks a path entirely her own. Unbending, untamed, and sovereign. Perhaps, like her, I too have struggled to release the past.

I took the name Dylan at my initiation into the Alexandrian Tradition of Witchcraft. The House name Raventree came to me on a pilgrimage to my birthplace, not long after the assay. On a jagged headland called Pen y Gogarth, high above Caer Arianrhod, I encountered a raven seated in an ancient, gnarled oak tree. I would come to understand the deeper meaning of that meeting years later, through the Sussex Tradition - the Oak and the Raven entwined in destiny.

I immigrated to Australia in the late 1950s with my parents. We settled in Sydney, where I was raised in the Christian tradition. I served as an altar boy by eleven and undertook Catholic confirmation as a teenager. But on the day I walked out of high school, I spat and cursed the Church's arrogance and hypocrisy, vowing never to return. My mother was mortified, but I could no longer walk a path that felt false.

For a time, I wandered without faith. I joined the State Police Force, later working my way to Detective. In those days, I wore cynicism like armour and bore little patience for politicians or pretenders. I faced the underworld with a grin and left more than a few of its worst in prison's cold embrace. It was all smoke, mirrors, and survival until someone, with unexpected grace, urged me to leave that world behind.

I transitioned into the public service and moved to the nation's capital. With the polluted air of the city behind me and the green hush of forest ahead, I softened. Perspective crept in. And it was there, amid those quiet woods and open skies, that I finally rediscovered what had always pulled at my soul: the Craft.

Since boyhood, I had dreamed of otherworldly things - of gods and lakes and luminous beings invisible to the adult world. I took flight across the Welsh mountains in dreams and played with faery folk in the liminal dark. My great-grandmother understood these visions; she whispered her tales of ancient ways and old magics. Still, I pushed it all down as I grew. Until I could not any longer.

Eventually, I found a teacher of the Old Religion. I endured the assay and stood at the gates of Initiation into the mysteries. The Alexandrian Tradition welcomed me, with its taste for ceremonial elegance and discipline beyond the garden variety of Witchcraft. My love of the Goddess led me across oceans to Clonegal Castle in Ireland, where I was ordained a priest of the Fellowship of Isis by the late Lady Olivia Robertson. Upon returning, I established the Iseum of Aradia in Australia, honouring the Goddess in Her countless forms.

Later, I was privileged to meet Lady Michelin, matriarch of the Sussex strand of British Traditional Witchcraft. Through her, I was elevated in a rarely seen ritual - an experience that deepened my vow to preserve the old mysteries.

And so now, as the wheel turns once more, I find myself not only as seeker, but also as teacher, guide, and guardian of these sacred threads. This is my journey. And it continues.

Beyond a Year and a Day

Introduction

This story is dedicated to the memory of Simon Goodman, whose legacy continues to shape the arcane tapestry of Witchcraft in the Alexandrian Tradition. Here we chart my journey of discovery into the mysteries of the Craft, guided both by whispered intuition and hard-won experience.

Most of the characters herein are inspired by real people. A few have been embellished slightly for dramatic or visual effect, and most names have been changed to protect the guilty (and perhaps the innocent). This is more than a memoir; it is a guided visualisation into the inner planes of the Art Magical, a quest to rediscover the Gods of old and explore how we might honour them in this modern age.

The material behind these pages comes from many sources. Chief among them are unpublished writings of Simon Goodman, whom I regard as the father of Alexandrian Wicca in Australia. Additional threads were drawn from Coven notes, manuscripts, and papers, some dating back to Coventus Quercus, the original Queanbeyan Coven, and Quercus Umbraofficio Coventus, as well as spirited conversations with Elders, Witches, Magicians, and Occultists. I've also relied on my notebooks and handouts, remnants of my first formal training in 'The Craft of the Wise' under my first teacher, Thomas. For his guidance, regardless of what may have passed between us (and now forgotten, at least by me), I remain profoundly grateful.

In writing this story, I have endeavoured to honour my oaths and preserve the sanctity of our trust. My aim is not to unveil forbidden truths, but to share the path of a seeker: the awakening, the challenges, the knowledge earned and bestowed. They say knowledge is power, so wield what you discover here with care.

Notably absent are the true keys to the Mysteries: the visualisations, passwords, and initiatory secrets. These are safeguarded by sacred oath and entrusted only through genuine Initiation. While many of the rituals described may stir something deep and resonate powerfully, without those keys, they remain somewhat hollow. And that is no slight, just a truth of the tradition. You may still benefit from walking this path… if your eyes and heart remain open. To glimpse the Mystery, one must be willing to endure. *'Hast thou the courage to make the assay?'*

The structure of this book follows the natural unfolding of my journey:

Part One explores the beginnings, how the Craft found me, my first year of trials, my training, and the founding of our first Coven.

Part Two delves into our beliefs, why we do what we do, whom we honour, and the purpose of our secrecy.

Part Three unveils our magical workings, the theory behind our Spellcraft, and how we apply it through herbs, tools, and healing practices.

Part Four turns toward daily life, how ritual and celebration thread through our mundane hours and elevate them into moments of magic.

I have no desire to argue doctrine or justify my truths. This Tradition, this Magic, this Religion, it works for me, for my Coven, and my Initiates. I owe no explanation outside the Circle. That said, thoughtful reflections and questions are always welcome.

The practices detailed within are accurate to the best of my knowledge and experience. But take heed: some may pose real risks if undertaken without guidance. Magic is not a toy, and the unseen has teeth. I strongly urge readers to research deeply, reflect honestly, and proceed with respect and caution.

And finally, a word from Thomas, passed on to me and now offered to you: *"Don't believe a word I say. Go and do your own research and corroborate my story for yourself."*

"Dare ye cross the veil, where certainty ends and legend stirs?"

Our Beginnings
The Path, the Pain, and the Pulse of the Craft

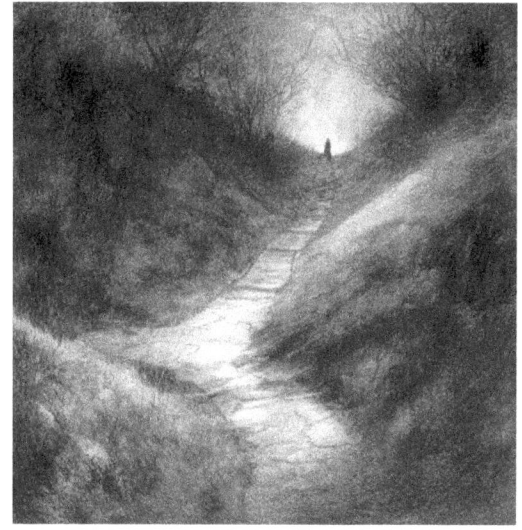

Before there were Gods, there was mystery. Before there was a path, there was the longing for one.

This book begins where every true journey must: in the unquiet silence of the soul. *Beyond a Year and a Day* is not merely a chronicle of rites and rituals; it is a memoir of becoming, a weaving of shadows and light, of aching questions and small, sacred certainties. It is the story of what happens when the veil thins not just on the sabbat, but also in a person's life, and what waits on the other side when it does.

Our Beginnings traces the spiralling path from spiritual hunger to awakening, from the first hesitant Circle to the formation of a living Coven. It is a pilgrimage through both initiation and doubt, where 'The Ordeal' is not a single event but a crucible that repeats and refines. It speaks of how ordinary coffee dates bloom into unexpected convocations; how sacred space is not only cast with salt and sword, but built over time, with trust and shared vulnerability.

Through chapters like *The Source* and *A Course in the Old Religion*, readers are invited to witness a transformation: a seeker stepping beyond folklore into lived Craft. There is humour in the pages (because the Gods have a wicked sense of timing), there is sacred discomfort, and above all, there is devotion, not just to the Old Ways, but also to community, service, and self-knowledge.

The title is no idle phrase. In Wiccan tradition, 'a year and a day' marks the time of dedication and preparation for those seeking initiation. But as this story shows, the real journey stretches beyond that threshold, into unexpected joys, deeper trials, and the infinite unfolding of purpose. What begins as a personal seeking becomes an offering: a map written in incense and ink, for others who wander in search of the divine.

Welcome then, to the fire at the centre. The Circle has not yet been cast, but the story is beginning. Let us walk it together.

Chapter One
The Ordeal

Let us commence this story at the end of the road, which is the beginning of a great adventure, and then go back to the start. The term *'beyond a year and a day'* should then make sense.

So, way back when, in the mists of time, between the worlds within that primordial soup of national politics known as Canberra, I was sitting at the kitchen table crunching on my Coco Pops and reading the morning paper when my lovely wife looked over at me and says, *"In two weeks you're going to be initiated."* I nearly choked, spitting a mouthful of my favourite breakfast cereal all over the table. Bloody hell, you could have waited until I swallowed! What a waste of a perfectly good mouthful of the most nutritious breakfast cereal on the planet!

Nevertheless, the statement still knocked me from left field weeks after I had asked the big question and was told to seriously think about it, and this coming from my wife! Even so, I sort of half expected it to happen, but it still knocked me over.

My pulse rate sharply increased, and a million images were instantly conjured up in my tiny mind. A feeling of childhood excitement came over me. This was not the end of over a year's training and study, but the beginning of a new life, a total commitment to some sort of inner, arcane feeling of belonging.

When? How? Who? What do I need to know, and a hundred other questions surfaced. I had an idea of what was to come. I had read all the necessary articles on initiation by the Farrars, Alex's lectures and the like, but did I know what was going to happen?

Evelyn had been initiated some months before. I remember dropping her off one night at the designated place and thinking, *"Luck lady, someday it will be me."* Then thinking, *"I wonder what is really going to happen to her in there, and who's in there anyway?"* What if the Book of Shadows (the so-called original version of Gerald's Book that was available on dark-site, secret bulletin boards) and other material I had read were all lies?

She might be sacrificed! No, I knew her initiator and trusted him implicitly. The thought did not enter my mind that my wife, lover and best friend in the world, was running around somebody's lounge room stark naked, and how many other people were there, I didn't know!

Now it was going to be my turn. Was the same thing going to happen to me? By the way, my wife was not sacrificed and survived the ordeal!

Evelyn then calmly directed me to start preparing myself physically and mentally for that special day. I had to be prepared to fast and cease all intake of alcohol, nicotine, caffeine, or other drugs. I was not allowed to talk Craft with anyone else until the day. I had to have a hot shower every night before bed and in the morning, a cold one – there was a mystery.

Mind you, Evelyn went through the same preparation before her Initiation, but I was oblivious to what she was experiencing back then. She has always been so good at keeping secrets!

If you continue reading my story, you are going to read the odd thing with the words, *'and there is another mystery you have to look forward to'.* You will be amazed at just how many secrets are contained in this story. And if you squint your eyes hard enough and look between the lines, you just might find something remarkable.

As the time got closer, I got more excited and maybe a little apprehensive. On the day of the initiation, I had to work. Fortunately, I was extra busy and did not have much time to contemplate my impending fate later that evening.

I was told to bring my Athame, a bottle of red wine (better make it a good vintage), and an apple, and be at the designated address at precisely 8.50 pm. Evelyn had not come home from work that afternoon. She had gone to the house of our teacher, the man who initiated her, and the man who was going to assist my wife to initiate me!

Now, some of you are going to say, *'But how can Evelyn initiate someone? She is only a First Degree?'* That is a very valid question, for within the Gardnerian, Alexandrian or British Tradition Witchcraft traditions, there is a general rule that says only a second or third degree can initiate, and that is true; except! Putting aside the father-mother exemptions, it can be done, and it was done. So I will leave it to your resourcefulness to discover the answer to that question.

I arrived home that afternoon to find the house quiet and empty, except for the cat. I had over three hours to keep myself amused before my initiation. Panic! Do I have everything I need? The little shopping bag contained my Athame, wine, apple, and towel so that I could have a shower when I arrived. It was all there! Check again. My mind was racing at a million miles an hour. I just began to realise I was hungry, having fasted all day, no, I was ravenous!

I retired to the study with the cat for a heart-to-heart discussion on initiation rites! Went through the paperwork again, and made sure I could write the Athame Runes and the first letter of my new name in Theban. Yes, I was sure I had everything down pat; it would not hurt to check again! What do you reckon cat? Do I look nervous? I had better check the time again. My watch might be wrong, better phone the time, and check (back in the day, before mobile phones). Some of you will understand that comment. Reset my watch; it was 18 seconds slow! Could never be late, never been late in my life! Time dragged on.

I only had to drive 10 kilometres. What if the car didn't start? Better leave at 8.30 pm, which will give me extra time if something happens on the way. What if I drive out of my street, and there is a major traffic accident, I have to detour, holy hell, that is going to take extra time. I start driving faster, no better not, cops might catch me and book me for speeding, which is going to cost more time, and then I am going to be late. Breathe, slow down, relax. Easy for you to say, you are not the one driving to a scary place to be sacrificed!

I eventually make it with three minutes to spare. Twice around the block should do it nicely, park the car outside a common-looking house on an average street. I walked up to the front door (I was told the door would be open and to walk right in, sit right down, baby let... sorry about that). It was a conspicuous-looking sign hanging on the door which said, *'Do not enter, mystic rites in session'*. I wonder if the Police pay any attention to that sign, if the neighbours hear me scream and call the cops.

I walk inside and leave my Athame, wine, and apple on a table at the door. I take my towel and follow a row of candles that lead to the bathroom. I strip off and have a nice warm soothing shower, then sit on a chair outside the bathroom. I wonder if I should have had a cold shower.

There is music playing, and I can hear a man's voice; the muffled tones sound like Thomas. Time marches on, and I am starting to get cold sitting in this deserted hallway stark naked. I wonder if Evelyn felt like this. Then, all of a sudden, a man appears in flowing red robes, his head half covered by the hood of a large cap. He asks me a question, I answer, and he disappears. Did I say the right thing?

He returns a few minutes later and tells me to stand and turn around. I comply and feel a blindfold placed over my eyes. *'Is that too tight? Can you see?'* No, No. My hands are pulled behind my back and tied together; then a cord is tied around my neck. They are going to hang me! Too tight? No, OK. Other cords are wrapped around my knees and ankles. I'm asked if I'm OK. As well as can be expected under the circumstances! I'm trussed up for the slaughter!

There is no turning back now! I'm spun around and led through the house, a doorway, probably into the kitchen, and the floor was cold. Then into another room, the lounge room, this is where it is all going to happen. I can feel my pulse starting to race. Who is there? How many people are looking at my naked body? I did not care, but it would be nice to know! I am told to stand still and not move.

Could not if I tried! I figured I was at the gateway, somewhere between the worlds. The usual place where willing sacrifices are told to wait before their execution!

I then heard the Circle being cast. Yes, I could hear Evelyn's voice, and I felt a little better. She was not going to let anything happen to me, or was she? After all, she was now one of them!

I tried to follow the ritual, but some things sounded slightly different, and they did not say the right words I was used to. This was strange. A new invocation I had not heard before, it was beautiful, and I let myself drift.

I felt cold, but I was sweating, my knees were knocking together, and I wanted to go to the loo, but I had just been a few minutes ago, no, that was half an hour ago. My bladder could not be full again; I had not drunk anything, must be my imagination. No, I definitely wanted to have a pee.

I shifted my attention from my cold, shrivelled penis to my bound wrists; they were starting to feel uncomfortable, and my right ear started to itch. Honestly, someone, hurry up, this is taking an eternity!

I start to drift again; am I in an altered state? I feel the Circle; I can sense the power being raised, then the Charge! I have never listened to the words as closely as I did that night. I felt the Goddess was talking to me alone!

I drift again, then I meet the challenge, I say, *"I do,"* and then the sword, it's cold and hard on my chest, have I the courage, yes. A kiss and I'm spun into the Circle, around and around. It's begun! I've made the step into the otherworld.

The Fivefold Kiss, sweetly I feel Evelyn's tender lips, but the words are wrong, again they are strange and not what I am used to saying or hearing. Then my measure is taken. Then my blood spot! A prick with a needle on my finger, squeeze. How much have you got? None, I found out later, I do not bleed. Yes, you do, then another prick, shit, how much blood do you want!

I'm told to kneel. Am I still willing? What happened next is one of our Coven secrets, I'll leave it to your imagination.

After regaining my composure my blindfold is removed, and I see my lovely wife standing in front of me, her face lit by a candle.

The room was strange, nobody else, Evelyn and her initiator. The tools are presented; I am starting to feel a little calmer, forgotten about wanting a pee. I was still cold, yet sweating all over someone's carpet!

The Sword, do not touch; there is something about dominating spirits. The Athame, mine! Evelyn places it between her breasts, and we push our bodies together with a kiss. For the love of all things sacred, don't drop it, I have more to lose than you, my lady! The Wand, the Boline.....

We kneel at the Altar. I have to write the Runes on the Athame handle. I get them wrong. Evelyn, *"If you're going to do them, let's do them properly."* We start again.

When I finish, I take my Athame around to the quarters. *"I call upon Earth to bond my spell."* Then East and South, and West. What now? I am taken to the Quarters, Dylan's a Witch, Dylan's a Witch, tell the world!

Let us eat. My hunger had vanished; however, I managed to gulp down a bowl of chicken soup! Evelyn thrusts something in my face, *"Read this now."* It was the script of the ritual we had just done. Then something else, words, I was still off with the Fairies. It's over, we banish.

Now I know what is meant by the phrase, '*hast thou the courage to make the assay*'.

Now it's time to go back to the very beginning, where my real adventure commences, but first, let me tell you another story. A story, I believe, has become folklore in my community. It tells of our real beginnings, back in the mists of time, the story of the birth of the Wida.

"Enter this space as breath into the unseen - where the veil thins and truth wears no name."

Chapter Two
The Source

The Atlantean Story

It is written in our *Books of Wisdom* that there was a Priest of the Sea; this was the Priest who brought the Priestess away from Atlantis when his knowledge told him that the final catastrophe was imminent.

Legends tell of the first Merlin who came to the shores of Wales and of the first Arthur, the King and the Priestess, daughter of Diana, the Great Mother.

It is Diana, the Great Mother, who is the Mother of our people. She was worshipped as the Moon; neither was she distant from them, but forever with them; for she dwelt within the secret heart of every woman.

The people of Atlantis had two main mysteries that were of the Sun and the Moon. The Solar mysteries belonged to the men, while the Lunar, which made up the older cult, belonged to the darkness, the Moon, and women.

It was the Great Mother, who was also the Earth beneath their feet, that had given birth to the Sun to be a guiding light to humanity and a symbol to which they could aspire.

In the beginning, they had risen within their spirits and yearned to be like the Sun; they longed that their souls should shine with the rays of the Lord of Light, but as their knowledge and power grew, some among them became corrupt and turned towards sorcery and power rather than Wisdom. They created monsters by the use of alchemy and enslaved the most primitive races with the power of their minds.

The Sun God saw this and determined to destroy the race that so defiled his lands; the earth would open up and swallow them, and the sea would obliterate their memory forever.

One of the great wheels of evolution was drawing to a close, and with it, a land and a people. Yet the Mother would not let their memory die; how could it die, for was not She the promise of Immortality?

The sacred city of Atlantis was built around a mountain that had become a volcano, just as Pompeii was built in historic times. Around it, the wide alluvial plain stretched away to a far range of mountains. Land made bare by the receding sea. At the very verge of the water, rose the Great Cone. The Cone was flat on top, not pyramidal, because in some previous cataclysm, it had blown off its crater, as volcanoes do. On this level, the crest were the white buildings of the Sacred Clan - the Great Sun Temple.

The Temple was a circular building, within, its open court was paved with black and white alternate marble and basalt, and its two pillars were the twin gnomons of a time dial as vast as the court, one for the Sun, and one for the moon, and calculations were made upon the way the shadows crossed the squares. All other temples of the Mysteries take after it.

The entrance to the Temple was rectangular. It was built of white, glistening stone. A stone which looked as if it were filled with mica and colour. The heavy crossbeam of stone that spanned the doorway had sculptured upon it a great raven with its head raised upwards. The Raven symbolises our secret and hidden knowledge; it is the protector and revealer of the Mysteries. The power of the Raven gives courage and protection to enter the Great Mysteries. Its blue-black colour contains an iridescence that speaks of magic and a changeability of form and shape that brings an awakening within the spirit.

There were groups of pillars composed of the precious white stone, which was bendable but could not be broken, which were moulded to form a perfect circular upright, and the steps were rectangular, in the same white glistening stone as the building itself.

There were no gates or walls to guard its gardens. The gardens were filled with blossoms: great beds of marigolds in their season, tulips, sunflowers, and many of the small, sweetly perfumed roses.

Around the temples were buildings with porticoes and colonnades; these were the houses of the Priests and scribes that served the temple, and beyond them was the House of the Virgins, built around a court, with no windows looking outwards. It was there that Morgan grew to womanhood.

Within were courts leading one into the other and surrounded by rooms and colonnades. There were sunken stone tanks with steps leading down to them where the sacred lilies grew, and over them leant trees, not unlike mulberry trees, ancient and gnarled, from whose bark oozed the fragrant resins they burnt in the temples. The young Priestesses sat under the trees spinning with the spindle and whorl that are more ancient than the wheel.

From the House of the Virgins, an underground way led to the Temple. Priests from whom all passion had gone watched over the upbringing of the young Priestesses in the care of the wise women. In this way, they were brought into the temple as the occasion required, never setting eyes on the outside world, nor any undedicated men; and by this way, they returned when their work was done.

Beneath the Temple was a way, led by the path of the lava to the very heart of the ancient volcano, and herein was hollowed out a crypt where a rising jet of flame burnt continually, telling those who had eyes to see that the mountain was not dead, but sleeping. This flame, lit by the Earth herself, was to them a symbol of their faith, for all fires are one in nature, though after three kinds: volcanic, solar, and terrestrial. It was the leaping of this flame that warned that long foretold catastrophe was at hand.

Out of the many, The Great Mother chose the few that would transmit the Wisdom to the younger races. She warned of the coming destruction that they might escape and take Her arcane knowledge with them.

The members of their missions were picked according to the symbolism of their craft; first, a King who was to be as the visible Sun surrounded by his men-at-arms who were the days of the year.

Secondly, a Magician who was to be a secret essence of the Sun, the Hidden One, was versed in esoteric lore and sciences. It was he who would lead men through the labyrinthine ways of the Underworld to find the Holy Grail of Immortality that was the source of all life and from which issued the shining inner sun that was the true self of the Initiate. Such a man was Merlin, whose name means literally 'Man of the Sea'.

Thirdly, there was the Priestess, the incarnation of the Great Mother to whom all power and all magic were attributed. The woman was the oracle and the medium by which the Priest's power took form. She was associated with the Moon and its triple aspects of Birth, Life, and Death. She was Morgan. She is also Aradia.

And when the time came that the leaping flame gave warning, the Great Mother gave into the hands of the Priest of the Sea, the secret scrolls, and sacred symbols. He and the King went by night by the underground way to the House of the Virgins and looked at the young girls as they slept in the moonlight, and chose one who had been prepared to serve Her purpose, and roused her and led her away in a dark cloak while the others slept.

And she saw for the first and last time by moonlight the wide spaces of the plain where the spearmen and javelin-throwers learnt their skill, and horsemen rode the two-toed horse, and she went down the winding processional way to the shore, and so to the sea. And the land wind blowing at dawn filled their sails, and they went swiftly. For a day, a night, and a day, they went. Then, upon the third morning, in the hour between the dark and the dawn, three great billows heaved their ship as the sea floor shook, and when the sun rose, they saw a dark pillar of smoke and cloud where once was Atlantis.

From Egypt, they went to Greece, America, and Europe to found their Mystery schools. Wherever they went, they built temples of worship according to the minds of the people they encountered; the pyramids of the Americas and Egypt and the Stone Circles of Britain were their handiwork; these were the Wicca, the wise ones. Well, they knew of the coming disaster and of their divine mission to preserve the ancient lore.

It was such as this that the first ships came to Britain bearing Arthur, Merlin, and Morgan. They landed on the shores of Wales and started to establish the culture that we now know as Witchcraft.

Merlin's life shows us the pattern of the Wicca initiation of his life on Atlantis, governed by the Great Mother. His crossing of the water, the first death, and his teaching of the mysteries. His marriage to Ellen and subsequent disillusionment, and finally his enchantment with the fairy Vivian, the Lady of the Lake, who shows him that Atlantis is not dead but lives on in a body younger and more beautiful.

His task is done; she tricks him out of the word of power that is life itself, and his spirit returns once more to the lands of the West, where souls find their resting place.

The land of Atlantis is no more, but men still go there in their dreams and on death, their souls still tread the ancient pathways to the Goddess whom they thought forgotten.

It is always Vivian who shall raise the sword of Endeavour above the waters that cover up the past, and to her it is returned when all is done, for she is the spring of eternal youth that shall come again, again, and again. She it is, who is the Secret Grail that is never empty.

It was the teaching of the Wicca that the pathway of the Initiate was to descend into the darkness of Anwyn beneath the waves to search for the grail. The Initiate may see many things there and learn many secrets, but they must remain silent lest they be trapped forever, unable to return to the world of men.

If they follow the instructions, they will find the grail that is the secret of life, the legacy of the amassed experiences of the previous cycle. Having found the grail, they must drink from it the waters of life and return from the Underworld to the world of men to do their will among the living.

They emerge from the waters as does the Sun with all the glory of wisdom and knowledge upon their brow.

If the Initiate remains true to their acquired knowledge, at death they go beyond the Sun into the future; they have escaped from the Glass Castle of the Seasons and are free to come and go as they desire. They need not incarnate for many cycles to come, but remain as one of the Wise Ones for the benefit of humanity.

Merlin belongs to the Sea out of which he came, yet his teachings have lived on; they are for us, the forms are different, but the spirit is always the same.

Comments: This story is a reproduction of a typed photocopy of a document I found hidden within my original course notes many years ago. Its source and author were unknown until recently, but I believe it was based on the works of Plato. It is also very similar to a story retold within *The Sea Priestess*, a book written by Dion Fortune.

I recently found that Alex had included this story in his lectures. I felt it fitted in nicely among the other myths and legends we use within our tradition. I wonder if he too thought the same. My apologies to the original author, whoever you are, if I have used this material inappropriately.

Chapter Three
The Beginning

So, the Legend of Atlantis and the birth of the Wicca; is it real or a fantasy? Do we believe, one day, maybe, we will see our home as we enter the Summerlands? I do, and why not? Nobody can definitively prove that a god exists or that there is a heaven or hell. So why not have a little faith and have a belief just like other religions?

The history of modern Wicca has been retold many times and is probably known to many who read this story, but just to summarise for those who do not know. In a nutshell, the birth of modern Wicca started in England in the 1930s. The man most responsible for its re-emergence as a modern-day religion was Gerald B Gardner. However, long before Gardner's reformation, a person named George Pickingill may have had a hand in changing things.

Old George, as he was known, has his detractors and his supporters. Many papers have been written concerning his actual existence and whether or not he was a cunning man who practised an ancient form of witchcraft. Some occultists believe he was a key figure in the nineteenth-century esoteric community, a member of an alleged hereditary witch cult.

It is claimed he led a Coven of Witches and formed nine other Covens across southern England. It is said he restructured the established English witch-cult by introducing new concepts from French and Danish witchcraft and Classical literary sources, and in doing so, created the structure from which Gardnerian Wicca is alleged to have emerged in the 1950s, and may be one of the sources of our Sussex Tradition.

In addition, of course, we cannot forget Alex Sanders, who definitely put his own twist on things. After all, he was King of the Witches, a legend in his own lifetime!

Nevertheless, at the end of the day, does it really matter where our current belief system originated? It is nice to think we have a history and genuine ancestors, but as far as I am concerned, my religion, my beliefs, my magic and my way of celebrating life and living work for me! I do believe Atlantis exists, and I do return to her when the veil is thinnest, and I will tread her path at the end of time.

Ian Watts (born 16 September 1951), known by his Craft name of Simon Goodman, was the father of the Alexandrian branch of Wicca in Australia that originated in Perth, Western Australia. Through Simon, it spread to Melbourne and country Victoria and finally emerged in Canberra. He was as charismatic and somewhat irreverent as Alex. The cheeky little bugger would often wear the suit of a Catholic priest, especially when he flew in aeroplanes – it always got him an automatic upgrade to business class. After all, he was a Priest - of the Wicca!

Some say that a woman named Betty Britton initiated him into Alexandrian Wicca in England. I do not believe that is quite right. My sources tell me that his initiation was a lot closer to Alex than is publicly known. The fact that he is a legitimate descendant of Alex Sanders is all that matters.

He was also a dear friend of Maxine Sanders and trained in her Coven for a short time. I spent an afternoon with Maxine not that long ago, sipping tea and eating cake (very British), and it was lovely to hear her say great things about Simon.

Simon undertook further magical training in England before returning to Australia. He was then instrumental in creating the first legitimate Wiccan Coven in Perth, Western Australia back in 1974.

Around 1965, before Simon found Wicca, he discovered a group that practised a form of Paganism that differed from that of the Alexandrian and Gardnerian traditions.

This form of witchcraft was allegedly practised in Etchingham in Essex in the UK until the 1940s and appears to be the precursor to a traditional form of witchcraft now known as the Sussex Tradition. The form of this tradition is, of course, highly controversial, very private, and really cannot be authenticated, but more about that later.

The Cockroach Papers

The complete history of the Craft in Australia through Simon's eyes was documented by him in a paper titled *'A True and Faithful Relation'*, more commonly known within our Circle as *The Cockroach Papers*.

The Cockroach Papers were written, with some editing from Simon, and compiled from notes and voice tapes made because of various discussions between Simon and several senior Craft members over the period July 1989 to May 1990. It documents the history of the Craft in Australia between 1965 and 1989, seen through Simon's eyes.

The Cockroach Papers was a restricted document only held by senior members of Simon's inner circle, or at least it was when I was handed my copy. If you are lucky enough to find a copy of this document, I guarantee it will make fascinating reading!

Ian Watts passed to the Summerlands on 23 September 1991. I knew him only briefly, but in my eyes, he was the most influential figure in the history of Wicca in Australia, a brilliant Occultist, High Priest, and Magister of the Art Magical.

This brings us back to the enigmatic Sussex Tradition, which was brought to Australia in the early 1960s and was practised in a Perth Coven known as Coventus Quercus – or simply *'The Covenant'*. Simon was initiated into this group and began his training in the magical arts around 1965.

The tradition at that time had no Book of Shadows and was a totally oral magical tradition. The concept of the tradition was oriented toward an idea of a priesthood, not unlike Wicca, but did not limit its activities to Wiccan practices alone.

The Sussex Tradition is part of my Coven's family heritage. Sussex is a potent and beautiful form of the Craft and connects us with the sense and energy of the Old Religion. The version that my group practices and teaches today is a melding of Sussex with Alexandrian.

Simon was a member of the original Perth Coven; he later became its Magister. The Coven closed in 1975. Simon and his High Priestess, the Lady Michelin, later passed the leadership of the Tradition onto another Magister and Lady who continues the tradition to this day.

Some say that Simon offered a Sussex Initiation (the Third Level) to only those Alexandrian Initiates who had been a Third Degree and performing the duties of an Elder for at least two years, and he deemed them worthy and capable of possessing the knowledge contained in the Sussex Book.

There are three levels of Initiation in the Sussex Tradition. The first Level corresponds to the First Degree Initiation in Gardnerian or Alexandrian Covens. The Second Level is the Initiation into the Craft proper. The Third Level is the Initiation into the High Priesthood.

The form of a First Degree Sussex Initiation is not much different to a normal Alexandrian Initiation, except the Witch does not receive the Sussex Book of Shadows. The Third Level is something altogether different, and that is when the Sussex Book of Shadows is revealed!

This story and our Coven training program and methods are primarily based on the Alexandrian system, with just a hint of Sussex giving us a flavour that is a little more 'earthy' and much easier to 'tune into' from a Wheel of the Year perspective.

Chapter Four
Coffee?

It's about time we started the real story this tome is all about. So without further ado, follow my path as I find a new life and work my way towards the Ordeal.

On a chilly autumn night, I found myself sitting in a trendy coffee shop in Canberra, looking over the table at my wife and thinking, *"What are we getting ourselves into?"* A few weeks earlier, I was reading the local newspaper and just happened to flick over to the advertising section; not that I made a habit of reading the wanted ads and for sale columns, but something compelled me to start reading the personal column.

'A course in the old religion of witchcraft starting soon. Write to PO Box 777 Canberra ACT' (not the real address). No other details, not even a phone number! They were the days before the internet and smartphones, when folks actually communicated using real language face-to-face, way before emoji and texting.

It caught my attention and I had to know more.

Ever since I was a boy, I had been somewhat intrigued by the unknown, the occult, magic, the fairies at the bottom of the garden – don't tell me you haven't seen them? I even went along to have my fortune told by an old gypsy woman in Sydney. I don't think it quite turned out like she predicted!

When I was a young boy of around 10 or 12 years,

I used to go to bed at night and lie there, look up at the corner of the ceiling, and I would get the feeling that everything around me would shrink or somehow seem far away. It was difficult to explain how I felt. Then I would somehow leave my body and all of a sudden be hovering in the corner of the ceiling looking down at myself in bed.

I would then go wandering around the house, floating just under the ceiling. I cannot remember being confident enough to wander too far from home. I realised years later that this must have been some form of astral projection, but at the time, it was my little secret, and I thought that if I ever told anyone, they would lock me away in Callan Park! (Those who grew up in Sydney in the 60s and 70s would know that Callan Park was an infamous mental hospital, a very scary place.)

My childhood was filled with dreaming. I would fantasise about flying, and in my dreams, I would often find myself flying and gliding over mountains and valleys.

I would walk into the bush, sit against a tree, and just dream, and I really did see fairies and otherworldly folk on my inner adventures. I remember doing the same thing when I was about seven before Mum and Dad emigrated from Wales to Australia. I would walk into the woods at the end of our road, hide in the deep undergrowth, and pretend I had entered the fairy realm.

It is a shame we have to grow up. For most of us, we tend to lose that child-like part of ourselves as we grow into adults and scoff at the thought of our imaginary friends. However, we really do not have to; all we need to do is find that child within us again, and we will find those magical realms we once knew as children.

I have one very vivid memory, sitting in my great-grandmother's kitchen. It was dark and gloomy. She lived in a solid stone granite cottage at least 120 years old (the cottage, not my gran; and then again, she might have been close to a hundred) with exposed oak ceiling beams and a Welsh slate roof. I must have been only six or seven at the time.

She was making me hot chips, cooking them in a pot of boiling lard. The one thing I remember was a great black pot or cauldron hanging on a chain over the huge open fireplace. I never saw what was in it; possibly stew or, as the Welsh called it, Cawl. Nowadays, I like to think it was something magical, something witchy, for it was rumoured she was the village wise woman – could I possibly be descended from a real witch? Probably not, but is it not nice to have that thought?

"So," I said to Evelyn, *"What do you think? Shall I write them a letter?" "It can't hurt. Sounds intriguing, we've got nothing to lose,"* she said.

She, too, had been somewhat intrigued with the occult in one way or another. Nevertheless, we were both very sceptical, having worked in a Police environment for a couple of decades; trust does not come naturally. A healthy amount of scepticism is best when you deal with the unknown.

Some days later, I received a telephone call from Thomas, who said he and his partner Vivienne, operated the Occult Heritage Collective, a library of occult learning, and regularly conducted courses in the old religion. Rather than talk on the phone, why couldn't we get together over a coffee and get to know one another?

So here we were, being everything an ex-cop was: back to the wall in the last cubicle in the coffee shop facing the door, scrutinising everyone that walked in, half expecting someone in a black pointy hat to saunter up to our table and say, *"Boo"*.

As it turns out, Thomas was in his early thirties, six feet tall with jet-black straight hair tied in a thick ponytail stretching halfway down his back. He wore black jeans, a black sloppy joe, and a three-quarter black tweed overcoat. He carried a black leather briefcase in his left hand and a black walking cane in his right. Did I mention the piercing black eyes? No, they were actually dark brown. Behold, the Prince of Darkness! (I will explain that statement later.)

Vivienne was half his size, petite, with an air of authority around her that made you think twice about answering back! I could tell she held some kind of power, authority, or influence. It was in her smoky grey-blue eyes. However, she also had a nurturing feeling around her; she was a mother as well. She had to be a Witch Queen or something like that! The Taurus in me instantly bonded with her.

As soon as they walked into the coffee shop, our eyes met, and they walked straight up to our table and introduced themselves. Vivienne sat ever so, looking like that queen, allowing Thomas to do most of the talking.

They handed us a flyer outlining what this *'Wicca'* course was all about, being careful not to divulge too much, and told us that if we were interested, the course would be about three to four months long, one night a week and would be starting in three weeks. There were already about half a dozen people committed, and for us to let them know within the week.

I looked at Vivienne and asked her how much it was going to cost us. To my surprise, she said, *"Nothing, we are not permitted by our Craft Laws to charge for knowledge that was given freely in the first place. I find it disrespectful when I see people charging for the Craft, even reading the tarot cards, it offends the Goddess."*

Over thirty years later, I have the same feeling and give exactly the same answer. *'Come and join us for a night of magic and drumming as we celebrate the Goddess and perform a full moon ritual in her honour. Only fifty dollars and you get a free cup of tea and cake.'* Advertisements like that really do offend me! The Craft is not, never was, and never will be for sale! Do not let anyone ever charge you for honouring the Goddess and learning the Old Ways, never!

As they were leaving, Thomas' parting words were, *"If you want to know more about the Craft and what you're getting into, do yourself a favour and get a book called What Witches Do by Stewart Farrar."*

The next day, I went to our local 'alternative' bookstore and found the book. To my amazement, in a little corner at the back of the store, a whole section on the occult and other witchy-type subjects, and the floor around these shelves was all types of flyers advertising occult courses, weekend workshops and a host of other subjects unknown to a mere uninitiated nobody! Where had all this stuff been hiding all my life?

That bookstore, just like similar ones around the country at the time, was typical of the place where you would find and meet people who were looking for an alternative. It was a time way before social media, and from that sprang Pagans in the Pub. I think every major city has one pub where the local university students, academics, and other strange types come together once a month to debate the occult and other things that go bump in the night.

I guess it wasn't much different back in the 1920s, 30s and 40s when the Theosophical Society, the Rosicrucians, the Golden Dawn, and people like Alistair Crowley came together to stimulate discussion on the paranormal. Secret societies were born from the mist created by occult energies, and so it still is in some places today. Teachers tend not to advertise. It is the student who finds the teacher. Except for Thomas' advertisement, which turned out to be an experiment to create a *Supergroup of Witches* – but more about that later.

Evelyn and I had spent long hours reading *'What Witches Do'* and some of the other material I had found in the bookstore, and discussing our options. And so, it still is today, 'What Witches Do' is compulsory reading for any student wishing to enter our Outer Circle.

Thomas eventually contacted us, and we were told where and when the course would start. One thing I remember Evelyn saying was, *"I'm not taking my clothes off for anyone. This skyclad stuff I've read about is not for me!"* Oh, how times have changed.

For those of you who are not aware of what the word 'skyclad' means, it is used in the Craft to refer to ritual nudity. In some instances, celebrations and rituals are performed naked, as well as the First Degree Initiation. *'And as the sign that ye are truly free, Ye shall be naked in your rites.'* But more about getting your gear off later!

And so, from an innocent-looking ad in the local newspaper to coffee with strangers, the journey began. Now, some 35 years later, the journey continues, for once you tread the path, there is no going back.

"Whispers bound in ink – enter the beginning of lost stories."

Chapter Five
A Course in the Old Religion

Half an hour's drive in the hills outside Canberra was a group of old weatherboard cottages on the banks of the Cotter River. One of those cottages was the 'Covenstead', the home of Thomas and Vivienne and the place we were to become very familiar with over the next few years. This was where we learnt our Craft and, unbeknownst to us at the time, the beginning of our involvement and eventual leadership of a *'Super Group'*, a very special and hand-picked group of people who were to become initiates of Thomas' vision of a professional band of witches! By 'professional', I mean businessmen and women, academics, and leaders, with a smattering of alpha males and alpha females thrown in for good measure - not your average seeker.

It is funny to reminisce today on what Thomas really had in mind back then and his vision of the future. Suffice it to say it did not happen; well, it did, but without Thomas. Some years later, a nasty parting of the ways between Thomas and me and our lives took separate courses. That being so much water has passed under the bridge, it is not worth talking about anymore. All is well, and our 'Super Group' became known as *Quercus Umbraofficio Coventus* (Coven in the Shadow of the Oak), part of Simon's original Coventus Quercus group.

I am not quite sure exactly what Thomas had in mind, but I believe he was following Simon's concepts of propagating the Craft using people who were somewhat academically trained and most of mature standing, not your average witchy type of that era. He wanted charismatic characters;

I guess something like Alex back in the '60s!

Do not for one moment think I am putting myself in the same boat as Alex; I do have a little charisma, but not that much! It was some years earlier that Simon conducted an experiment in country Victoria, attempting to turn predominantly Christian country townsfolk into Pagans. That is another story, suffice to say the Maypole is still erected at Beltane in the local park with a healthy attendance of locals dancing and singing the summer in!

Thomas took a lead role in the training and delivering lectures, with the Lady Vivienne stepping in to talk about the Goddess, all things feminine and Circle Casting. For it was she who cast our first Circle and sealed my fate when I felt the power of the Craft at my fingertips, and she who lifted me to the Second Degree, and she who performed the Handfasting to celebrate Evelyn and my tenth wedding anniversary. There is a saying in our tradition, *'Behind all is the Mother'*, behind my Craft life has been the Lady Vivienne; and such is true of all High Priestesses, for it is they who rule the Coven – but the High Priest owns the Sword – there also lies a mystery!

I should say at this point that Simon's way of teaching and initiating was very different to that practised in the UK by Alex. The British used to, and still do, I believe, undertake a thorough vetting over numerous cups of coffee and exhaustive discussions to assess the suitability of an applicant. It was only then that they initiated the applicant, and then commenced their training in the Art Magical. They kind of did it back to front: get them in the door first, then train them up.

We here in Australia tend to offer a course that covers most of the topics, as you will shortly see, then the applicant is assessed and initiation is only given if the student has learnt all the lessons to the required standard.

Our course lasted all through winter and into spring, and during that time, I met Simon and went to my first Wiccan Conference. Evelyn and I run the same course today, nothing has changed, and we still meet potential neophytes in a coffee shop and recommend reading *What Witches Do*. Although our current course has a little bit of Sussex Tradition thrown in just to confuse the issue!

The object of the course is to provide an overview of Witchcraft, its beliefs, and practices and define a cohesive view of Wicca in general. The course provides a comparison between various occult traditions and practices and establishes a benchmark against which a student can evaluate literature concerning the Craft, especially today, with Mr Google and Wiki whatshisname throwing curveballs from every direction, confusing the crap out of students!

Please, please, please, do not believe anything you find on the internet unless you either have been directed to the source by a teacher or have been able to confirm its authenticity yourself through alternate means or research.

Just like my first teacher, today I strive to provide a course that is an authoritative resource centre for the study of Wicca, witchcraft, and magic and provide training in occult and psychic practices.

On the first night of our course, Thomas explained

that the course aimed to deliver the training necessary for a student to evaluate the validity of the Wiccan path. He added that completion of the course also prepares a student to the level required by most Covens for Initiation. You little ripper, did that mean I could become a real initiated witch if I passed my final exam? Believe me, some people really think that way!

In the car on the way home from the Cotter, Evelyn and I had a mind full of information to digest and to truly decide if we were going back the following week. *"Absolutely,"* said Evelyn, *"But I'm still not taking my bloody clothes off for anyone but you."*

So, what did we learn? Thirteen formal lessons plus practical Circle casting and an invitation to a real Coven Sabbat ritual, where we met many strange-looking people who later became family. In addition, the highlight was dancing with Simon around a Maypole and watching Evelyn nearly garrotte him with her cord! He died the following year. I am sure Evelyn had nothing to do with it.

So, the course started. How excitement, as the saying goes! There were eight of us altogether, me, Evelyn, Kevin, Nicolas, Stuart, Sharon, Tracey and Aaron, who later was to become my Man-in-Black.

The Man-in-Black, sometimes called The Summoner and on others, The Devil, is the public face of the Coven. He is the envoy who delivers messages between Covens. He is the second in charge to the High Priest and the protector of the High Priestess. He can stand between worlds – one foot in the Circle, one foot out – there be another mystery!

The first few meetings could be considered mundane to the now, new-age pagan-type person. But back then, we were all bright-eyed and bushy-tailed because none of us had ever experienced anything like what we were hearing, seeing and doing. That is the impact of this technical revolution, this age of man, where everything is just a mouse click away. That is one of my current difficulties when I teach new students the Craft, for most of the knowledge is out there on the internet, well, people think it is, for what they find is the outer covering, but it is enough to taint a seeker's impressions.

I forever find myself hearing things like 'I did a Google and found such and such written by the High Priestess for the Covenant of the Whatever, who said that, blah, blah, blah.' Then I have to explain that the High Priestess is a fake and what she has written is a plagiarised copy of a plagiarised version of a plagiarised story of something that was written by a self-made magician from the planet Pluto.

Once in a while, a student will find me who hasn't been tainted by the works of charlatans, one who is prepared to learn the real ways of the Old Religion, one who is ready to open their soul, one who is willing to suffer to learn. It is then that I am content with the feeling that I have fulfilled my role as a teacher. And at the time of writing this story, I have one such student, and if the tides are right, she will face the Guardians and make the assay.

During the first few lessons, we discussed the history of the Craft and how the Gardnerian Reformation influenced modern witchcraft. We talked about the concept of paganism and the beliefs, customs, and etiquette of various traditions and denominations of the Craft. This history lesson was most interesting, for back in the day, there were very few books that explained the Craft. Today, the history from Gardner forward has been well documented, and it is of little surprise to most, so we tend to tell the stories between the lines, the little Craft titbits that are known only to those who were there at the time.

The BBC and British television, back in the 1960s and 70s, made some remarkable documentaries about witchcraft and occultism. You can discover interviews with Maxine and Alex Sanders, a couple with Gerald and of course, the Alex phenomenon, all worth finding on YouTube. Our own Neville Drury made an interesting documentary called *'The Occult Experience'*, another one worth discovering.

I am lucky enough to be able to retell some of those stories today, for many years ago, I undertook a journey, a pilgrimage if you like, to find my roots in Celtic Britain. During that journey, I visited many ancient sites and met a gaggle of the 'original Craft' at gatherings like the Pagan Federation's annual conference and other similar get-togethers. I was lucky enough to meet and spend time with Stewart before his passing. Alas, I fear the original characters will soon become memories.

Just thinking about Stewart Farrar. On our travels around the Emerald Isle, Evelyn and I intended to visit Newgrange and other Celtic sites. Before we left the Farrar's they presented us with a note addressed to the British Heritage Society, the people who operated the sacred sites and charged tourists entry fees. The note demanded that Evelyn and I be given free entry to any pagan site in Ireland, as we were Initiates of the Old Religion and therefore it was our right to freely enter the sacred sites of our ancestors! A get-out-of-goal card that let us in! Moreover, it actually worked! Fair dinkum, we were treated like royalty.

Back on track, we then moved onto the subject most seekers desire to know and the subject most believe Wicca is all about; that is, Goddess worship, the Divine Mother, and women's spirituality. Before the Craft, I had never been one to think too much about femininity, feminism, and anything that might hint at the subject. I was an ex-cop, a guy who rode a Harley, a typical bloke, and those issues had never really crossed my mind. Oh, how my feelings have changed since that time!

However, the Craft is not just centred on the Goddess; it is a balance of God and Goddess, male and female, good and bad, yin and yang, black and white, within and without. Get the idea? It is about polarity. Yes, polarity, for without it, there is no Craft. Is there sex in the Craft? Yes, of course there is. Without it, we do not exist.

Then we identified with the God; the mighty Karnayna, the Horned One, Pan, Herne and the ever-loving Cernunnos and understood that balance. This is another one of those things that is difficult to document. It is not so much a mystery, but a feeling, an enlightenment of such that all of a sudden rings true like someone turned on the light. When you understand the life cycle of the Gods and work that into the green world and your everyday life, all becomes clear.

Later on in our lessons, Thomas taught us about the Priesthood and what it was like to be part of a Coven. We learnt there is no congregation in the Craft, all are of the Priesthood, and all are equal in the eyes of the Gods. We identified the different levels of the Craft. What was involved in progressing from a Neophyte to a Third Degree?

He very quickly discussed Initiation, and what could be expected during that ritual – for that was a mystery, and a mystery has to be experienced, not taught! Evelyn still insisted she was not going skyclad for anyone, especially for some of those funny-looking people she met the previous weekend during a friendly Coven get-together.

We learnt that the Wheel of the Year, the annual Festivals of the Craft, was not only a celebration of the agricultural cycle of nature but also overlaid the cycle of life, death, and rebirth of the Gods. A merger of the real world and the otherworldly cycle was at the heart of all that is Wiccan and all that we believe and live by.

It was about now in the course that everything seemed to fall into place. We had not even touched on magic or other mystical topics at that time, and for me, I suddenly felt in harmony with everything; I was one with the universe, and I was balanced. I could see Initiation somewhere down the track and becoming a member of a very elite club!

Actually, just saying the word 'elite' brings a smile to my face. As far as the rest of the Craft community is concerned, especially in Canberra and eastern Australia, anyone descended from Simon's line (and that's through Thomas and Vivienne in Canberra) has been labelled as 'elitists' just because we are strict and hold our ideals and Craft beliefs in very high regard. There is a right way to do things and a wrong way, right? As far as I'm concerned, that is a good thing, for did not the Goddess say, *'Keep pure your highest ideal. Strive ever towards it: let nought stop you or turn you aside.'*

So, back to the course again, and we learnt about our myths and legends and how they are incorporated in ritual. Atlantis is my favourite, but a little later, I will tell you about some more stories. All tied into myths and legends are the subjects of meditation, guided visualisations, together with the practices of invocation and evocation and my favourite, pathworkings.

Another term that is fundamental within Craft workings, a pathworking is a technique derived from the Qabalistic Tree of Life. A visual excursion along one of the 22 paths, each of which incorporates a variety of tools as keys, including Tarot images, numbers and colours, specific landscapes and other symbolism.

Then we moved on to the most amazing subject I had ever studied – Magic! We learnt about the power of the Pentagram, the laws and basic rules of magic, the use of correspondences and building a ritual framework to perform magic. Other topics included: the Futhark runes, natural magic, the major arcana, Sephiroth colours and elements, oils and herbs, planetary correspondences and talismanic magic, healing, aromancy, magnetic healing, and herbal preparations.

On the final night of the course, Vivienne again spoke about Initiation, but in a very religious sort of way that made me think deeply about the way forward. She reviewed everything we had experienced and offered suggestions for making contact with other Crafters and alternatives for future study. Back in those days, it was bloody hard to find anyone in the Craft who was willing to talk to you – it was challenging to find anyone in the Craft, period. Nobody advertised his or her presence. You will hear the saying often, *'they find us; we don't go looking for them.'*

Then Thomas spoke, *"You have all done well. You have learnt your lessons and are now armed with the knowledge to make a choice. Do not ask us for Initiation; there is no room in our current Coven. You must find your way. I want you all to leave this place and none is to return for at least 40 days. If, at that time, you have questions, feel free to return for guidance. Till then, may you Blessed Be."* He abruptly left the room, leaving the Lady Vivienne to offer us all her heartfelt thanks and other words of encouragement.

WTF! Was that the hugest letdown and kick in the arse out the door, thank you, ma'am, bugger off, I don't want to see you for 40 days, or even ever! What just happened?

On the way out the door, the Lady Vivienne quietly stopped just Evelyn and me after the others had toddled off like dejected school kids, and with a slight smirk and a twinkle in her eye whispered, *"Call me next week."*

That little piece of theatrics was Thomas's way of attempting to kick off his supergroup, with very little subtlety involved!

On the way home, Evelyn was livid, *"That arrogant know-it-all. Who does he think he is – king of the bloody witches in Australia? He's no Alex Sanders, and what I know about Simon, he doesn't deserve to wipe his arse!"*

Whoa, slow down sweetheart. It's not the end of everything. Vivienne wants us to call her. There still might be something or a way forward. Let's just wait and see what she has to say.

About a week later, we met Vivienne in our now favourite yuppie coffee shop and who walked in behind her, the man-in-black, Lucifer himself, Satan with horns, the Prince of Darkness – his lordship, Thomas! Again, WTF was going on.

No, how are you? Nice to see you, an apology for being such a prick, straight to the point, *"I want you to start your own Coven. To act as High Priestess and High Priest, I want you to bring into your group all the members of the course. I want you to initiate yourselves, then initiate the others."*

Riiiight. Why? With a genuine smile on his face, Thomas said, *"You guys are the most outstanding group we have ever trained. You all have so much potential. You can stand on your own. You are professionals, and you two are alphas. You are leaders and you are going to create something special, and we're going to guide you."*

Well, beat me with a pineapple! Holy shit! Ummm. I am speechless!

Over the next hour, the Prince of Darkness explained how we should go about this project. You have all the course handouts (an arch-lever folder full) plus your notes. You have the Farrar's books and also Vivian Crowley's, Dion Fortune, Leland, Crowley, and Starhawk (see the reading list in the Annexe). You have everything you need to run a Coven.

Did you all take note of that? You, I'm talking to, you who's reading this story. There is a lesson to be learnt here. But what about Initiation I asked. He said. *"Use a dedication ritual for yourselves and the others. That is all you need for now. Start writing your rituals; create your Book of Shadows. Use the Sabbat outline in Eight Sabbats for Witches. Perform a monthly lunar ritual and get together to teach and learn from each other."*

And so the journey began.

It was not until years later that, as Second Degrees, Evelyn and I with the help of various other Elders in our tradition, expanded and further developed the standards that Simon had originally created. These were eventually adopted by all Covens in our immediate family lines. A system that allowed for pre-initiations like Paganings and Craftings that lead up to the real Initiation to the First Degree in the Alexandrian tradition or the First Rite of the Sussex Tradition.

I might add that what Thomas did to us, we have never done to any student. We have a system in place that allows students to continue their training after the formal course has been completed and eventually find their paths. Even if we cannot place a student with a working Coven, they always have the choice to ask for Initiation and become a solitary and still maintain that lineage with our tradition.

Footnote: Now is probably a good time to explain the Prince of Darkness thing. Everywhere Thomas went, he was dressed in black, always carrying his black leather briefcase and black cane. If he wasn't a Satanist, he should have been. You know that archetypal look of something evil. Evelyn gave him that name after our messy altercation and break-up. Sorry mate, but it suited you.

"He walks not in shadow but as shadow - crowned with silence, robed in mystery."

Chapter Six
The Supergroup

The next day, Evelyn and I invited Kevin, Nicolas, Stuart, Sharon, Tracey, and Aaron over to our home, which became our new Covenstead. It took us all night to review our course notes and other material. We eventually agreed that Evelyn and I would act as the Priestess and Priest of our new Coven. At that point, we did not see the need to give ourselves a name – apart from *'The Supergroup'* – just kidding.

The first thing we did was decide on some sort of Initiation or dedication. Evelyn and I had some ideas, and the others decided to leave us to our own devices so that they all could be surprised during their 'Initiations'. And so we wrote our dedication ritual, which was compiled using Simon's notes, which we believe he sourced during his research into British Pagan rites.

We were later given a copy of a dedication ritual our Progressive Wiccan friends in the UK used to introduce new students to the Craft during their training course, and this was very similar to the notes Simon had been using. Thomas gave us a little input, also, and so our *Circle Cross Ritual* was born.

There are no secrets or special visualisations in the following ritual, so please feel free to use it as your way of dedicating yourself to the Goddess and the Craft if you have no other way of joining an established group. This ritual is a traditional method of self-initiation, much better than those that can be found on the internet today.

Aaron was the first of our clan to step over the threshold. He was instructed to attend the

Covenstead the following Friday night and to bring a robe, a bottle of Claret, an apple, and an Athame. The wine formerly known as Claret can no longer be called that; it is now known as Cabernet Shiraz. The original Claret is a red Bordeaux, a specific style of red wine from the Bordeaux region of France. Just like the champagne style of wine can only be labelled Champagne if it originates from the Champagne region of France. Very confusing.

Just remember, if you are ever asked to bring a bottle of red to an Esbat, get a good bottle of Cabernet Shiraz unless you can find an original French Claret! And the reason for that? It's one of those special little secrets you find out from your Priestess the first time you attend a Coven Esbat. So I will not spoil the surprise.

Back on track, Aaron was told three days before the ritual that he was to have no stimulants (tea, coffee, chocolate, drugs, alcohol, etc.), he was to have no contact with other Crafters, no sex, and was banned from eating any protein for the last 24 hrs. The reason for these will become clear later when we talk about the meaning of ritual and initiations.

The following Friday, Evelyn and I prepared our lounge room for our first real Circle and 'initiation'. We had no proper tools back then, so we improvised. Fingers for Athames, a saucer for a Pentacle, kitty litter with a charcoal block sitting on it in a wooden bowl for the Thurible. A couple of candles around the room to set the mood, we were ready.

Another point that will become clear as we travel on this journey of discovery is that you do not need elaborate tools to conduct rituals or perform magic; in fact, you don't need tools at all if your mind is attuned and focused. However, more of that later.

At exactly 8.50 pm, Aaron knocked on the door. He was greeted by Evelyn and asked to change into his robe and wait in the kitchen in the darkness. His Athame (he had one before me!) was taken from him, together with a vintage bottle of Claret and a shiny red apple. Why Claret and an apple? There be a mystery! And don't forget the slice of cheese!

Are you getting pissed off already? All these little secrets and hints I have been dropping! Doesn't it just make you want to offer yourself to the Scourge? Relax, they are not all secrets for the Initiate alone; they are little surprises and Coven mysteries that, when revealed, make your passage a little more enjoyable. Just something else to look forward to in your voyage to the dark side. I really did not say that!

Evelyn returned, and we prepared the Circle. I then went to the kitchen where Aaron was seated and in my sternest, most authoritative voice said: *"This rite is voluntary, an offering of yourself to walk in the ways of the Craft, and to discover the path of myth. Do you wish to proceed?"* With a huge smile on his face, he said, *"Yes."*

I said, *"This Rite confers no authority or degree recognised by any other than the witnesses here tonight. It gives no status within any other system of witchcraft. Is this absolutely clear?"* His answer was *"Yes."*

I then said, *"Will you vow to remain silent about all hereafter experienced or seen, or heard by you within this rite to any outside those of this Circle?"*

Again, he answered *"Yes."*

I then asked Aaron to stand, and silently I secured his hands with Cords and slipped a blindfold around his head. Evelyn had secretly left the Circle and walked up silently behind Aaron and whispered in his ear, *"Wherever I lead you, you must follow. Wherever I stop, you stop. Whichever I turn, you turn. Only when you are asked anything by name, answer, else remain silent and listen."*

She then walked Aaron from the kitchen to the lounge room and stopped at the northeast boundary of the Circle, where he was told to wait. Evelyn and I then cast the Circle silently, but making enough noise so that Aaron would get some sort of idea that a Circle or some sort of sacred space was being created. The first clear words he heard were when I then invoked the Elementals.

Standing at the Eastern quarter, I said, *"For the East, all-wise eagle, great ruler of tempest storm and whirlwind, master of the heavenly vault, great prince of the powers of air, be present we pray thee and guard this Circle from all perils approaching from the East."*

I moved to the South and said, *"O thou lion, lord of lightning, master of the solar orb, great prince of the powers of fire, be present we pray thee and guard this Circle from all perils approaching from the South."*

To the West, I went and said, *"O thou serpent of old, ruler of the deeps, guardian of the bitter sea, prince of the powers of water, be present we pray thee and guard this Circle from all perils approaching from the West."*

And finally to the North, saying, *"Black bull of the North, horned one, dark ruler of mountains and all that lies beneath them, prince of the powers of earth, be present we pray thee and guard this Circle from all perils approaching from the North."*

Whenever I have invoked the North Watchtower, my whole being seems to change. I am an old-fashioned Taurus, and Earth is my realm. My voice always gets deeper and more forceful. The same applies when I vibrate BOREAS in the North; it is deep and hollow and seems to pulsate somehow. Evelyn always encourages me to say the line *'Beam on us of joyous Bacchus...'* when giving the toast. I have noticed the same with other Crafters, how they change when dealing with their inner elements.

Evelyn then cuts a doorway in the northeast. She then holds Aaron by his bound hands. Using Aaron's Athame, I press it over Aaron's heart and challenge him in an irate tone, *"Who is this whom thou hast brought, unclean and unknown, to the fellowship of this Circle, O Priestess?"*

Evelyn says, *"'Tis one who seeks the way of myth, the grove of pagan dreams. He has vowed to silence and a willingness to learn. I have brought him to be within our Circle."* I said, *"Do you know him to be worthy?"* She answered, *"He is, in so much as human frailty allows me to judge."* I said, *"Then let him be cleansed."*

Evelyn sprinkles Aaron with water, scented with lemonbalm. As she does so, she says, *"From darkness shall ye be reborn as light. With salt water from the womb of life, with essences grown to grant thee love, walk thee in the way of myth, to life and love and light."*

I then said, *"Enter thee this place that is not a place, a time that is no time, between the worlds to exist, to be born into the way."*

Aaron is then guided into the Circle by Evelyn, and the Circle is closed. Evelyn and I then guide him to the East, where I say, *"O thou wise eagle, lord of the Watchtower of the East, master of the heavenly vault, Aaron comes before you seeking the fellowship of this Circle."*

We then move to the South and say, *"O thou lion, lord of the Watchtower of the South, master of the solar orb, Aaron comes before you seeking the fellowship of this Circle."*

To the West, we go, and I say, *"O thou serpent of old, lord of the Watchtower of the West, guardian of the bitter sea, Aaron comes before you seeking the fellowship of this Circle."*

And finally, to the North, I say, *"O thou black bull, lord of the Watchtower of the North, dark ruler of mountains, Aaron comes before you seeking the fellowship of this Circle."*

Aaron is then made to kneel at the North, facing South. A Wand is placed in the East, the Sword in the South, the Chalice in the West, with the Pentacle on the Altar. Evelyn stood in front of Aaron, and I stood behind him. She invokes, *"Lovely Goddess of the bow, lovely Goddess of the arrows, thou who wakest in starry heavens, with the moon in thy forehead. Fair Goddess of the rainbow, of the stars and the moon. Think for an instant of Aaron, who awaits here."*

After the space of three heartbeats, she continued, *"Queen of night's enchantment, of moon and stars, of all fate and fortune, thou who art mistress of the ocean, sailing heaven high in thy crescent ship, sailing in reflection upon the waters, ruling life's tides. Grant this sleeper understanding."*

I then challenge Aaron once again with his Athame at his heart and say, *"Do thou, Aaron, freely, solemnly and for this mortal life, choose to walk the way of the Sun as is recorded by tradition, and to serve our Lady, the Great Mother?"* He answers, *"Yes."*

Evelyn rewarded him with a kiss. She has a great time kissing all the boys, and I have an equally fine time kissing all the girls – such is our Craft.

She stands back, holding a light between her and Aaron as I remove the blindfold and cords. She says, *"You can see me now. If you reach out, you can touch this form. Yet truly, I have always been here and always will be. Follow me."*

She puts the candle down and leads Aaron to the East, showing him the Wand. She says, *"This is the Staff of Air. Let its knowledge bring you light."*

She and Aaron move to the South. Evelyn picks up the Sword and says, *"This is the Sword of Fire. Wield energy with care, as it is two-edged. As is truth."*

She and Aaron move to the West. Evelyn picks up the Chalice and says, *"This is the Cup of Living Water. Its draught brings both forgetfulness and memory."*

She and Aaron move to the North. Evelyn picks up the Pentacle and says, *"This is the Stone of Destiny. Upon which my throne is based. Without it, you are baseless."*

Aaron turns and faces me. I point his Athame at his

heart once again and say, *"Aaron, do you vow to walk the way of myth, to draw the sword,* (pointing his Athame to the South) *from the stone*, (pointing his Athame to the North), *and with your last breath,* (pointing his Athame to the East) *cast it into the lake of memory,* (pointing his Athame to the West), *and so live the Circle Cross?"* He said, *"I do."*

Evelyn kisses his heart and lips, saying, *"With my lips, I seal thee within the fellowship of this Circle, a great mother's child, and brother."*

I then say, *"Take your Athame and present it to the Quarters."*

Aaron takes his Athame and presents it to each quarter, starting in the East, saying, *"Bless this knife and the intent by which I wield it - only in the Lord and Lady's service."* He does the same for the South, West and then North.

Evelyn then presents him with a White Cord and says, *"I welcome you to our Covenant."*

All three of us, relieved, we sit down for a feast, and a very good Claret if I remember.

Over the next two weeks, we initiated the rest of the group, and we started to write our Sabbat Wheel and Esbat rites. But first, we dedicated ourselves to the Goddess in a Coven Dedication ritual.

"… and so live the Circle Cross."

Chapter Seven
Coven Dedication

Now that we were 'initiates' of our own little tradition, we thought it appropriate to formalise our new identity and give birth to our new Coven. This is one of those ceremonies you might consider, even if you are self-initiating and dedicating yourself to a pagan way of life.

Evelyn and I cast a Circle with the group's support. Standing in the centre of the Circle, hands joined, Evelyn said, *"I invoke thee and call upon thee, Mighty Mother of us all. Bringer of all fruitfulness. By seed and root and stem and bud, by leaf and flower and fruit do I invoke thee to bless this rite and to admit us to the company of Thy Hidden Children."*

I said, *"Karnayna and Aradia, hear our call. We are simple pagans holding Thee in honour. Far have we journeyed and long have we searched seeking that which we desire above all things."*

Sharon said, *"Grant us that which we desire. Permit us to worship the Gods and all that the Gods represent."*

Aaron said, *"Ever will we protect you and that which is yours. Let none speak ill of you."*

Tracey then said, *"Forever will we defend you. You are our life, and we are yours from this day forth."*

Nicolas said, *"We give our sacred promise that we will abide by our chosen path and will seek to do the will of the Gods without hesitation."*

Kevin said, *"We shall keep silent all things entrusted to us by the Gods."*

Stuart said, *"We call upon the Guardians of the Watchtowers to witness this, our sacred promise."*

Everyone said: *"So mote it be."*

Evelyn then blessed a cup of wine and offered it to the Coven in turn with a kiss and two questions: *"What is it you seek of the Goddess?"* and *"What will you give in return?"* Each had their own special answer.

We were now officially legitimate, as legitimate as you can be without going through a proper Initiation. But for us at that time, it worked, and I guess looking back at the hard knocks we took, the frustrations and some setbacks, the politics that later came into play and the bitchcraft, we turned out alright in the end. I can look back today and not change a thing because the mistakes made us stronger and more focused.

Again, I recommend anyone reading this story who is not in a position to find a teacher or a training Coven, to find your own way and follow your instincts. Please feel free to use this material as an aid in finding your own path, but please, do not join an eGroup or an Internet Hogwarts or something just as crazy. Find real teachers and learn the Craft face-to-face.

Chapter Eight
The First Esbat

Now that we were a legitimate group, it was time we constructed our monthly Esbat or Full Moon rites. This was to be an important ritual. The one we would use every month. The one we would use for all magical workings, so it was important we got it right from the start.

We used the Circle casting learnt in our course and stuck together snippets from other course notes and handouts with some of the Farrar's works. It was some years later, to our surprise, that we found that the result of our efforts was very close to the Esbat ritual that Simon had been using in his Sussex rites. So, consequently, nothing much has changed from that day to this.

Our ritual occurred on the night of a full moon sometime way back in 1990. Everyone brought food and drink. We cleared the lounge room and covered most of the furniture with bedsheets – this helps us focus on the ritual and stops our eyes from wandering.

We placed large white candles in the East, South and West quarters. We used an old TV/video mobile unit for our Altar. It was a perfect size, about 60cm x 40cm x 90cm high. We covered it with a black cloth.

On the Altar, we had two candles, one for the North and the other as the 'One Light'. An image of the Goddess (which at the beginning of the ritual is covered with a small veil) and some fresh flowers are placed between the candles. We had a Pentacle, a bowl of water, a bowl of salt, a container to hold a charcoal block, some Three Kings incense, a small bell, a taper, and some anointing oil.

No Athames at that stage, so I used a Wand I fashioned from a local willow tree. We had not made our ritual robes at that time, except for Aaron, who already had a robe and Athame, so we changed into some fresh, clean casuals, no shoes or socks, of course! Later, we found an obliging tailor, some black cotton fabric, and a kaftan pattern from the local Spotlight store, and we all had matching robes.

The Three Kings incense is a combination of

frankincense, sandalwood, and benzoin, and the best is only available at your local Catholic Supply Store. This blend is the one we use for all Esbats and Initiations; various other blends are used for Sabbats. The Catholics do come in handy occasionally.

I'll discuss the Tools and how and why a Circle is set up a little bit later, but for now, it's important to remember you do not need proper tools to cast a Circle. The most important thing is your intent. Use a teacup and saucer, a kitchen knife, or anything at all to improvise. You will learn later that you do not need any Tools to cast a Circle, for the Circle is cast not on the physical but on the inner planes. The same can be said for Divination, casting the Runes and reading the Tarot; you do not need the cards or runes to divine, you just need yourself, your focus and your intent. The Tools simply aid that focus, but I digress; let us continue with how we did things in the old days.

I walked around the Circle widdershins (anti-clockwise), ringing a small bell to frighten away any lurking spirits. Evelyn then lit the Altar candle, saying, *"From fire above to fire below, from fire within to fire without, may Michael's spear from there to here make the magic fire appear."* The Altar candle is also known as the One Light is always placed on the right-hand edge of the Altar; the other, the North candle, is placed on the left-hand edge of the Altar. Michael is not the bloke next door, but the Archangel Michael (pronounced Mikha'el) and is the Guardian of the South and keeper of fire.

We all then pay homage to the image of the Goddess, and those of us who had them, presented our Athames to show our intention. We then anointed with anointing oil to take on our magical personalities.

When presenting an Athame, Boline, Sword or Wand, always use two hands with the point or end pointing to the East. Our anointing oil was made using a combination of essential oils and herbs that were special to our group. Anointing oil can be anything you like that suits your purpose. And how do you anoint? We have a very special way; suffice it to say it involves Pentagrams! Use whatever way is best for you.

Aaron, Kevin, Stuart, Tracey, Sharon, and Nicolas then left the Circle and stood near the northeast boundary.

Evelyn then traced the Circle boundary using her finger (later she would use our Coven Sword). Starting in the North and walking deosil, pointing her finger to the ground, she walks around the Circle finishing in the North. Again, I will explain the theory and practice of the intricacies of casting a Circle a little further in this story, but for now, let us follow the actions and take note of the dialogue.

The blessing of salt comes next. Standing at the Altar, I pour a small amount of rock salt onto the Pentacle (do not use table salt because it is not pure, unadulterated chunks of unprocessed rock salt are best).

Facing North, I raise the Pentacle and say, *"Blessings be upon this creature of salt. Let all malignancy and hindrance be cast forth hencefrom and let all good enter herein. Wherefore do I bless thee and consecrate thee in the names of Karnayna and Aradia."*

Everyone repeats, *"Karnayna and Aradia."* I replace the Pentacle on the Altar and stand aside to let Evelyn approach.

The exorcising of the water is next, for water contains contaminants and is not totally pure; therefore, those impurities have to be purged. Evelyn puts the tip of her finger (later she will use her Athame) into the bowl of water and says, *"I exorcize thee oh creature of water of all the impurities and uncleanliness of the spirit of the world of phantasm in the names of Karnayna and Aradia."*

All repeat, *"Karnayna and Aradia."*

She then pours the salt from the Pentacle into the bowl of water and stirs it with her finger, saying, *"But remember and ever mind, as water purifies the body, so the scourge purifies the soul. Wherefore do I bless thee that thou mayest aid me. In the names of Karnayna and Aradia."*

All repeat, *"Karnayna and Aradia."*

Next comes asperging the Circle and the boundary with the salt and water mixture. Evelyn sprinkles the salt water around the perimeter, together with everyone present, starting in the North and says three times, *"Earth and water thou art cast, let no evil purpose last. If not in accord with me, then as I will, so mote it be."*

The Circle is then sealed with incense. I approach the Altar and add incense to the Thurible. I elevate it, saying, *"The four winds are the breath which doth purify our sacred land. Be far from us, forces foul and thoughts of evil."* I then carry the smoking Thurible around the perimeter, stopping at each Watchtower to present it to that element.

Sealing the Circle boundary with fire is next, together with the lighting of the Watchtower candles. After returning to the Altar, I take a taper and light it from the Altar candle. I then carry it around the Circle boundary, lighting the Watchtower candles starting in the East. The last candle I light is the North candle (the left-hand one on the Altar).

Evelyn then traces the Circle boundary again using her finger (later she will use her Athame, not the Sword) and seals the Circle, cementing the four elements together.

She then conjures the Circle. Standing in the centre of the Circle, arms outstretched, she allows her etheric body to expand to the delineated boundary of the Circle. She turns around three times as she conjures the Circle, saying, *"I conjure thee, oh Circle, that thou beist a boundary between the world of men and the realms of the mighty ones. A guardian and a protection that shall preserve and contain the power, which we will raise within thee. Wherefore do I bless and consecrate thee in the names of Karnayna and Aradia."*

All repeat: *"Karnayna and Aradia."*

Evelyn then cuts a doorway in the northeast and brings in the boys one at a time with a twirl and a kiss. I then bring in the girls in the same manner. Always, female, male.

I then stand together with Evelyn in front of the Altar and say, *"The place of this ritual is now consecrated to the honour of the Old Ones. This is a time that is not a time, in a place that is not a place, on a day that is not a day, between the worlds and beyond."*

Evelyn says, *"Let this world stand apart from time, for we now dance with the Old Ones."*

We all join hands (alternating the best we can, man then woman – it's important to try and keep the balance) and dance the Witches Rune, moving deosil, *"Darksome night and shining moon, East, then South, then West, then North, hearken to the Witches Rune, here I come to call ye forth! Earth and Water, Air and Fire, Wand and Pentacle and Sword, work ye unto my desire, hearken ye unto my word! Cord and Censer, Scourge and Knife, powers of the witch's blade. Waken all ye unto life, come ye as the charm is made! Queen of Heaven, Queen of Hell, Horned Hunter of the night - lend your power unto the spell and work my will by magic rite! By all the power of Land and Sea. By all the might of Moon and Sun, as I do will, so mote it be. Chant the spell and be it done! Eko Eko Azarak, Eko Eko Zomalak, Eko Eko Karnayna, Eko Eko Aradia."*

We dance and spin faster and faster, repeating the last few lines over and over again: *"Eko Eko …."* It felt like forever until Evelyn decided it was time, and then she orders, *"Down."* We all drop to the floor, dizzy and exhausted! That is one good way to raise energy within a Circle, and warm the place up on a cold winter's night!

It was then time to invoke the Lords of the Watchtowers. Starting in the East, I draw an invoking earth pentagram using my finger and say, *"Ye Lords of the Watchtower of the East, I do summon, stir and call Thee forth to witness these rites and to guard the Circle."* I then vibrate the elemental name, *"EURUS."*

We all turn to the South, and again I draw an invoking earth pentagram and say, *"Ye Lords of the Watchtower of the South, I do summon, stir and call thee forth to witness these rites and to guard the Circle."* I then vibrate the elemental name, *"NOTAS."*

We all turn to the West, and again I draw an invoking earth pentagram and say, *"Ye Lords of the Watchtower of the West, I do summon, stir and call thee forth to witness these rites and to guard the Circle."* I then vibrate the elemental name, *"ZEPHYRUS."*

Finally, we all turn to the North and again I draw an invoking earth pentagram and say, *"Ye Lords of the Watchtower of the North, I do summon, stir and call thee forth to witness these rites and to guard the Circle."* I then vibrate the elemental name, *"BOREAS."*

The Circle is now complete, and we are secured in our sacred space.

As this is an Esbat, it is time to perform the Drawing Down of the Moon. Evelyn stands at the Altar facing South in the God position. I kneel in front and give her the Fivefold Kiss, saying, *"Blessed be thy feet that have brought thee in these ways. Blessed be thy knees that shall kneel at the sacred Altar. Blessed be thy womb, without which we would not be. Blessed be thy breasts formed in beauty. Blessed be thy lips that shall utter the Sacred Names."* I kiss each foot, both knees, her womb, both breasts and her lips.

(The Fivefold Kiss? Eight kisses! Another mystery! Not really, wait till the end of this chapter and I'll explain.)

I then take the Wand from the Altar, kneel, and

with it, point and lightly touch Evelyn on her right breast, left breast and womb; the same three points again and finally the right breast. Why? To show respect to the Goddess she will become when the Moon is drawn down.

I remain kneeling as Evelyn turns and faces North with her back to the Coven. The rest of the Coven also kneel, and I reach out and call, *"We call to thee Lady, the Lady of Night. The Lady of power, the Lady of might. Who sails the heavens in silvery barque, Lady who guides us in sacred dark. Lady of laughter and Lady of tears. Lady on high, much older than years. We, your people, stand here and call. Come down to us Lady, Your children all."*

The Coven then reach out and call, *"Lady of Moonlight, Lady of Night. Come at our call, and send us your might."*

I then say, *"We call to Thee Lady, the Lady of Night. The Lady of Magic, the Lady of Sight. Who knowest the secrets, and in Esbat time. Reveals as of old, in mystic rhyme. The way of all working, the bending of mind. The Lady of freedom, with Power to bind. We your people stand here and call. Come down to us Lady, your children all."*

The Coven say, *"Lady of beauty, Lady above. Come at our call and give us your love."*

I say, *"We call to Thee Lady of Death and of Birth. Daughter of Sun and daughter of Earth. Ruling the lives of woman and man. We call to Thee Lady as only we can. From the sky, we draw Thee your children who know, the ways of all magic, how green things grow. How animals breed and why all things must die. We know your secrets, the how and the why. We your people stand here and call. Come down to us Lady your children all."*

The Coven say, *"Lady of silver in Esbat hour. Come at our call and give us your power."*

Evelyn then removes the veil from the figure of the Lady and turns to face the Coven in Full Moon position and replies, *"As you, My children, gather below, and round about the Altar go. I know your wishes and answer your call; I know that you calling are witches all. Meet me in forests, meet on a hill, or meet Me in moonlight and dance as ye will. Dance round my Altar, or round the oak tree, dance all ye naked, to show ye are free. Dance by the seashore, or dance round the stone, keep ye My Secrets, and dance ye alone. Tell naught to others these Rites of Mine, for what I tell you are Mysteries Divine."*

She then changes her stance into a Pentagram position, arms outstretched and says, *"Call to me shining when days gone to rest, for you, my children, with power I've blessed. I'll teach you of morthwork and I'll teach it with love. You see that I answer, I come from above."*

She reaches forward and says, *"I come to My Children in Witching Hour, and with My coming, I bring ye power. Now do I come to witches all, I come to my children and answer your call."*

I then give The Lady the Fivefold Kiss.

The Coven then file past the Lady and bow before Her. She raises each in turn, kisses them on the left cheek, and asks if there be any boons that She will grant or deny as appropriate.

You will notice I now refer to Evelyn as The Lady, for she is no longer mortal; she takes on the persona of the Goddess and speaks as the Goddess.

The Lady then delivers the Charge. The Coven kneel and I say, *"Listen to the words of the great Mother, who was of old also called among men Artemis, Astarte, Dione, Melusine, Aphrodite, Cerridwen, Dana, Arianrhod, Bride, and by many other names."* The Lady continues with Her message to Her hidden children. The full Charge can be found later in this story under the chapter dealing with the Goddess.

From this point forward, it is usual for The Lady to ask what work there is to be done. For now, is the time to perform magic or other Coven work like healing or performing a guided visualisation of other teachings.

But for now, our first Esbat is complete. To celebrate, we do 'cakes and wine'. I say, *"All is ready save the wine."* Evelyn says, *"Let the wine also be blessed."* I kneel and hold up the chalice of wine and offer it to Evelyn. She places the point of her finger in the wine and says, *"As the Athame is male."* I say, *"So the cup is female."* She says, *"Conjoined they bring blessedness."* I say, *"And become one in truth."*

Evelyn takes the cup and drinks, and then gives it to me with a kiss. I drink and hand it back with a kiss. She then takes the cup to each Covenor with a kiss.

We all sat around the Circle, eating, drinking, and discussing our work. This night was to be one of many more over the next few years, and our Circle casting was to become better and different as time went by.

Just an afterthought, usually during Sabbats or other rituals, we eat Sabbat Cakes and the HP is usually the one who blesses them, after the wine has been blessed. The blessing goes like this: *"O Queen most secret, bless this food unto our bodies. Bestowing health, wealth, strength, joy and peace and that fulfilment of love that is perpetual happiness."*

During Full Moon Rituals, instead of Sabbat Cakes, we eat slices of apple with a slice of cheese on top (we prefer the crumbly, tasty, tangy type). It is then eaten in one mouthful. The taste is quite different, and for future reference, it becomes another one of those triggers in your brain that always makes you relate to an Esbat.

When we had finished, it was time to banish. But before we did, the Lady stood and decreed, *"You, my children, take heed and bear my words. You have trained in the ways of the Craft; therefore shall you honour the Great Goddess Aradia and Her Consort Karnayna. You shall follow the Traditional Path, the ways of Old and heed the Laws well. You are Children of the Gods, your life is for the enjoyment and understanding of love and beauty through the Goddess, and you shall strive towards the development of mind and body, in balance and harmony, to better serve the Gods. You shall invoke the Gods of Old and shall follow the cycle of nature and celebrate the seasons. You shall meet at Esbats and remember the Goddess. You shall rekindle thoughts lost in time, that era of mystery. You shall practice magic, the magic of healing, of love and the magic to help your brothers and sisters of the Art. You shall walk in the halls of the Gods and learn from Their teachings. You shall drink from the Cauldron of*

Cerridwen and work in harmony and love, teaching and learning from one another for the benefit of all. Take heed my words when I say remember always; I am thy Mother and thy Queen, and thy Guide. On those that love Me I will shower with Blessings, and curse those that oppress My Children, and those that do Evil in My Name."

We then started the banishing; starting in the West, I drew a banishing earth pentagram in the Air and said, *"Ye Lords of the Watchtower of the West. I do thank Thee for attending these rites and ere Ye depart for thy lovely realms, I say Hail and farewell."* All said, *"Hail and farewell."*

I extinguished the Watchtower candle. We did the same at each of the remaining Watchtowers moving in a widdershins direction.

Our Lady then returned to the Altar, turns, faces the Coven, and says, *"Earth Children, let My cloak enfold and warm thee against the cold hearts of the Other Places wherein ye hide in darkness. Let My light ever shine over the Path ye see with faery sight. Return now in time, and may ye Blessed Be."* She extinguishes the Altar candle and replaces the veil on the Lady.

We all join hands and sing, *"We've danced and sung our sacred way, between the worlds twixt night and day, hand to hand and heart to heart, merry we've met now merry we part."*

And with that final word, the lights come on and we return to the mortal, mundane world.

Notes on the Fivefold Kiss:

The Fivefold Kiss is a sacred blessing ritual, often performed during Initiations, Sabbats and Esbats. It is deeply symbolic, honouring the Priest/Priestess as a vessel of the divine and aligning them with the elemental and spiritual forces represented by the pentagram.

The ritual consists of five kisses, each accompanied by a spoken blessing. These are traditionally given by a Priest to a Priestess (or vice versa).

The five points and their associated blessings are:

The Feet - *"Blessed be thy feet, that have brought thee in these ways."*

The Knees - *"Blessed be thy knees, that shall kneel at the sacred altar."*

The Womb or Phallus - *"Blessed be thy [womb/phallus], without which we would not be."*

The Breasts or Chest - *"Blessed be thy breasts/chest, formed in beauty/strength."*

The Lips - *"Blessed be thy lips, that shall utter the Sacred Names."*

Each kiss is placed on the corresponding body part, symbolising reverence, humility, and the Priest/Priestess' connection to nature, spirit, and the divine. It's a beautiful example of how Wicca blends ritual, reverence, and personal empowerment.

The term "Fivefold Kiss" refers not to the literal number of kisses, but to the five sacred body parts being blessed. These correspond to the five points of the Pentagram, representing the elements of Earth, Air, Fire, Water, and Spirit. It's a poetic naming convention, much like how a 'threefold law' isn't about counting but a karmic principle.

Chapter Nine
Our Sacred Space

We now know how to cast a Circle, but let us look closely at the how and the why.

Firstly, a Circle is not a circle, it is a sphere! How can you create a secure space by just drawing a circle on the ground? Things can get in and out above and below the circle.

The Circle is three-dimensional; it is a protective barrier for two reasons: to keep energy in, or to keep what you may have conjured out!

Conjuring something outside a Circle is not usually something that Wiccans do; it usually falls within the realms of the Ceremonial Magician, but having said that, most Alexandrians tend to inject a little Ceremonial Magic into their workings more than a Gardnerian does. For the time being, let us just focus on keeping things inside our Circle.

So, a Wiccan Circle protects us from forces outside our sacred space from getting in and disturbing our working. It also allows us to focus and raise energy within the confines of our sacred space, and that is our prime goal.

When we raise energy, we call it *'Raising a Cone of Power'*. That energy must be finely focused and then released. However, before it is released, it must be created, intensified, and directed. All that must be done in a confined space, the Magic Circle.

The most important thing to remember is, you are not actually creating a Magic Circle on the ground. The Circle you physically create is created on the inner planes, the Astral. The one you physically create is a representation; that is why it is so important to visualise and focus your intent.

As I said before, you do not need Tools to create a Circle; you only need your intent or your will. Everything you do on the physical plane is mirrored on the Astral, and that is where the real magic is undertaken.

So, let us work on the physical aspects of creating the Circle, remembering that the action you perform is happening on the Astral.

Firstly, decide why you want to create a sacred space. Do not create a sacred space, wasting energy for the hell of it. Something as simple as a personal meditation is enough, but if you are going to perform a Coven ritual, you need to plan it beforehand. You need to select an area big enough to perform your ritual and in a place appropriate.

Once you have selected the location, it needs to be prepared. I mentioned before that at our first Esbat, we covered the furniture with bed sheets; that was to help us focus so that we were not distracted by paintings, lamps, colours and shapes. So, unless you have a dedicated Temple you use only for ritual, it is best to prepare the room by removing anything likely to distract.

If you are working outside, it is just as important to select the area that is appropriate for the ritual. A public park, on the top of a hill, next to a river, are all places that would be suitable for ritual. Whatever the place, you mustn't be disturbed.

As time goes by, if you use the same spot outside, it becomes charged, and you will find it becomes very special the more you use it, just like places like Stonehenge and other magical sites. We had a special spot in the mountains outside Canberra, just next to a fresh spring. The local wombat loved it and used to shit on the altar stone in between our visits. Every time we came back, there was a little present for us left by our favourite friend. Maybe there is a deep and meaningful explanation behind this story, or just the fact that it was a nice place to have a shit!

It was certainly a special place to conduct our Sabbats, away from prying eyes, in the middle of a forest with a gentle freshwater stream flowing past. No commercial noise from industry or motor vehicles, no people, a back-to-nature feeling, even primordial. I wonder sometimes if that place still holds its charge. I would be surprised if it had not been for the amount of energy we raised in our fabricated stone circle.

The size of the Circle is important. If you are just casting a Circle for yourself, a five or six-foot Circle in the middle of the lounge room is good. For a Coven of a dozen people, maybe a twelve-foot Circle in the backyard. An open public ritual would need something big enough to hold all the people expected to attend. For Coven or solitary work, the Circle must not be bigger than you can cast and maintain.

Once the area has been prepared, the next step is to set up your Altar and place your Tools in the appropriate positions, together with quarter candles and any other items you need to create or use in your sacred space.

Later in this story, I will discuss the Tools in detail, together with how they are arranged on the Altar. Depending on the type of ritual you are conducting will depend on what Tools you need and where they are specifically placed on the Altar. This may be different each time, depending on the position you place your Altar within the Circle.

Once the area has been laid out, the area needs to be cleaned. We do this in a number of ways, depending on the circumstances. Sometimes we use a broom, and other times a bell or even a horn. Whatever you use, you must walk around the area in an anti-clockwise (widdershins) direction, sweeping the ground clean, ringing the bell or blowing the horn.

This act starts the chain of events that will create your sacred space. It frightens away any lurking spirits or any nasties that might want to disrupt your ritual, at the same time sending out a message to the Gods or other friendly beings that something is about to begin.

Fact be known, this process starts the minute you take your ritual bath or shower and dress in your ritual clothes. This is when your intent begins, and another reason we talk about Circle etiquette is that you should stop all thoughts of the mundane world when preparing for ritual; no chitchat, smoking, drinking or anything that will distract your focus on what is going to happen.

Keep in mind that during this whole process, the stronger your visualisations are, the better your Circle will be. Your intention is everything. So focus, focus, focus.

Now that you have completed your preparations, it is time to start the ritual; it is time for your first circumambulation, to trace the Circle boundary either using your finger, an Athame or a Sword. Contrary to popular belief, Wands are not used to cast Circles. They are used to invoke, not create.

This process requires you to visualise an energy as a white light, flowing from your body through the Sword and touching the ground. Think of it like digging a moat, which you will fill in with water in a little while.

When Evelyn and I cast a Circle, she uses the Sword, and I stand behind her, focusing my energy on hers, thereby doubling the white light or energy that creates the moat. I place my hands, palms forward, fingers facing upwards towards the centre of her back and focus the energy through my hands into the back of her body.

If you have an Altar that is usually set in the North, the Altar is placed directly and evenly over the imagined Circle boundary. The Altar is both in and outside of the Circle.

The first circumambulation starts at the right-hand or eastern edge of the Altar, working your way steadily around the Circle boundary in a deosil direction and finishing at the left-hand edge of the Altar.

As with all the Tools or implements you use to cast your Circle, you must first present each to the Gods before using, and again after its use. Therefore, with the Sword, which is usually sitting on the front of the Altar, the point facing East, you pick it up in both hands and raise it to the North, showing your intent to use it. Then, holding it in the left hand with the right a little way down the blade, balancing the Sword, start to move deosil.

Never use a Sword in one hand, always two, always. Never show your ignorance and lack of balance in anything you do before the Gods; otherwise, be prepared for their wrath.

Now is the time to create the amalgam that will fill

the moat with earth and water. This is created by blessing salt and exorcising water. The Priest usually blesses the salt; it need not be exorcised because it is already pure. The Priestess usually exorcises the water and blesses it. These two acts are done at the Altar, remembering to once again show your intent by presenting the salt and the bowl of water to the North and the Gods.

The next step is to join both elements by pouring the salt into the bowl of water and mixing. The mixture is then taken around the Circle, again starting at the right corner of the Altar. The Priestess visualises the moat being filled with the amalgam as she sprinkles water around the boundary with her fingers. When she finishes at the left-hand edge of the Altar, she turns and flicks water on anyone who may be inside the Circle, a kind of blessing if you like. Pax vobiscum!

Next, the Priest builds a wall around the Circle. This is done by taking the smoking Thurible around, again in the same manner, but this time stopping at each quarter and presenting it to the element of that quarter. The Priest visualises the rising incense smoke creating a wall.

The kind of incense is important, for it is usually the first stimulus that starts your brain getting into gear. Different incenses are used for different Circles or rituals. We use Three Kings for all Esbats and First Degree Initiations. At every Esbat after your Initiation, you are taken back to your birth by that simple smell.

Once the wall has been built, it is time to activate the final element, fire. The Priest takes a fresh candle or taper, presents it and lights it from the Altar candle (the one on the right). He then walks deosil holding the candle out from his body over the Circle boundary, visualising fire filling in the moat and streaming up the wall. He stops at each quarter and presents the candle, lights the Quarter Candle, and then continues his journey around the Circle.

At the Altar, he presents the candle, lights the North Candle, and then snuffs out the taper using his thumb and index finger; never extinguish a candle by blowing it out! That is our tradition, and I cannot give you a definitive reason why. It is just another one of those things that have developed over time, and I guess the reason has been lost. Some say it is supposed to be an insult to the candle to blow it out, others are taught that you must not use Air to put out Fire, as it insults Fire, and yet others say you blow away all the positive energies of the rituals. I suppose at the end of the day, whether to blow out, pinch out, or use a candle snuffer is a matter of personal choice, but for now, I snuff with my thumb and forefinger! You can always tell a snuffer from a blower – all the little spots of candle wax stuck to their robes!

The Circle now needs to be sealed. The Priestess, using her Athame (never the Sword for this part of the Circle creation), traces the Circle boundary, visualising the four elements combining to make a solid boundary. Again, if Evelyn is casting, I will stand behind her, focusing my energies just as before on hers.

The physical work is now complete. The Circle has been cast using the four elements. It is now time to add the fifth! The Priestess will stand in the centre of the Circle. She will visualise her etheric body expanding to fill the whole Circle. She will turn three times around whilst speaking the conjuring invocation. This is the most important and final aspect of creating the Circle on the inner plains.

The Priest usually stands aside or kneels in the South out of her way as she conjures. It is a good idea to stay away from her reach as she is still holding her Athame – you do not need to draw blood during this part of the ritual!

The Magic Circle is now complete, save two very important things: the raising of energy and the calling of the Elements or Watchtowers.

To seek assistance in any magical work, the Elements must be called, not on the physical, but on the Astral. To do so, we need to increase our energy level to invoke the Elements. We do this by dancing the Witches Rune or any similar method of dance and song. This increases the heart rate and the temperature in the Circle, and believe me, if done correctly, the temperature skyrockets, great on a winter's night!

Once the Circle, and everyone in it, is charged, the Watchtowers are invoked. This can be done in a number of ways, using a variety of Entities or Gods or Elements. It matters not, the intent is to call that guardian and ask it to guard that particular portal or direction; to help contain the energy within the Circle and to stop any malevolent force from disrupting the proceedings or entering the Circle. Remember, this is not happening on the physical plane; it all happens on the Astral, where all magic is created.

The Watchtower is invoked by using your Athame and making an invoking Earth pentagram in the air at each quarter, starting in the East. Remembering to 'seal' the pentagram by finishing with a sixth stroke at the same time, invoking that particular element. See my chapter further in this story on Pentagrams and Watchtowers – it explains the details of sealing a pentagram.

Once the pentagram and invocation are complete, you must then visualise the element being forced to come to the edge of the Circle. This is best done by imagining the pentagram being drawn at infinity or on the horizon and physically using your Athame to pull it towards you and the edge of the Circle, seeing it get bigger and bigger as it approaches the Circle edge.

Each quarter is done, finishing at the North. Now the Circle is cast, on both the physical and the Astral.

A couple of things to keep in mind. If someone needs to leave or enter the Circle once it has been created, the one who cast the Circle can create a door, usually in the northeast quarter. This is done by using an Athame and creating three lines to outline a doorway, starting on the floor on the left edge, tracing it upwards, across to the right and down to the floor. The person, if going out, does so quickly and the doorway is closed by invoking an Earth Pentagram over the doorway.

If a person or persons are entering, as is usually the case when there are too many people to cast a Circle with everyone in at the same time, a major Sabbat, for example. The doorway is cut in the same manner, and each person is invited into the Circle by a person of the opposite sex with a kiss and a twirl, always deosil. The doorway is again closed as before.

The other special thing about a Circle is the fact that the Man-in-Black can come and go as he pleases. He does not need a doorway because he always stands between the worlds! There is one Sabbat that he stands across the Circle during the ritual to protect all within and without!

So, there you go, you now know what to say, and what to do to create your own sacred space. The theory behind the creation of a Circle does not change irrespective of where you are on the planet. Some think that because they are in the northern hemisphere, things have to be done differently from those in the South. Some change the system upside down and back to front because they think it is based on the direction of the Sun – absolute and utter rubbish! The Sun has nothing whatsoever to do with the casting of a Circle. The inner planes do not have a North and South; for that matter, I do not believe the place has a Sun, it just is!

End of rant!

'Raising a Cone of Power'

Chapter Ten
The Wheel of the Year

We learnt in our course that the Wheel of the Year is a continuing cycle of life, death, and rebirth. Thus, the Wheel reflects both the natural passage of life in the world around us, as well as revealing our connection with the greater world.

To a Wiccan, all of creation is divine, and by realising how we are connected to the turning of the seasons and the natural world, we come to a deeper understanding of how we are connected to the God and Goddess. Therefore, when we celebrate our seasonal rites, we draw the symbolism that we use from the natural world and our own lives, thus attempting to unite the essential identity that underlies all things.

The Wiccan Wheel has two great inspirations; it is both a wheel of celebration and a wheel of initiation. As a wheel of initiation, it hopes to guide those who tread its pathway towards an understanding of the mysteries of life and the universe expressed through the teachings of the Old Ones and made manifest in the turning of the seasons.

For a Wiccan, the Gods and nature are one; humanity is a part of nature, thus humanity and the Gods are one. In exploring the mysteries of the seasons, we are seeking to penetrate more deeply the mysteries of the God and Goddess.

As a wheel of celebration, Wiccans accord to the words of the Charge of the Goddess, where She says, *"Let my worship be within the heart that rejoiceth, for behold, all acts of love and pleasure are my rituals"*; and that, *"Ye shall dance, sing, feast, make music and love, all in my praise."* And so we put together our own interpretation of the Wiccan Sabbat Round and made each Sabbat a time for us to come together and make the festivals a time of joyful merrymaking.

We celebrate eight festivals, roughly six to seven weeks apart, which are pivotal points in the solar cycle. Four of the festivals are called the Lesser Sabbats: these are the Spring and Autumn Equinoxes and the Winter and Summer Solstices.

The other four festivals are called the Greater Sabbats and relate to particular seasons when, in bygone days, certain activities would have been undertaken (and still are if you work or live on the land), usually followed by a party of some kind, such as during the harvest or planting time of the year. There are variations upon the names by which these Greater Sabbats are known, but we refer to them as Imbolg, Beltane, Lammas, and Samhain.

To put a slightly different viewpoint on the traditional Wiccan Sabbat round, here is an explanation from a Sussex perspective.

The Old Ones are the Earth Mother and the Sky Father. From the sky comes the power to make fecund, and from Mother Earth comes all life - the plants which give food to all, and the water without which all would die is given by the Sky Father and nursed by the Earth Mother.

As all life comes from the female, the Earth must be female; and as the Source of Life, the Earth must be the Mother.

Her moods alter as Her Husband, the Sky Father, moves across Her. We see in the changing of Her moods the four-fold state of Magic - Her moods of Fire (summer), of Water (autumn), of Earth (winter) and Air (spring), and we try to understand our own changing life patterns in the Lesser Sabbats of the Changes - the Solstices and the Equinoxes.

The life of The Mother in change is one of the Greater Mysteries. From Her, in Spring, is born the Lord, the Sun. With His awakening to manhood at Beltane, the Lord courts our Mother Earth, wedding Her at Midsummer, and our people celebrate the marriage feast.

The honeymoon ends with the consummation of the marriage at Lammas. Our Lady takes from Him His Power, and discards Him, for She is ever Queen. She stands by as He is laid to rest in the earth at Michaelmas, and follows Him in sorrow into the Underworld. Her tresses of leaves falling down upon Her heaving bosom, and Her grassy cloak pales in mourning.

Withdrawing from the world, a Widow, She waits until we, Her people return to Her the Spirit of Her lover, consumed by us in the Eaten Flesh.

Life stirs in Her Womb, potent and pregnant on our surrender at Yule. Her breasts fill at Oimelc as She enters labour, and all animals join Her in preparation to feed the coming God.

Her travel ends with the breaking forth from the Womb, and to show Her joy, She dons once again Her cloak of Nature.

We laugh and cry with Her in Her Ecstasy, the Spring Festival being merely the outward show of our hearts. And the Great Cycle goes on . . . This is the great Wheel of the Year.

Chapter Eleven
Our Sabbats

The following ritual outlines became our annual festivals we performed between 1990 and 1993. Evelyn and I assumed the roles of High Priestess and High Priest for the first two years; by then, our group had grown, and we had another male and two females. We were now a Coven of eleven and growing with a few neophytes waiting in the wings.

Eleven was a good number; it allowed us to partner up, male to female, and our energies were balanced. But what of the eleventh, you ask? The Man-in-Black, always standing between the worlds!

Over the years, we stepped back and allowed others to work as a High Priest or High Priestess, each organising the Coven and acting their roles. It gave us a break, but also allowed others to hone their management skills and develop their magical abilities, taking on the persona of the God and Goddess when required.

So, this first round we put together ended up being a pretty solid system of celebrating our Wiccan ways. Looking back, we were lucky enough to have been given most of the right material during the course and with a little more research, thanks to the Farrars, we had a system that worked. In addition, I might add, that this same Sabbat round can be worked today with absolutely no changes; so please, by all means, give it a go if you wish.

Remember also that the more you perform a particular ritual, over and over again, the more power is embedded in the ritual and the more magical it becomes. Especially performed in the same place at the same time in exactly the same conditions. That is how a place can be magically charged and how a simple celebration becomes a magical link to the Gods. We have been using the same invocations for over thirty years and find no reason to change them, now, or ever, for that matter, because they work!

Winter Solstice: Let us start with Yule, the winter solstice that is celebrated on 22 June. This festival celebrates the Conception – the God of the Underworld enters the Goddess, and the Virgin becomes a Maid. Yule marks the rebirth of the sun after the longest night and initiates a period of leisure, solitude, and making plans. It is a time for socialising and celebration. Rituals focus on birth and rebirth; fires may be lit during a working which began in relative gloom, and gifts are exchanged – our Christmas!

Since becoming part of the Craft, we dispensed with celebrating Christmas in December. We stopped giving presents and sending out cards, except for my mum. She has never forgiven me for defecting, so I always wished her a Merry Christmas with a card and a pressie.

Some of our non-Craft friends felt sorry for us and thought it very sad, but when we explained our Christmas was in June and we had a monster celebration, they thought differently and asked if they could come along. We throw some great parties, all in the name of the Old Ones! None Greater! There be another little mystery.

Remember, as we cover the eight festivals, that we are overlaying the cycle of the Goddess and God over the natural cycles of the earth, the four seasons. These celebrations are a fabulous way to meld the two cycles into a lifestyle and become closer to our Gods. Wicca is a living religion, and the Sabbats connect everything together.

Getting back to the Winter Solstice. The land remains fallow at this time of year, awaiting the planting of grain crops. It is a time of ploughing and fertilising the soil. It is the shortest day and the longest night. Heavy rains fall; fruit trees are pruned; the sap starts to flow in plants, they start to come back to life, the buds start to swell; some root and winter crops are harvested late in the season, and our sheep, cattle, and goats are pregnant.

In organising our Circle, the Cauldron of Cerridwen (symbol of immortality) is placed towards the South of the Circle, wreathed with holly, ivy, and mistletoe, and with a lit candle in it. There is no other light except the Altar candle and those about the Circle, which should be red and green. The High Priestess wears a gold cord. All others wear their usual cords. The Circle is cast as usual.

From this point forward, I will refer to the High Priestess as the HPS and the High Priest as the HP. We will also assume we all now have our robes, Athames, and a full set of working Tools.

The HP stands behind the Cauldron facing North, the Coven form a ring facing inwards, alternating men and women. The HPS stands in the North, facing the HP.

The HP holds a handful of unlit candles and the Book of Shadows. One of the Coven stands beside him with a lighted candle so that he can read. (I think this is where my BOS got burnt – but more about that later).

The HP says, *"Tonight we celebrate the festival of Yule. During this season, the soil is ploughed and* fertilised. The land remains fallow, awaiting the planting of grain crops. It is the shortest day and the longest night. Heavy rains usually fall, and fruit trees are pruned.

"As the season progresses, the sap starts to flow in plants, they start to come back to life, and the buds start to swell. Some root and winter crops are harvested late in the season. Livestock are pregnant.

"This celebration marks the God in the Underworld entering the Goddess. The Virgin becomes a Maid. Yule marks the rebirth of the Sun after the longest night and initiates a period of leisure, solitude and making plans. It is a time for socialising and celebration."

The HPS says, "Before rebirth, there must be death. This is the cycle of nature. Plants die off during winter to flower again in spring, and many animals hibernate. It is now midwinter, and the sun is at its weakest; it is the time of great darkness. But through this time, the Goddess as Mother Nature protects the seeds of life so that all can flourish again in the New Year."

The Coven starts to move slowly deosil around the Circle, as each one passes the HP, he lights a candle from the fire in the Cauldron and hands it to the Coven member.

The HP then reads the incantation, "Queen of the moon, Queen of the sun, Queen of the heavens, Queen of the stars, Queen of the waters, Queen of the earth, bring us the Child of Promise! It is the Great Mother who giveth birth to Him. It is the Lord of Life who is born again. Darkness and tears are set aside when the Sun shall come up early.

"Golden Sun of the mountains, illuminate the land, light up the world, illuminate the seas and the rivers; sorrows be laid - joy to the world! Blessed be the Great Goddess, without beginning, without end, everlasting to eternity. Io Evo! He! Blessed be! Io Evo! He! Blessed be! Io Evo! He! Blessed be!"

During the incantation, the Coven Circle slowly. They join in the chant of 'Io Evo! He! Blessed be!' and finally, the HPS joins the dance, leading it with a quieter rhythm.

The Cauldron is pushed into the centre of the Circle, and the dancers jump over it in couples. The last couple over before the fire goes out should be well purified, three times each, and may pay an amusing forfeit as the HPS may ordain.

For the non-initiated, place your interpretation on the preceding, and please have fun purifying each other and playing whatever games you deem appropriate.

The Great Rite is performed in token, then Cakes and Wine. When the food is served, we give the following toast: *"Hail to the returning Sun. We drink to the Old Gods, to the Holly and the Oak and the Lady. A merry Yule to all."*

Now might be a good time to explain what the Great Rite is and what 'in token' means.

The Great Rite is one of the most revered rituals in Wicca, symbolising the union of the Goddess and God, the feminine and masculine aspects of divinity. It is not merely physical intimacy, but a sacred act that embodies cosmic principles of creation, polarity, and divine union. It is often performed during fertility festivals like Beltane, when the energies of growth, passion, and life are at their peak. Think about the Maypole!

There are two forms of the Great Rite. The actual and the 'in token' form. Nowadays, the actual form is rare and typically reserved for private rituals between consenting adults, usually the High Priest and High Priestess or the couple performing the ritual. It is also used by Initiates or practitioners who are deeply experienced and spiritually bonded.

The act is seen as a sacrament, not casual sex. It is performed with reverence, intention, and spiritual alignment. In this form, the couple channels the divine energies of the God and Goddess, becoming vessels for their union. The goal is not personal gratification, but spiritual communion, transformation, and the raising of magical energy.

In Token, it is the symbolic form of the ritual. This is the most common and widely practised version, where the HP and HPS enact the rite using an Athame (representing the masculine) and a chalice of wine (representing the feminine)

The Athame is plunged into the chalice. This symbolic act represents the creative union of the divine forces, echoing the generative power of nature and the cosmos. Those present at the ritual may then share the wine, imbibing the sacred energy of the rite.

This version is deeply poetic and powerful, emphasising balance, harmony, and sacred polarity, without requiring physical intimacy.

The philosophical and magical significance of the Great Rite reflects the hieros gamos, the sacred marriage found in many ancient traditions. It honours the duality and unity of life: light and dark, sun and moon, seed and soil. It is a celebration of eros as a divine force, where sexuality is not taboo but holy, and as Doreen Valiente wrote in The Charge of the Goddess: *"All acts of love and pleasure are my rituals."*

Imbolg: The next festival is Imbolg, also known as Candlemas, which is celebrated on the 2nd of August. It is the time of the Quickening when the God grows in the womb and the Maiden goes into labour. Imbolg celebrates the end of darkness and the reaffirmation of growth. Purification rituals are often performed, not as a cleansing of sin, but to cast away redundant or unwanted aspects of our lives. Yet another time to play silly games. I bet you are beginning to like this Craft stuff, go on, admit it!

On the land, the days lengthen; winter veggies are harvested together with the fruit of the citrus tree. Flowering blossom trees, the last of winter frosts, fields are ploughed in preparation for planting, ewes are lactating, late pregnancy of some livestock and sheep are sheared.

In the Temple, the Altar is decorated with white flowers. The Cauldron is filled with soil, and one burning candle is placed in it in the South. Beside the Cauldron are a few dried evergreen twigs such as Holly, Ivy, and Mistletoe.

The Circle is cast as usual, then a meeting dance whilst singing, *"We dance the Ring of Imbolg, we dance the round of Spring. We dance tonight to invoke the hope that it will bring."*

The HP stands in front of the Altar, carrying a Wand and Scourge in the Osiris position. The

Wand is held in the right hand, Scourge in the left, arms folded across the chest, right over left with both Tools crossing each other, pointing outwards in opposite directions (Scourge towards the left, Wand towards the right).

The HPS gives the Fivefold Kiss and then invokes an Active Spirit Pentagram on the HP.

She says: *"Dread Lord of Death and Resurrection, of life and the Giver of Life; Lord within ourselves, whose name is Mystery of Mysteries. Encourage our hearts, let Thy Light crystallise itself in our blood, fulfilling in us resurrection. For there is no part of us that is not of the Gods. Descend we pray thee, upon thy servant and Priest."*

The HP draws an Invoking Earth Pentagram in the air towards the HPS using the Wand and says, *"Blessed Be."* All greet the HP with a Solar Salute.

The Solar Salute is performed with the index and little finger pointing up and the other two fingers and thumb closed into a fist – like a heavy metal salute. The other salute, which is sometimes given, is the Lunar Salute, where the thumb and little finger are pointed up with the other three fingers rolled into the fist, like the old Hawaiian 'how you going' salute. What an analogy – almost irreverent!

The HPS then takes up a broomstick and ritually sweeps the Circle clear of all that is old and outworn. The HP then goes to the Cauldron and picks up each twig, burns it with the candle, blows it out and puts it in the Cauldron beside the candle. As he does this, he declares, *"Thus we banish winter, thus we welcome spring; say farewell to what is dead, and greet each living thing. Thus we banish winter, thus we welcome spring."*

The rite is finished in the usual manner with Cakes and Wine, and more silly games; the sillier the better!

Spring Equinox: The next festival is the Spring Equinox or Lady Day, celebrated on the 21st of September. This is the time of the Birth of the God and the time when He grows to manhood, and the Maiden grows to womanhood. Light is mastering darkness, for that which began at Imbolg is gathering momentum by Spring: birth and growth are celebrated with an emphasis on fertility.

On the land, day and night are equal. All blossoms are out. The crops have been planted, and seeds have been sown. Bulbs are flowering. The rains have come. Animals are born.

The Circle should be decorated with Spring flowers. The Cauldron is placed in the centre of the Circle with a candle inside it. Place Spring flowers around the East candle. Cast the Circle as usual. The HP invokes the Watchtowers and then purifies all with incense.

The Man-in-Black says, *"This is the time of the Spring Equinox. Where night and day are equal. It is a time of growth and awakening. In our tradition, this is the time the Maiden gives birth to the God. From this time onwards, He shall grow towards manhood, and the Maiden grows to womanhood. As He is reborn, so the land is reborn. That which began at Imbolg has gathered momentum and has now come forth as a renewed life. Let us focus our minds on the rebirth and reawakening of the land and celebrate the beginning of new life and growth, and fertility in all living things. Let the rite begin."*

The HP stands in the East, the HPS in the West facing each other across the Cauldron. The HPS carries the Phallic Wand in her right hand.

The Phallic Wand is usually a normal wand made from the branch of an oak tree with a small pinecone stuck on the end. As its name suggests, it represents a phallus.

The Maiden stands in front of the Altar facing South. A helper stands in the South, facing the HPS. All others are around the Circle boundary.

The helper faces the HPS and says, *"We call upon thee, O Diana, Huntress of the woods, Lady of bright imaginings, Silver Star of our desire, Crescent Moon of midnight clear. Diana the wild, Diana the pure, Virgin Huntress, white as snow. Fair thou art as the music of the harp, radiant thy smile as moonlight on water. Light thy step as a blossom on the wind. Thy womb is the Cauldron of Creation that shall bring forth all hope to men. O Lady of the word of power who makes the shadows flee. Turn thy ear, Diana, as we call upon thee."*

The HPS facing the HP says, *"We kindle this fire today in the presence of the Holy Ones, without malice, without jealousy, without envy, without fear of aught beneath the Sun but the High Gods. Thee we invoke, O Light of Life. Be Thou a bright flame before us, be Thou a guiding star above us, be Thou a smooth path beneath us. Kindle Thou within our hearts, a flame of love for our neighbours, to our foes, to our friends, to our kindred all, to all men on the broad earth. O merciful Son of Cerridwen, from the lowliest thing that liveth to the Name which is highest of all."*

The HPS invokes a Fire Pentagram on HP, then holds the Phallic Wand high, and walks deosil around the Circle to stand in front of the HP. She says, *"O Sun, be Thou armed to conquer the Dark."*

The HPS presents the Phallic Wand to the HP and then steps aside. The HP holds the Wand up in salute, then hands it to the Maiden, who replaces it on the Altar. The Maiden lights a taper from the Altar candle and hands it to the HP. He then lights the candle in the Cauldron, hands the taper back to the Maiden, who extinguishes it and replaces it on the Altar.

Everyone then forms a Circle around the Cauldron, alternating man and woman, and linking hands. They circle deosil and chant: *"Isis, Astarte, Diana. Hecate, Demeter, Kali. Inanna!"*

As they chant, each couple jumps the Cauldron - not forgetting to make a wish!

With the jumping over of the Cauldron, the party begins. Remember to banish the Watchtowers after the party!

Beltane: The next festival is Beltane on the 31st of October. It is the time of the Maturation when the God courts Mother Nature. The Maiden blushes at the chase, as the Lady and the Lord commence their courtship, the world veils are again made thin. Major projects are being worked on. Bonfires, flowers and fertility symbols (Maypoles) are traditionally associated with Beltane. Ecological work is apt, and the Great Rite should be celebrated by lovers. Handfasting could not be better timed.

Next time you see a Maypole, remember the pole symbolises an erect phallus, the red ribbons held by women (menstrual blood) and the white ribbons held by men (semen). The folks you see dancing and holding their ribbons are symbolically performing a fertility or mating ritual. Now you have that picture in your mind, I guess you will never see a Maypole dance in the same light again!

In addition, I hesitate to bring it up, but that image is a little disturbing when you see it in modern society (those folk that are not of the Craft), young children dancing around the Maypole, having a great time! However, having said that, I guess in olden days, children were an integral part of the community and were fully aware of religious pagan rites intertwined in their daily lives, so the Maypole image and ritual would not have been thought of as inappropriate. I guess modern society has lost a lot over time.

On the land, the crops are starting to sprout. The soil is warmer. Flowering bulbs are starting to die. Fruit trees are pollinating, the flowers falling and fruit starting to set. Baby animals are suckling.

Before our ritual, the Cauldron is placed in the centre of the Circle with a lit candle (to be lit when the Altar candle is lit). A green scarf is on the Altar, then the Circle is cast as usual.

After all are in the Circle, the HP takes the green scarf and slowly pursues the HPS around the Circle while the Coven claps their hands rhythmically and hinders him in his pursuit. The HP is attempting to throw the scarf around her shoulders and pull her to him. After several times around the Circle, the HPS allows herself to be caught, and they kiss in front of the Altar.

The HP then gives the scarf to another Priest, and he pursues his partner in the same manner until she is caught. He then hands the scarf back to the HP.

The HP again pursues the HPS, but this time in a slower and more dignified manner. No one intervenes until the HPS places herself behind the Cauldron in the South and the HP in the North. They embrace over the Cauldron and kiss. The HP lets the scarf drop. He then takes a step backwards and drops to his knees.

The Maiden takes the scarf and places it over the head of the HP like a shroud. All kneel around the Cauldron.

The HPS extinguishes the candle in the Cauldron and says, *"The Bel-Fire is extinguished and the King is dead. He has embraced the Great Mother and died of his love; so has it been, year by year, since time began. If he is dead, the fields bear no crops, the trees bear no fruit, and the creatures of the Great Mother bear no young. What shall we do so that the King may live again?"*

All say, *"Rekindle the Bel-Fire!"*

The HPS says, *"So mote it be."*

The HPS takes a taper, rises and goes to the Altar, lights the taper from the North candle, returns to the Cauldron, re-lights the candle and says, *"Friends, light the brands you hold (they do) for here we celebrate the sacred night of Beltane and the flowering forth of the woods and meadows."*

The Maiden then goes to the HP and removes the scarf from over his head. He rises and says, *"I am a stag of seven tines. I am a wide flood on a plain, I am a wind on the deep waters, I am a shining tear of the sun. I am a hawk on a cliff, I am fair among flowers, I am a god who sets the head afire with smoke."*

HPS leads the dance around Cauldron, all carrying tapers and chanting, *"Oh, do not tell the Priest of our art, or he would call it a sin. But we shall be out in the woods all night a-conjuring summer in! And we bring you good news by word of mouth, for women, cattle, and corn - for the sun is coming up from the South with oak and ash and thorn."*

Repeat, *'With oak and ash and thorn'* till the HPS blows out her taper and places it in the Cauldron. Others follow her and join hands and circle faster then jump the Cauldron in pairs.

It became common practice for us at this Sabbat to consecrate (and re-consecrate in future years) the Guardian of the House. Our Guardian is a concrete statue of a lion that has always been placed at our front door.

The Guardian is placed near the East candle. The HPS lights an incense stick and places it near the Guardian.

The HP says, *"Guardian of our house, watch over it in the year to come till again the Bel-Fire is extinguished and relit. Bless our house and be blessed by it, let all who live there and all friends who are welcomed there prosper under its roof. So mote it be."*

Cakes and Wine, as usual, and the Great Rite in actuality is normally performed at this time of year. You can incorporate this into the ritual or wait for cakes and wine, or perform it in private later, after all have left.

Summer Solstice: The next festival is the Summer Solstice, held on the 22nd of December. This is the time of the great wedding. The God rules the sky, and the crops ripen under His smile. The Lady waxes under his attention. Summer is the realisation of life, maturity, and consummation, the sacred marriage of the Sun and Earth, the most magically potent time of the year. The Worlds are never closer. Fire is again a major theme. Sexual magic is obviously very appropriate to the Summer Solstice.

On our land, the grain harvest is completed. The feed is dried off. Droving animals and hand feeding. Everything is growing to completion: crops, fruit, and animals. The young are weaned. Trees are in full foliage, and fruit is swelling.

Our Altar is placed in the North and decorated with summer flowers of red and white. The Cauldron is in the centre of the Circle, filled with water and a floating candle. An aspergillus is placed beside the Cauldron. The HP wears a red robe with a gold cape. HPS wears white and silver. The Circle is cast by HP and HPS as usual.

The Aspergillus, which, according to the Grimorium Verum, should be composed of mint, marjoram, and rosemary, is bound about with a thread woven by a virgin girl. It should be made on the day and in the hour of Mercury on the moon waxing. In practice, we use just a sprig of rosemary taken from our garden just before the ritual begins.

The meeting dance is the Clover Leaf as we sing, *"Round the Circle, we will go, where it will lead, no one may know. Round and round and round we go, binding ourselves in the Sacred Bow."*

The MIB introduces the Sabbat, saying, *"Today we celebrate! We celebrate the sacred union of marriage. The marriage of the Lord and the Lady: The Sun King and the Earth Mother. The Horned Lord has left the verdant shades of the greenwood, now ruling the sky. He is crowned: The Sun at his brow. Under his dominion and protection, the animals and plants which came forth in Spring now grow and mature. The crops set fruit and seed and ripen. As the earth grows, so the Lady grows. All life rejoices in the Sun King's glorious zenith."*

The HP stands in front of the Altar, holding an Arrow and the Sword. I managed to get my hands on a hunting arrow made from wood and feathers with a triple-bladed point. I painted the whole thing with gold paint.

The HPS stands behind the Cauldron, holding a Phallic Wand, facing the HP and imagines a golden glow surrounding him. She draws the Invoking Pentagram of Fire upon him with her Phallic Wand, then invokes, *"Great One of Heaven, Power of the Sun, we invoke Thee in Thine ancient names. Michael, Balin, Arthur, Lugh, Herne; come again as of Old into this Thy Land. Lift up thy Shining Spear of Light to protect us. Put to flight the powers of darkness. Give us fair woodlands and green fields, blossoming orchards and ripening corn. Bring us to stand upon Thy Hill of Vision, and show us the Lovely Realms of the Gods."*

She then removes the gold cape. The HP raises both his hands and says, *"The Spear to the Cauldron, the Lance to the Grail, Spirit to Flesh, Man to Woman, Sun to Earth."*

Then plunges the Arrow into the Cauldron and extinguishes the candle. The HP lays the Arrow and Sword on the ground in front of the Altar, then salutes the HPS over the Cauldron and rejoins the people.

The HPS takes the Aspergillus and stands by the Cauldron. The Coven, all led by the HP, start to dance deosil around the Circle.

The HPS sprinkles each as they pass her with water from the Cauldron, saying, *"Dance ye about the Cauldron of Cerridwen, the Goddess, and be ye blessed with the touch of this Consecrated Water, even as the Sun, the Lord of Life, ariseth in his strength in the sign of the waters of Life."*

Cakes and Wine as per usual, and the Circle banished.

A word of warning for the male who performs the duty of the HP. When the HPS invokes a fire pentagram, be prepared to get hot and energised! Believe me, that feeling will not subside after you banish the Circle, and even after a hearty meal to ground yourself. If performed correctly, it is one of the most energising rituals you can experience - so you must be prepared! If you are lucky enough to perform the Great Rite during or after the ritual, both partners will want to celebrate the Summer Solstice every day henceforth!

Lammas: The festival of Lammas or Lughnassad is next, celebrated on the 1st of February. It is the harvest festival the time of the Consummation of the Sacred Marriage. Lammas celebrates the Harvest, the sacrifice of the God, which is necessary to fertilise the land, and his death, which liberates him to the challenge of conquering a new kingdom, that of the Underworld.

It is the time of increased plenty and decreasing light, of acknowledging the death of the God, a time for rededication and celebrations relating to harvest, a time of working and feasting. In ancient times, this was the Feast of Bread, the time of year when the divine Priest-King was sacrificed in the fields and his body scattered. The grain made into bread represents his body.

On the land, the final grain harvest is stored. Planting winter crops of peas, cauliflower and root crops. Brewing, preserving, and winemaking. Harvest stone fruit. Fruit falling, apples, pears and peaches. Preparation for winter starts, stocking the larder. Killing and salting meat, lambs, mutton, yearlings, and chickens. The leaves are starting to brown on trees, and the sap slows. A corn dolly, which is traditionally made from barley straw, should be hung up in the home to attract health and wealth.

Our Circle area is cleared, and the Altar is in the North. The area is decorated with seasonal flowers and ears of corn. The Cauldron is placed by the eastern candle, the quarter of rebirth and decorated with stems of grain and a Corn Dolly. A small loaf of bread is placed on the Altar, and a Sabbat Cake in the shape of a man is placed on the Pentacle.

Cast the Circle as usual. Circle Dance and Chant, *"Corn rigs, an' barley rigs, an' corn rigs are bonnie; I'll ne'er forget that happy night, amang the rigs wi' Annie."* The Watchtowers are then invoked.

The HPS introduces the Sabbat, saying, *"Lammas is the beginning of the harvest. At this time long ago, our ancestors went out into the fields to collect the first ripened ears of corn. These were brought back to the tribe with great rejoicing, and the women ground the seeds to make the first bread of the season. This loaf was held to be particularly sacred, and a festival of the first loaf was consecrated. The whole tribe was given of this, the first fruits of the gathering.*

"Today, we celebrate also, and we acknowledge the part played by the Lord. We also remember our younger brothers in life. They, too, are beginning to collect their stores for the coming winter, as the migrating birds leave us. The summer has been hot and sunny, yet Our Lady Mother, the earth, has given us abundance. The days are getting shorter, and we know that after the harvest is completed, autumn will be advanced, and with it, the last of the fruit and berries. The corn is ripe, and the grass is lush and green.

"We, the Children of the Goddess, look forward to the harvest. The great wheel is turning towards the mists of autumn, and we gather in the bountiful fruit of the earth as we begin to gather in ourselves."

The Coven then spread themselves around the Circle and start a rhythmic clapping. The HP starts to move towards the HPS and chases her around the Circle, the HPS avoiding the advances of the HP and teasing him. After three laps of the Circle, the HPS allows the HP to capture her. They kiss and fall to the ground and embrace. Haven't we done this before? Boy chases girl. Girl allows boy to catch her. Girl allows boy to kiss her. And so it goes, the same old story, over and over again – but how much fun is it?

The HPS stands in front of the Altar facing South in Goddess position.

The HP then draws an invoking Fire Pentagram on the HPS, saying, *"O Mighty Mother of us all, bringer of all fruitfulness, give us fruits and grain, flocks and herds, and children to the tribe, that we may be mighty. By Thy rosy love, do thou descend upon thy servant and Priestess here."*

There was one part in our historic past that 'children' became 'chickens' in the above invocation. That is a very funny story for Initiates only – something else to look forward to!

All salute the HPS. (Use a Solar Salute – index and little fingers pointed up, the rest folded into the palm.)

Then the HP stands in front of the Altar and falls to his knees, head bowed.

The HPS says, *"This is the time of the year when the Divine Priest-King was sacrificed in the fields and his body scattered. Today, we scatter the grain made into bread to represent his body. The God must die to be reborn."*

The MIB takes the Pentacle with the Sabbat Cake on it and presents it to the HPS. She draws her Athame and stabs the Sabbat Cake several times.

The Coven says, *"Give us to eat the bread of life."*

A murder among us! No, a willing sacrifice.

The HPS takes the Sabbat Cake and walks around the Circle, giving a piece to each Covenor. As she does, she says, *"As the Sun disappears in the dust of night, as the Old Moon dies to be reborn. As the flower gives way to the fruit, so the seed can be replanted in the soil. So the God must die and descend to the Underworld, that the Earth may be fertilised to bring forth new fruit. But although the God has gone from the face of the Earth, we of the Wicca know that He lives on within us. For we believe that there is no part of us that is not of the Gods."*

The wine is blessed and taken around. If outside, a little wine and a couple of pieces of Sabbat Cake are thrown to the earth, just as the body of the sacrificed king was scattered into the fields to generate next year's harvest.

Autumn Equinox: The next festival is the Autumn Equinox or Michaelmas, celebrated on the 21st of March. It is the Funeral when the God rests in the earth, the bosom of the Earth Mother. The Widow searches for her husband and becomes a virgin.

The harvest is complete, well stored, and we prepare for the Winter season. Thanks are given to the Providers for whatever was harvested and preparation is made for the quiet time ahead, for study, for strength to hold firm resolutions and for guidance in using the fallow period well.

On the land, the livestock are being hand-fed. Bare earth. Hope for April rains and cooler nights. The last harvest and harvest of nuts and berries to make jams, cider, and mead. The fruit trees have finished. All are preparing for winter. Animals are starting to grow winter coats. Leaves are starting to change colour due to restricted sap flow.

The Altar is decorated with pine cones, grain, acorns, red poppies, other autumnal flowers, fruit, and leaves. The Circle is cast as usual.

The HP stands in the West and HPS in the East holding the Phallic Wand, she says, *"Farewell, oh Sun, ever returning light. The hidden God, whoever yet remains, who now departs to the land of youth through the gates of death, to dwell enthroned, the judge of Gods and men. The horned leader of the hosts of air, yet, even as he stands unseen about the Circle, so dwelleth he, within the secret seed, the seed of newly reaped grain, the seed of flesh, hidden in the earth, the marvellous seed of the stars. In Him is life, and life is the light of man. That which was never born, and never dies, therefore the Wicca weep not, but rejoice."*

HPS goes to the HP, hands him the Phallic Wand and turns to the Coven, and she says, *"We came together this night to mark the passing of the Sun, the Hidden God from this earth into eternal light. As the Sun now sinks into darkness, may we have the faith to follow him through darkness so that we may be born again."*

The Coven says, *"Without darkness, there is no light; without cold, there is no heat. There can be no flow without the ebb, and only through death can life be renewed."*

HP and HPS lead the dance and all chant, *"Now the darkness is descending, light our way, oh love unending. For His death is a beginning, for His dance is just beginning."*

The HPS then says, *"As we enter this darkest of seasons, may our fear be replaced by faith in the eternal light in whom the God and Goddess are one."*

Cakes and wine as normal, and the Circle is banished.

Samhain: The last festival of the year is Samhain, the Gaelic Fire festival celebrated on the 30th of April. It is the Descent, as the God rules as Lord of the Underworld, and the Virgin greets the Lord of Death and Resurrection. Being the end of the Wiccan year, it is also the beginning. The Worlds are very close, boundaries thin; the dead are remembered and the elders honoured. Fires may be lit and love made to reaffirm life in death.

On the land, we await the new season. Early rains, the first working of the soil. The remains of the chaff have been ploughed into the fields. Harvest of pumpkins and some other vine crops. The trees have lost their leaves. The ground is dry and hard. Animals have grown their full winter coat, and all are preparing for winter.

The Altar is decorated with seasonal foliage and fruit, among which apples, and if possible, nuts on the twig, should feature prominently. On the ground beside the Altar rests the HP's Horned Helmet. (We made a horned crown from a couple of goat's horns tied to a leather strap and worn on the forehead.) The Cauldron is placed in the centre of the Circle with a candle in it.

The HPS says, *"We welcome you in love and trust to our festival. It is yours to enjoy. Give what you can and take what you need."*

Cast the Circle as usual.

HPS says, *"All is ready. Let the Bale Fire be lit!"*

The HP proclaims, *"Hurrayah!"*

The candle inside the Cauldron is lit. The HP leads the HPS; he carries the Phallic Wand, and she the Broomstick.

The rest of Coven follows. Slow dance to Black Spirits and White – *"Black spirits and white, red spirits and grey, come ye and join us, come ye that* may. Around and about, within and without, the good come in and the ill keep out."

The HP, with his back to the Altar and the HPS facing him, says, *"As the summer draws to a close, so begin the dark months of winter. Gracious Goddess, we thank you for the joys of summer, for the crops, the harvest; for life and love."*

The HPS takes up the Horned Helmet, holds it high, and says, *"Here do I hold the symbol of Karnayna the Mighty One, Lord of Life and of Death. As he will guard us and guide us through the months to come, so will his servant and Priest here."*

She places the Helmet on the HP's head and says, *"Now do you (name of HP) represent Karnayna. For Him you speak; for Him you act. Lead us, we ask you, through the hardships that lie ahead, that again we may see the glory of spring and the love of the Goddess Aradia."*

The HP and HPS kiss. The HP and HPS invoke each other with Athame using Earth Pentagrams, and the HPS says, *"Dread Lord of the Shadow, God of Life and the Giver of Life. Yet is the knowledge of Thee, the knowledge of death.*

"Open wide, I pray thee, Thy gates through which all must pass. Let our dear ones who have gone before return this night to make merry with us.

"And when our time comes, as it must, Oh Thou the Comforter, The Consoler, The Giver of Peace and Rest, we will enter Thy Realms gladly and unafraid, for we know that when rested and refreshed among our dear ones, we will be reborn again by Thy Grace, and the Grace of the Great Mother. Let it be in the same place, and the same time as our beloved ones and may we meet, and know, and remember, and love them again. Descend we pray Thee on thy servant and Priest."

The HPS then gives the Five Fold Kiss to the HP.

The MIB walks to the West Watchtower and says, *"Behold, the West is Amenti, the Land of the Dead, to which many have gone for rest and renewal. On this night, we hold communion with them, and as I stand in welcome by the Western portal, I call upon my brothers and sisters of the Craft to hold the image of your loved ones in your hearts and minds, that our welcome may reach out to them.*

" There is mystery within mystery; for the resting place is also Caer Arianrhod, the castle of the silver wheel at the hub of the turning stars. Beyond the West wind, here reigns Arianrhod, the White Lady, whose name means silver wheel. To this in spirit, we call our loved ones. Let me lead them in, for the spiral path inwards to Caer Arianrhod leads tonight. May all who visit here this night remain in peace and love. So mote it be!"

The MIB walks slowly with dignity, in a widdershins direction around the Circle, spiralling inwards, taking 3 or 4 circuits to reach the centre. He stops before the HPS.

She says, *"Those you bring with you are truly welcome to our festival. May they remain with us in peace. And you may now return by the spiral path to stand with your brothers and sisters; but deosil - for the way of rebirth, outwards from Caer Arianrhod, is the way of the Sun."*

The MIB walks back, spiralling, to the edge of the Circle. The HP and HPS stand at the Altar together.

The HP says, *"As Lord of Life, of Love, of Death, I bid you have no fear. With my Lady at my side, know ye always that there be light. I tell thee that there is hope of life to come. I will lead thee happily, as I have led those who have gone before, yet are here now. Whenever there is a festival for the dead, we must also celebrate life and achievement."*

The HPS hands out to each Covenor a small piece of incense. The Thurible is placed in the centre of the Circle next to the Cauldron, and all sit around.

The HP says, *"Each of you should now meditate on your grain of incense, charging it with the main things you want to achieve this year. Then declare silently to your inner self what it is exactly, and cast the incense into the fire to seal the spell."*

Each person, in turn, casts his or her spell.

Any divination that may seem appropriate is performed. Cakes, wine, and the Great Rite in token. HP and HPS should celebrate the Great Rite as soon as convenient, privately in reality.

And so ends our Sabbat Round. What is missing from this round is the keys, the visualisation, and various other correspondences that have a magical effect on the rituals and very special meaning to our Coven and Tradition. This should not deter anyone from performing these rituals as they are written; they will work, and maybe with your intuition, you might just find those special keys; after all, we did back in the day!

"Dance we now to raise the power."

Chapter Twelve
The Priesthood

During that first year, I assumed the role of High Priest, I undertook further training before I entered the Priesthood as an Initiate. I realised that the Craft is a religion and a way of life centred on the natural cycles of the Earth, fused with the magic of the life cycle of the Gods. The only way to enter that Priesthood was to live and experience the cycle of the Gods as the wheel of the agricultural year turned.

Just think back, or re-read the last few chapters about the Sabbats. Look closely at what is happening in the green world and understand our description of what the spiritual cycle of the Gods is telling you. That is one of the main reasons most Traditions require that a Neophyte spend a year and a day studying before Initiation; to give them the chance to experience a full year of Sabbats. Believe me, somewhere along that journey the penny drops!

I use the word 'religion' because the Craft is a religion, a faith, a belief system. When we sometimes describe the Craft or Wicca specifically, we compare it to the analogy that Catholicism is to Christianity, like Wicca is to Paganism, if that makes sense.

Catholics, Protestants, Methodists, and the like are divisions of Christianity. Wiccans, Witches, Pagans, Druids, and similar groups are subsets of Paganism. I dislike that analogy because it rather puts me in the same group of folks who call themselves Pagans. Maybe twenty or thirty years ago, I would have been happy being called a Pagan, but not today. I am not a Pagan; I am a Priest of the Wicca.

Most Pagans I know are an eclectic bunch of folk who would not describe their path as a religion but more of a spiritual path. Truth be known, a lot have a foot in both camps. They are neo-Christians who celebrate Christmas, Easter, and other Christian holidays with their family and friends. They sometimes pray to the Goddess on a full moon, and most dismiss the existence of a Pagan God. They dance in circles, chant and pound a drum; nothing wrong with that, but most have to pay someone for the privilege, and that pisses me off. As I said earlier in this story, the Craft is not, never was, and never will be for sale! That is the difference between calling yourself a Pagan and being a Priest of the Wicca.

They say that there is no congregation in Wicca; all are said to be of the Priesthood because we are all Initiates. That is somewhat true, but in most Traditions, there is a hierarchy, a pecking order from Neophyte to Magus, and each has their place; so really, there is a kind of congregation.

Divinity is inherent. The essence of the Creator is present in the material world; therefore, our bodies, our land, and our homes are sacred. Our awareness of the Creator manifested as the God and Goddess within ourselves is enhanced when we act in harmony with the cycles of nature.

We honour both God and Goddess and recognise the divine polarity as the primary creative force of the universe. The energy, harmony, and divinity of sexual polarity between Goddess and God are part of our religious practice, as it was in the ancient Temples.

The Priesthood is a way of life necessitated by a certain level of spiritual responsibility, a lifestyle, or tradition that focuses on both achievement and ambivalence towards universal enlightenment.

And how do we find this priesthood? For some, it is evident from childhood as a growing natural interest in matters of the spirit. For others, the call comes in a blinding moment of revelation, but for the larger number of the spiritually aware, the call to the Priesthood manifests as a course of action arising from one's own developing wisdom gained from progress along the Initiatory path. It can sometimes be found in the classified section of your weekend newspaper, on the floor of an alternative bookstore, or even in the last cubicle of a yuppie coffee shop!

Chapter Thirteen
Our Coven

A strong Coven usually develops a group mind or persona with its purposes and direction. The orientation can be quite varied, with some Covens concentrating on healing or teaching and others leaning towards psychic work, trance states, high magic, or simply throwing great parties.

With a group mind, group power develops. In the Craft, power is another word for that energy, which is the subtle current of forces that shapes reality. A powerful person is seen as someone who draws power into the group, not out of it. The sources of inner power are unlimited. One person's power does not diminish another's; instead, as each Covenor comes into his or her power, the power of the group grows stronger.

As the Coven grows stronger, it starts to develop its consciousness. One of the laws of magic is that as thoughtforms are fed regularly, they grow into self-sufficiency. This is why religious sites that have been abandoned for ages still affect sensitive people who visit them. And why rituals performed the same way repeatedly become more powerful with each repetition.

I remember in the early days some Coven members complained that we always performed the same Sabbat ceremony, and it was becoming boring. It wasn't until a few years later that it became evident that the rituals were becoming more and more powerful each time we performed them; more so with our Esbats – the same old thing each month. Absolutely not! Each one becomes ever so more powerful and magical each time we draw down that Moon!

Once the thoughtform is fully formed, it is brought into manifestation through repeatedly re-forming it, and the consciousness begins. Again, this is why rituals are performed repeatedly in the same way.

You are following a blueprint for a thoughtform, and deviation produces a distorted thoughtform.

Once a Coven has found its orientation, it begins work on forming a thoughtform of the work it wishes to do. Eventually, the Coven actualises its thoughtforms, and the group consciousness becomes a reality and a reservoir of power that any Coven member can draw on in need.

Our first Coven was a group of people fresh out of Canberra's version of Hogwarts and thrown together out of necessity. Our heads were full of so many ideas pulling us in various directions, for we each wanted to try something different. It took us a long while to find our group mind and many Esbats to develop that magical spark.

We found that we were very good at healing spells and making talismans. Over time, we created a Book of Correspondences; a list of herbs, colours, oils, planetary influences, the chakras, the Major Arcana, Runes, and the list goes on. Each of those elements corresponds in one way or another to one of the other elements or something significant belonging to a feeling, an emotion, a desire or some other issue, problem or need. We put together data from modern and ancient texts and grimoires, scientific lists, and Crowley's 777 was a great inspiration. We found that planetary attributes corresponded to desires and feelings, and combined with paths on the Qabalistic Tree, injecting the appropriate colour and shape, you had the beginning of a magical formula.

We experimented, studied, and eventually became a very cohesive group that found we were pretty bloody awesome at creating magical talismans for our friends and family who required help or our assistance in some way or another.

We had requests to help with getting a job, overcoming an ailment, finding a new home, a protection against mental and physical attack, overcoming financial issues, and the list goes on.

As our Coven got older and members came and went, the persona changed. We went from creating magical talismans and rituals to developing a different Sabbat Round that involved more guided visualisations and pathworking. Rituals that allowed us to invite outsiders and make them more public, which in turn brought more seekers to our Craft and eventually turned our group into a teaching Coven and each of our members into teachers.

And so the wheel turns.

Part Two
Our Wiccan Ways
Structure, Spirit, and the Sacred Design

If the first part of this journey was about finding the path, the following chapters are about learning to walk it, with purpose.

In *Our Wiccan Ways*, I shift from experience to explanation. From the chaotic beauty of beginnings to the sacred geometry that underpins the Craft. It is one thing to cast a circle with instinct; it is another to understand why that circle matters, how it holds, and what it opens.

These chapters explore the scaffolding - the beliefs, rituals, and cosmology that anchor our practice and guide our communication with the divine.

Modern witches often bristle at the notion of rules, and I understand that. Structure can feel like a cage until you see it as a vessel. What follows is not rigidity for its own sake, but a blueprint, earned through devotion, and shaped by the needs of those who came before us. From The Laws to The Magic Circle, from The Tools to The Gods themselves, this is the theology behind the practice, the dogma behind the dance.

Yes, dogma. We even have it. Structured initiatory traditions within the Craft do carry philosophy, expectations, and oaths, not to limit the soul, but to protect the sacred and steward the mystery.

You will step with me into the liminal threshold of Initiation, witness The Ordeal Revisited with new eyes, and finally glimpse The Book of Shadows - not just as a record, but also as a living spirit.

By the end of this section, you will see not just how we built the framework of our Coven, but why we built it the way we did.

This is the architecture behind the altar. The deeper pulse beneath the dance. The bones beneath the beauty.

Let us open the circle and begin.

Chapter Fourteen
The Craft

Back in Alex's day, there probably was not a great emphasis put on the theosophical side of Wicca; its philosophy and ethics. I probably think most of it was practical and celebratory. Today, as the Craft has evolved into somewhat of a structured religion, thanks to the work of people like Simon, we have a religion like any other that has a system of philosophy and dogma that includes a pantheon, worship, ethics, and the use of magic.

Yes, magic is used in other religions – next Good Friday or any time the Catholics are performing a High Mass (not just your normal Sunday gig), take yourself along and look very closely at what the Priest does; I mean very closely at the minute details – you will be surprised at the things that are lost on the general congregation.

The Craft has its origins in the nature worship and sympathetic magic of prehistory and has been in a state of constant evolution ever since. Most traditions place their emphasis on various aspects of their belief system. Our Alexandrian Tradition, thanks to Simon's input and borrowing from older traditions such as Sussex, has given us our viewpoint as to the design of the philosophical aspects of the Craft.

So, to quote Simon, *"The Craft in general places importance on the feminine aspect of our creation.*

Given its origin from nature worship, the heart of the Craft today is, of necessity, the worship of the Creator through his/her creation."

As we have discussed, most Covens have a specific purpose, usually depending on the types of members and their skills or preferences. Today, our Coven has morphed through various identities to become a teaching Coven. Our purpose is to attempt to preserve the ancient mystery knowledge and to identify with the Old Gods through worship.

All Covens identify with the cycles of our environment through observing the Sabbats and Esbats and developing their psychic and mental control, healing and magical ability through training, thereby developing their spirituality.

The Craft in general is organised into Traditions or Systems, and most into Covens, there being groups of between four and twenty Initiates. The lower limit is set by the fact that it takes four Elders to perform a Second Degree Initiation.

A High Priestess, a High Priest, and one other working pair of Elders represent the minimum for a fully self-supporting Coven. Thirteen is more flexible, being set by the largest number of people who can work easily in the size of the Circle used, which, in turn, is set by the space available in the Temple, Covenstead, or meeting place.

Thirteen might sound like an odd number; it is. The Coven is balanced with male and female couples, and that statement is not sexist; it has to do with polarity, the actual magnetic attributes (positive and negative) of male and female. The odd man out is the Man-in-Black because he always stands between the worlds.

In past times, we worshipped in the greatest temples when the overall organisation of our religion had its public and reputable existence. During the persecution, the Covens deliberately lost contact with each other so that the discovery of one did not lead to the discovery of another. It was only the Man-in-Black who knew the identity and location of other Covens, and his job alone was to pass communications between Covens.

Today, each Coven is very independent and guards that independence jealously. Although having said that, Covens belonging to a specific system or tradition sometimes have to conform with respect to system rules and regulations. That is where bitchcraft raises its ugly head and can sometimes result in the destruction of groups.

The interpretation of perfect love and perfect trust is sometimes lost during witch wars.

So, from my perspective, the following description of the Craft Pantheon is the belief of an Alexandrian, melded with the philosophical ideals of a Sussex Initiate. It is a practical view of life that values the importance of the cycles of nature linked to the God and Goddess cycles of birth, death, and rebirth; it has four levels.

The First Level

The first level we identify as the Creator, which has two faces. The giver or Bountiful One that provides all things, and Fate or destiny, the maker of laws. Being the innermost self of every created thing, the Creator may not be known, save in the mirror of the universe, as a thing may not observe itself directly. In other words, our puny minds cannot understand what the Creator is. It transcends reason to attempt to know what 'god' is. Worship in the Craft is therefore directed towards the next level.

The Second Level

At this level, we can attempt to understand. As creation comes through the conjunction of male and female, the second level consists of the male and female principles, the God and the Goddess. This is the primary reason Wicca is a fertility religion; it cannot be anything other! So those who pretend to worship the Goddess to the exclusion of the God are fooling themselves.

The Goddess has three aspects corresponding to the state of the mood that represents Her. The Virgin Maiden corresponds to the waxing moon, the Bountiful Mother corresponds to the full moon, and the Hag of Death corresponds to the waning moon.

The God has two aspects: The Lord of Light

corresponds to day, and the Lord of Death and Resurrection corresponds to night. As the balance of night and day alters through the year, so one or another aspect becomes dominant. Since the God started as a hunting deity, He is horned.

The Universe is created and held in being by the conjunction of these two aspects of the Creator, and together with the Creator, they lie beyond Creation.

The Third Level

The third level can be defined as the Mighty Ones of the Quarters, the Lords of the Watchtowers, and the Kings of the Elements. They represent the highest principles of creation. Air in the East, Fire in the South, Water in the West, and Earth in the North. The Circle, lying between the Worlds, represents the fifth element, the quintessence of Spirit, in other words, the Triad of the Creator, the Goddess, and the God.

The Fourth Level

The fourth level is the Universe. The logical and sincere method for the worship of the Creator through creation is the experience of joy in creation, such as one may feel on a good day when the whole world seems to be singing! In one of the most important parts of the Craft's rituals comes the phrase *'All acts of love and pleasure are my rituals'*. This state should be natural to humanity, but as the natural condition in people is much overlaid, various techniques are used to assist the process.

These may include mental exercises and any other means of removing the obstacles between a person and the universe that then tend to lead to a joyful state. Ritual nudity inside a Magic Circle combined with dance. Sex obviously leads to this state of joy; however, the rite (The Great Rite) has fallen mainly into disuse, and nowadays we do the rite 'In Token', such is the impact of today's culture. The most common way these days is to call the God or Goddess to manifest through a member or members of the Coven, generally known as Drawing down the Moon.

We believe that it would not seem possible for any part of a universe created by the Creator to be evil. The concept of good and evil, therefore, would appear to be invalid. Furthermore, the laws of the physical level of the universe are immutable, and we have no reason to suppose otherwise of the other laws of the Creator. Sin, the breaking of these laws, is, therefore, impossible, and the concept, together with the corollary of judgment, seems to be an attempt to impose upon the Creator all the peculiar imperfections of human law.

Human beings, possessing free will, may choose to act in awareness and alignment with these laws, or to disregard them, whether knowingly or unknowingly. In either case, the operation of law brings to the individual and others the consequences of those actions. This process may span lives. Thus, the true dichotomy is between wisdom and unwisdom. Thus, the word 'Witch' is derived from the Anglo-Saxon word 'Wica', meaning both the knowledge of the way and the will and the ability to act in conformity with the knowledge.

The universe operates by virtue of the harmony between its parts, and hence the first and only injunction of ethics given by the Craft is, *'An it harm none, do what ye will'.*

This injunction that is given in the First Degree Initiation covers so much that it is not possible to make further generalities. Beyond this, the use of one's 'Will with Wisdom' is so dependent on one's peculiar abilities and the qualities of the particular situation encountered that no man or woman is competent to direct another.

Thus, the Craft is, in general, more permissive than most other religions, and places upon the individual the responsibility of acting wisely according to their wisdom and ability.

Having discussed the philosophical aspects of our religion, let us now be a little more practical and look at our structure and how things actually work.

Previously in this story, I have covered how we developed our Esbat ritual and our Sabbat Wheel. So, just to recap, we have two kinds of meetings, Sabbats and Esbats. The Sabbats, as you now know, celebrate the Wheel of the Year and follow the life cycle of the Gods. Some are agricultural celebrations, and others are Solar. The Sabbats are Yule, Imbolg, Spring Equinox, Beltane, Summer Solstice, Lammas, Autumn Equinox and Samhain.

Esbats are lunar celebrations and take place monthly, usually when the moon is full. They contain all or some of the following elements: Drawing Down of the Moon; reading of the Charge; works of Magic; Cakes and Wine; and general discussions on Craft or Coven matters.

The members of a traditional Coven are the High Priestess, High Priest, Man-in-Black, Maiden, Elders (Second Degrees), Initiates (First Degrees), and Neophytes. A Neophyte can be either someone who is following a Pagan path, a Pagan who has undergone a Paganing, or a student who has finished a formal training course and has undergone the Crafting ritual.

The High Priestess is the spiritual leader of the Coven. She represents the Goddess and sometimes speaks with Her voice. The High Priest is the governing head and controlling force behind the Coven, the manager, if you like. It is he who owns the Sword, but allows the High Priestess to wield it. If, for whatever reason, a Coven is disbanded, the HPS, usually as part of a ritual, will hand back the Sword to her HP. He then maintains control of it until it is needed again.

The Man-in-Black is second-in-command to the HP and assumes all responsibilities and duties of the HP in his absence. As I have already hinted, he is also the Coven messenger and sometimes the public face of a Coven.

The Maiden is a High Priestess-in-training. She is usually a First Degree and assists the HPS when required. She also assumes all her responsibilities and duties in her absence.

The Coven Elders are Third and Second Degree Initiates. They sit on governing bodies, councils, and committees and speak on behalf of the Craft.

The Second Degree is given after at least 3 years of training after the First Degree. The initiation includes several tests to see that the lessons of the First have been well learned, a vow of service to the Craft and its Gods, and the acting out of the Legend of the Goddess.

The Elders are organised in working pairs that, as to be coupled closely with this sort of work, are strongly conducive towards affection, always male and female. Instruction does not end with the Second Degree, but rather each Elder finds him or herself in the position of a research student to develop their understanding of reality, and to share it with others.

Initiates are First Degree Initiates who make up the general membership of a Coven. They may specialise in certain skills and help organise meetings and rituals. The First Degree is given a year and a day after Paganing (or 40 days after Crafting). The Initiation is the adoption of the Initiate into the family of the Coven; it involves an oath of mutual assistance and secrecy over certain details of Craft practice.

First Degree Initiates are under instruction from the High Priestess in the case of the men and the High Priest in the case of the women. They attend all meetings inside the Circle except when Second and Third Degree Initiations take place, and they undertake various mental training exercises that should have been commenced when the Goddess gave Her decree to accept them for Initiation.

They are also expected to make their own set of ritual implements, doing as much of the work as possible with their own hands so that something of themselves may be present in the finished article.

Neophytes are aspiring members who are studying a formal training course and may have undertaken a Paganing or Crafting ritual. A Paganing is given to someone who has done no formal training. It is an 'Initiation' into the Circle Cross, an introduction to the elements and the Mighty Ones. The aspirant gives their mind to the Goddess.

The Crafting Ritual is taken by someone who has completed the System Course. It is designed to enact an Oath of Secrecy from the Initiate and prepare them for the First Degree.

The Third Degree is given when required. The Initiation is held in the presence of the Elders. It consists of the God and Goddess manifesting through a particular working pair. They become High Priestess and High Priest representing the Goddess and the God in that Coven. The High Priestess and High Priest preside at all meetings; they also share equally in the work of teaching and that of maintaining contact with other Covens.

In British Tradition, a male and female couple who are taken to the Second Degree are usually given the Third at the same time as a matter of course. This, for some reason, has not occurred in the Australian scene, at least not in our Alexandrian Tradition. I believe mainly for the fact that older Elders of the Craft in Australia have strictly adhered to the hierarchical systems they were brought into and wanted to remain at the top of their trees!

Suffice it to say this does not occur today. When the Second Degree is given, especially to a working pair, the Third is also given. That is not quite the correct term; a Third is never given, it is always 'taken' by the working pair as a celebration of their Craft.

As Maxine most eloquently put it, *"The First is the initiation into the Craft, the Second is the penetration into the Craft, and the Third is the celebration of the Craft."*

Chapter Fifteen
The Laws

"The Laws were created to give our lives form and order, so that all might be balanced throughout all of the planes. In truth, there are two sets of laws which govern us: one set forth the way of the Wicca, and the other the ways of the Universe. Both are important, and both should be observed with respect and treated with honour. The Laws were shaped and moulded to teach us, to advise us and to counsel us in our time of mortal life on earth." (An extract from The New Book of the Law by Lady Galadriel.)

The first time most Initiates or even Neophytes hear about the Laws is when there is a problem in a Coven. Today, the Laws are hardly ever used, and some even say they are arcane, sexist, racist, and downright inflammatory. Even so, they are part of our history and one of the great books of the Craft that should never be forgotten.

The Laws appear to have become part of Gerald Gardner's Book of Shadows shortly after Doreen Valiente left his Coven in 1957. The Laws are one of those books that are kept by the High Priest or Priestess and are not usually seen by First Degree Initiates. However, in our system, we allow the Initiate to read the Laws at the same time they are copying their own Book of Shadows. This allows them to know what the Laws are and how they should be used. Not only by the governing body of their Tradition or Coven but also by all members, especially when a crisis or critical event has been reached.

In my case, I first saw the Book of Laws the day I was taken to the Second Degree, and I spent the next few weekends writing them at the rear of my Book of Shadows.

As a general rule, the Laws are formally given to a newly ordained Second Degree Initiate or a working couple. Depending on which book you read, there can be anywhere from a couple of dozen to a couple of hundred laws in one to maybe five or six different books. If you ever have the fortune to read a Goodmanian Book, you might find that Simon replaced some of the Laws with his own. Another little something to look forward to!

The Laws are another of those books that have already been published in one form or another, and Lady Galadriel has done a fine job in condensing them to suit today's climate, if you like. Therefore, this might be one occasion you could do a Google and find her version or even Gerald's published version. But that is not going to be better than the surprise you might get when you see and read an original Alexandrian copy.

Here are a couple of extracts I have summarised; the ones I feel worthy of discussion, but maybe another time, but for now, consider these.

Should someone do you harm or cause you injury or be malicious, never seek revenge or return the hate with evil acts. Any transgression or malevolent act will destroy your spirit; the other will eventually pay the price. The price of evil will rebound threefold, if not in this life, the next. However, it is lawful to reverse the flow of evil and nothing more.

Never use your knowledge selfishly for material gain or to harm another; always use the Craft for good. Never boast about who you are or what you can do, for most will be lost on those not of the Craft.

Never accept money for using the Craft, for it often denigrates and weakens your character, making you corruptible.

All of nature, including animals, birds and plants, all living things are part of our life equally. Do not mistreat or exploit Mother Nature. Kill only for food or in time of need or self-defence, never for amusement.

Remember that you own nothing; your only true possession is knowledge, so use it wisely and honourably.

Finally, remember the Laws are not set in stone, and they are not the Ten Commandments. They are there as a guide in a time of need and to assist you in focusing your energy on the bigger picture, your development.

"And the Wicca shall be properly prepared and purified to enter in the presence of the Gods."

Chapter Sixteen
The Magic Circle

The Magic Circle is the Temple of the Wicca, wherein the Wida worship and draw power to do their work. To cast a Circle without correct knowledge and ritual can be dangerous, since from the first moment you begin to lay out your Circle, certain factors are released to strike at triggers deeply rooted in your subconscious.

As you have been preparing your candles, incense, Altar, etc., you have begun to condition and program yourself to the concepts of eternal truth and wisdom. They were already there, but you had begun to release them when you made the preparations for the Magic Circle – *'the meeting place between the worlds of Gods and men.'* The foregoing is an extract from *'The Magic Circle of the Wicca'* by Alex Sanders.

There is a very strong tradition that is consistent throughout all magical systems. Except for certain types of Banishings, or rituals that utilise a chaotic energy, all movements to cast and consecrate the Circle, and all movements subsequently made within the Circle, are made in a deosil direction, i.e. any movement made in a clockwise direction. The opposite direction to deosil is widdershins, i.e. in a direction opposite to the usual; the wrong way or in an anti-clockwise direction.

The speculative viewpoint concerning the words Deosil and Widdershins adopts the notion that they relate to the direction of the sun. Deosil means sunwise or according to the course of the sun, and Widdershins means to take a course opposite the apparent motion of the sun. That being true, some of us of the Craft choose to disregard the formal meaning and prefer to use the concepts of clockwise and anti-clockwise. These concepts become evident when we perform magic and use the relationship of the elements and the quarters in our Circles. I believe this to be a problem that southern pagans fail to realise, or at least choose to ignore, when some transpose Fire and Earth for North and South. In my view, a very dangerous mistake when performing any type of ceremonial magic.

Wiccan philosophy does not subscribe to the viewpoint that widdershins is either evil or unlucky, but it is most definitely seen as a contrary motion. Certain types of banishing, or rituals to mark the decrease of something, could justifiably use a widdershins motion.

The Circle is divided into four elemental quarters. North for Earth, East for Air, South for Fire and West for Water, and these elements are totalled or combined in Aether.

North is the direction to which the Wicca pray, the home of the Mighty Ones and the place of greatest darkness. It is the quarter of binding, and to it are attributed the Pentacle and Cords.

East is the direction to which the solar worshippers pray. It is the place of the rising sun, the rebirth of the sacrificed god and the place of illumination. The tools used to cause enlightenment are the Scourge and the Wand.

The South is the direction of the hottest wind, the burning deserts, and is the realm of fire. The tools of fire are the Sword and the Thurible.

West is the direction of death and the Summerlands, the domain of the Goddess of Death and Love and Rebirth, the direction from which the original Wida arrived in Wales from Atlantis. The working tools of this quarter are the Athame and the Boline.

The final element, the fifth quarter, should be considered as the quintessence of all four other elements combined. This element is Aether, called Akasha by Eastern esoterics. It is symbolised by the Pentagram, whose manifestation is Spirit, and whose Tool is Man.

My first Sussex Circle experience was when I undertook the Ritual of Initiation into the Craft. This was after I had taken my Alexandrian Third Degree. The rite constituted an Initiation into the Third Level of the Sussex system, when a Witch, through their learning, ability, and intent, showed their commitment to the way of our people, and had indicated their desire to serve the High Gods within the Priesthood. Only those who have shown themselves to be truly dependable and trustworthy in all respects may be so inducted.

So, I was honoured when I received a telephone call from the Lady Michelin instructing me to be at a certain place, on a certain day, at a certain time and be ready to enter the Sussex family. And so it was, blindfolded and bound, I stepped between the worlds.

The ritual follows the same constructional format as most other Initiations into the Mystery Schools at the same level. The candidate is initially blindfolded, is declared as 'Prepared to undertake the Initiation', an ordeal is enacted, an oath is exacted, a Mystery is revealed, and the candidate is consecrated as a Priest/ess.

The Initiation is regarded by our people as a True

Initiation into the Craft proper and is also recognised as such by most other Traditional Covens, as the hallmark of traditional induction - the passing on or handing down of power by sexual congress - is observed. *'Joined in Mystic Rite, from darkness of earth, advance to the light!'* This ritual is secret, just like any other type of initiation, and should only be experienced by those undertaking the mystery.

After returning home, I took Evelyn on her journey to meet the High Gods, and later, we developed the framework of a Circle, not traditionally Wiccan in the strict sense, but more old-style in a Traditional Witchcraft way.

This became our Sussex Circle, not strictly how it was written by Simon's Coven, but one we changed that was suitable to share with our Coven and friends. As you will see, this Circle is not cast by the HPS and HP, but by everyone present within the area, each becoming a critical element in the creation of our Sacred Space.

The Sussex Circle (Raventree variant)

The Altar is set in the North, and all the usual Tools are placed in their corresponding positions. The quarter candles are placed in their respective positions with the addition of four Magical Weapons. Those weapons are: the Stone of Destiny, the Sword of Air, the Cauldron of Cerridwen, and the Spear of Victory.

The Stone (we use a large round smooth stone about 10" long, we sourced from the local beach) is placed on the ground in front of the Altar (it needs to be big enough to stand on, or at least get your ten toes over the top).

The Sword is placed on the floor in front of the East candle (we use our own Coven Sword).

For the Spear of Destiny, we use a hunting arrow painted gold, and it is placed in front of the South candle.

In the West, the Cauldron (a large copper cauldron we found in an antique shop serves the purpose), filled with water and placed in front of the candle, represents the Cauldron of Cerridwen.

With everyone prepared and spaced around the Circle, a bell is rung around the room by the HP to signal our intent to begin a ritual and frighten away any lurking spirits.

The HP says, *"Who comes here?"*

The Coven replies, *"We who seek the Old Ways."*

At this time, the whole Coven is inside the area that will become our Temple or sacred space or Circle; for this is a Circle all create, not just the Priest and Priestess.

The HPS says, *"Then be ye prepared, for this time is no time and this place is no place and this day is no day, for ye stand now between the Worlds!"*

The Altar candle is lit by the HPS as she says, *"From fire above to fire below, from fire within to fire without, may Michael's spear from there to here, make the magic fire appear."*

All members of the Coven then approach the Altar in turn, present their Athames and anoint, saying, *"My mind honours Thee, my body serves Thee, my heart adores Thee, my spirit is Thy Spirit, for we are one."*

The HPS moves to the West and the HP moves to

the East, then both face inwards. The Coven joins hands and circles moving deosil, encompassing in a figure-of-eight the HPS, the HP, and the central point of the Temple.

The Coven chant, *"The Lord above and Lady below, as round about the ring we go. With sacred blade from quarters four, the power to aid our work we draw. From castle far, in place alone, we dance before the Devil's throne. We dance our ring on moor or hill, and raise the power to work our will."*

The HPS and HP join the Coven as they circle and again repeat the chant until the HP orders, *"Banish the Evil Ones!"*

The Coven slows and walks in a stately manner. They all point their Athames into the centre of the Circle and call, *"Lords of Power of night and day, harken to these words I say! Earth and Air and Fire and Water, be within your son and daughter. Earth beneath and sky above, join with us our rite to prove. Banish evil, welcome calm; keep this Temple from all harm!"*

On saying the word *'harm'*, all raise their Athames to the sky.

Sheathing their Athames, the Coven then join hands and start to dance deosil faster and faster as they chant, *"Spin we now to raise the power! Dance with the Old Ones. Dance! Dance! Here! Now! We raise the power! Dance with the Old Ones! Dance! Dance! Dance with the Old Ones! Dance! Dance! Dance with the Old Ones!"*

The Coven continues circling, faster and faster, chanting the last line, until the area is effectively charged.

Just on the point of collapse, all fall to the floor still with joined hands and pause, their heartbeats become one.

The foregoing can be compared to creating a Circle using the traditional means of water, salt, fire, etc. This way, everyone joins their energies in creating a powerfully charged space ready for the Quarter Guardians to help protect the area.

The HP then calls, *"Let us present our Magical Weapons. Let us enter the realms of the Mighty Ones."*

The HP remains in the North whilst the HPS goes to the East. She raises the Sword and invokes, *"All wise Eagle of the East, Great Ruler of tempest storm and whirlwind, Master of the heavenly vault, Great Prince of the Powers of Air. We await Thee."*

She turns inwards, raising the Sword and says, *"I bring the Sword of Air."*

She then replaces the Sword on the ground in the East.

She then goes to the South, raises the Spear and says, *"O thou Lion, Lord of lightnings, Master of the solar orb, Great Prince of the powers of fire. We await Thee."*

Turning inwards, she raises the Rod and says, *"I bring the Spear of Victory."*

She replaces the Spear and walks to the West.

She raises the Cauldron and says, *"O thou Serpent of old, Ruler of the deeps, Guardian of the bitter sea, Prince of the powers of water. We await Thee."*

Turning inwards, she raises the Cauldron and says, *"I bring the Cauldron of Cerridwen."*

In the North, the HP raises the Stone and says, *"Black bull of the North, horned one, dark ruler of mountains and all that lies beneath them, Prince of the powers of earth. We await Thee."*

Turning inwards, he raises the Stone and says, *"I bring the Stone of Destiny."*

The HP then places the Stone on the ground in front of the Altar. Facing North, he steps on the stone with both feet; arms outstretched and says, *"The Stone is the Gate to the Old Ones, the Old Ones that are, the Old Ones that were, the Old Ones which always shall be. For we are of them and they are of us. The Gate is open, let us sound the names. Great Lady of Victory, Mother of our tribe, we honour Thee."*

The Coven together vibrates the Goddess name *'Aradia'*.

The HP continues saying, *"Bull Horned Hunter, Keeper of our herds, Ruler of the Sky. We honour Thee."*

All vibrate the God name *'Karnayna'*.

The HP joins the Coven, and the HPS says, *"We are now sacred within the Holy Heart. We are gathered here tonight in the presence of the Mighty Ones to celebrate ... (gives a reason) ... Let the ritual begin."*

So there you have it, not quite a conventional Circle Casting, but one that has the input of everyone in the Coven. It is very well balanced and extremely 'earthy'.

The HPS can also be replaced by Covenors for calling the East, South and West.

We find that this sacred space is perfect for performing any ritual involving the elements, together with any form of ceremonial magic, the creation of talismans, or other very practical work.

The Circle is banished with the HP standing in the centre of the Circle with the Coven behind him, facing each Quarter in turn, saying, *"Powers of Water, I release you and bid you farewell. Powers of Fire, I release you and bid you farewell. Powers of Air, I release you and bid you farewell. Powers of Earth, I release you and bid you farewell."*

The Coven sing and dance, *"We've danced and sung our sacred way, between the worlds twixt night and day. Hand to hand and heart to heart, merry we've met now merry we part."*

Chapter Seventeen
The Tools

So, now it is time to talk about the Tools which are the same within our Tradition as any other Magical system which recognises the use of Eight Working Tools, which are presented to a Witch on their First Degree Initiation. These Tools are the Sword, the Athame, the Boline, the Wand, the Pentacle, the Thurible, the Scourge, and the Cords. Some Traditions do not use all eight. The Tools have practical, mystical, and magical uses.

The following notes are extracts from *'The Working Tools of a Witch'*, a series of articles on the Magical Weapons of the Craft of the Wise published in various witchcraft magazines by Simon circa 1979. It now forms one of the Books in our tradition that is handed to a student upon their Initiation.

We will examine each of these Tools, their methods of use, and their relationship to the symbology of the Circle. This will be done by considering the elements of the Circle and their various attributes. You might remember I discussed the issue of North and South and Fire and Earth with regard to pagans working in the Southern Hemisphere. The following is the reason why we work the way we do.

The Circle is divided into four elemental quarters. North for EARTH, East for AIR, South for FIRE, West for WATER and these elements are combined in Aether.

North is the direction to which the Wicca pray, the home of the Mighty Ones, and the place of greatest darkness. It is the Quarter of Binding, and to it are attributed the Pentacle and the Cords. The North Wind, Boreas, living behind the Watchtower, is often invoked. Lying inside the Watchtower is the sacred symbol of the North, the Stone of Destiny. In ceremonial magic, the northern Quarter is ruled by the Archangel Uriel.

As you are reading, remember that the Alexandrian Tradition and, to some degree, the Sussex System both contain a quantity of traditional witchcraft and, more importantly, several different ceremonial magical systems. So the correspondences you will see attributed to different Quarters, Tools and other aspects of a Magical Circle are very important, for they reflect specific energies in precise positions.

East is the direction to which the Solar Worshippers pray, and this includes Western traditional ceremonial magicians. The East is the Place of the Rising Sun, the Rebirth of the Sacrificed God, and the Place of Illumination. The Tools used to cause enlightenment are the Scourge and the Wand. Eurus is the East Wind, and to the East lies the Watchtower wherein the Sword of Light rests. In ceremonial magic, the Eastern Quarter is ruled by Raphael.

South is the direction of the hottest wind, the burning deserts, and the realm of fire. The Tools of Fire are the Sword and the Thurible. Ceremonial magicians invoke Michael with his Sword of Flame, corresponding to the Celtic Spear of Victory, which lies within the Southern Watchtower. Notas is the South Wind.

West is the direction of death and the Summerlands, the domain of the Goddess of Death and Love and Rebirth, the direction from which the original Wida, arrived from Atlantis, and the Working Tools of this Quarter are the Athame and the Boline. The Western Watchtower has the distinction of being the repository for two of the Sacred Celtic Treasures - the Cauldron of Rebirth, guarded by the Goddess Cerridwen, and the Crystal Chalice of Healing Waters. The West is the Quarter of Water. Ceremonial magicians invoke Gabriel.

The final element – the 'fifth Quarter' – should be considered as the quintessence of all four other elements combined. This element is Aether, called Akasha by Eastern esoterics. It is symbolised by the Pentagram, whose manifestation is Spirit, and whose Tool is Man.

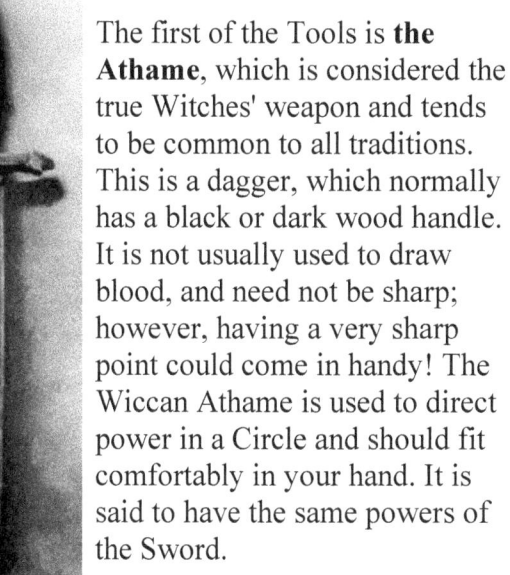

The first of the Tools is **the Athame**, which is considered the true Witches' weapon and tends to be common to all traditions. This is a dagger, which normally has a black or dark wood handle. It is not usually used to draw blood, and need not be sharp; however, having a very sharp point could come in handy! The Wiccan Athame is used to direct power in a Circle and should fit comfortably in your hand. It is said to have the same powers of the Sword.

I think the Athame is probably the first Tool a witch makes or purchases; I know it was mine. Let me say from the start that all tools that are created to become Magical Weapons are better for being fashioned or created by their owner. If you are lucky enough to have a workshop, garage or other place filled with hammers, screwdrivers and other normal tools, with a little bit of ingenuity, it is not difficult to set your mind to creating your own Tools.

Here's an idea: get an old circular saw blade, a piece of angle iron or old leaf spring from a car, any decent piece of steel that can be cut, ground and drilled into the shape of a dagger. Clean and sharpen it using some elbow grease and various grades of sandpaper. If you can find a forge, even better. Then find an appropriate handle, usually wood. I used a piece of ebony, black as, and hard as let me say. It took hours to sand that handle, with each stroke putting a little bit of my soul into it. A bit of horn can also be used; deer is good, and it can be stained or painted black.

If you can't find the time to make your own Athame, and really, you should, why not get a friend to help? Failing that, go hunting in the antique shops to find something appropriate. If you do buy an Athame, even if it is one from a witchy shop, put the effort into making it your own. Re-sand the handle, re-sharpen the blade, anything that will put some of your being into it, thereby making it yours and yours alone.

The White Handled Knife or **Boline** is the magical partner of the Athame and is used for all cutting or shaping functions within the Circle, like inscribing runes on a candle or cutting herbs. Our Coven Boline is a tiny 1 ½" long folding blade with a white bone inlay handle. It's a modern knife I found in a hunting store. Traditionally, the Boline is a small replica of a sickle, a curved blade used for cutting crops. Again, this is another Tool that could also be forged or made from scratch, remembering that it should be small enough to use like a pencil.

The Wand is used to invoke certain entities, usually Angelic and is used in place of the Sword in circumstances where it would be considered improper to use the Sword. Normally, of wood and traditionally the length of your arm from the elbow to the middle finger point. There are many kinds of wands and including the classic magician's wand of black and white, a phallic wand, a plain piece of wood, a staff, a walking stick, and even a phallic bone. Now that's a story for another time.

Although the classics go to great lengths to describe the preparation of the Wand and how it is to be inscribed, the Wand, when used in insular Craft, is quite simple. At either dawn or sunset, go to a willow tree that has grown for many years. Select a limb that is suitable for your working, and offer a prayer to the tree. Break off the length you require, about 1" thick, then pack the end of the break on the tree with fresh mud to preserve the tree's tissues. Knock on the tree three times in thanks and place a silver coin in the ground under the tree as payment. The Wand is trimmed to the length from the elbow to the middle fingertip when the arm is crooked. No other preparation is necessary, as the Wand carries the Earth charges from its source.

The Pentacle is a disc of wood or metal used as a talisman to invoke certain forces. In some traditions, the Pentacle is replaced with a stone. We currently have three Pentacles in our Coven. The first one I ever made was from a piece of common radiata pine, cut into a circle about 7" in diameter and ¾" thick. A pentagram was carved into the wood, and some runes I found on a similar Pentacle in one of the Farrar's books was later added. That one served us quite well back in the days before we were initiated.

The next one I made was from a piece of copper plate. Here we go again, talking about 'making' your Tools. Believe me, it means much more to you in the end, having put your blood, sweat and tears into the work. The copper I sourced from a local metal store. They were kind enough to cut it into a 10" square ready for me to file into a round disc! It was 1/8" thick. Again, it was one of those projects that took forever to file and polish. Once I had it round, I carved a pentacle on it, with the five points touching the edge. The third Pentacle is our Stone of Destiny, of which we have already spoken.

The Cords are another mystery of the First Degree. However, used as a cingulum tied around the waist denotes the level to which a witch has entered the mysteries of the Craft. The colour, length, and number of knots tied in the cord are mysteries to particular traditions. Common colours signify rank: black as Pagan, white as Neophyte, red as Witch, blue as Priest/ess and red/white/blue, mixed as High Priest/ess.

It was not that long ago that to enter the Magic Circle at one of the Australian witch's gatherings, you had to show your red cord. The number of knots and their position on the cord denoted who

and where you were from, just like a fingerprint! The Prince of Darkness once told Evelyn that he would unknot her Cord if she did not toe the line! Bet you can guess what the outcome of that was.

The Thurible is used to banish evil spirits and welcome good spirits. The particular incense used determines the type of entity that is attracted, and sometimes to stimulate our senses to assist meditation or alter consciousness. We have a few Thuribles, most are copper bowls filled with sand or other material, kitty litter is good, which will help disperse the heat from the charcoal blocks when fully lit. You used to be able to buy a flower-arranging bowl that had a criss-crossed wire top to keep the flowers in place; ideal for turning upside down and holding the charcoal blocks, but I have never been able to find another in the last 20 years or so. Whatever type of Thurible you use, be aware that it needs to be somewhat insulated, because it gets mighty hot as you walk around the Circle building that wall!

Some Covens use a Sword, but its use is optional. **The Sword** must be double-edged and cruciform. It is used to cast the Magic Circle and as a command over invoked entities in ceremonial rites.

Traditional Wiccan Covens usually have a Sword, like our own, basically to denote we belong to a system or tradition, and it represents the leadership of the Coven. The mystery of the Sword is the fact that it is wielded by the High Priestess but owned by the High Priest, and when taken back by the High Priest, the Coven is dissolved. Again, it's

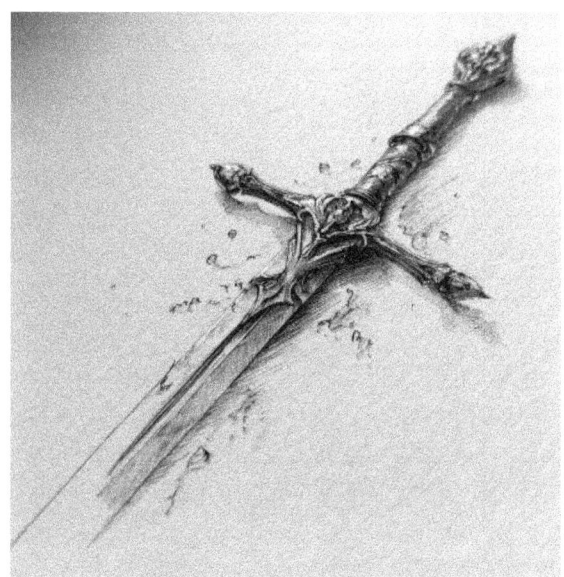 

another Tool at could be made by your hand, but we were again lucky enough to find ours in an antique shop made from genuine Toledo Steel.

The Scourge is the most misunderstood of all the weapons. The use of the Scourge is one of the mysteries of the First Degree and is used to cause purification and enlightenment. So I will leave its finer details to be another one of those surprises for later! This last Tool is another that should be made by hand, this time by the HPS of the Coven. With a little bit of imagination, a wand or something similar, and some supplies from your local Spotlight store, put together in a specific way, and hey presto, you have a Scourge!

All Tools are charged and consecrated in a specific manner relevant to each. It is not good manners to touch any working tool unless specifically asked to do so. Many Tools are marked with sigils or runes that relate to particular Mysteries. In some traditions, the runes are placed on the Tool using Indian Ink that can be washed off after the consecration. That way, an everyday object can be secretly used as a Magical Weapon, and no one would ever know!

The Eight Tools are placed on the Altar before working. They represent the four aspects of the Witch, and the Altar focuses the attention of the Witch on the Tools. The Altar supports the Tools.

The Tools are so-called for they are that with which the Witch works, but they are also called Magical Weapons for they protect the Witch from the fallacy of belief that he/she alone is important in the Universe. A Witch must have help if they are to work effectively; for *'There is no part of us that is not of the Gods.'*

Beyond a Year and a Day

The Altar is the connecting place between the worshipper and Deity and displays the Tools. The Tools must be in balance with each other. The Altar does not act on the Tools, but on the Witch, for it will show a lack of balance. So remember why things have a place, for disturbing that balance only disrupts energy.

The Altar is normally covered by a cloth to show that the true basis from which we work is concealed by a veil of illusion. Black is the preferred colour, for its neutrality does not detract from meditation upon the Tools. The cloth must not be used for any purpose other than to cover the Altar.

The Altar displays the Tools necessary for any ritual or specific operation. In most Craft workings, it also supports a Goddess and/or God image, and candles for illumination.

The Altar may be placed at the centre of the Circle, or more usually at the North. If a particular element is to be worked, the Altar may be placed in the Quarter corresponding to that element (e.g. if the Sylphs are to be contacted, the Altar may be placed in the East).

If the Altar is central to the Circle, the Tools are to be arranged so that each Tool is in the respective Elemental Quarter. This means that on facing each Quarter, the Tools opposite to the Quarter being worked are immediately visible, reminding the Witch that for every act there must be an act of balance with its opposite.

And so, the Circle exists as a Gateway between the World of Men and the Realm of the Mighty Ones. As the Circle connects the Four Quarters and Four Elements, it embodies within itself the Eight Working Tools. To cast a Circle is to declare oneself at one with the Circle and through its correspondences, with the Tools displayed upon the Altar. The Altar is the connecting point between the Witch and the Circle they cast.

I hope you can now see the importance and relevance of having the Tools in their correct positions and having the elements in their precise corresponding quarters. If you do not, you only show your ignorance, lack of balance and disrespect for the Gods and the power of the Elements.

Chapter Eighteen
Ritual

In general discussions concerning Craft philosophy and background information, we are often asked questions about ritual work. What is the aim of ritual? How rigid are rituals? Can you write them yourself? It is not always easy to give a ready-made answer, but I will attempt to set down a few ideas that may clarify some parts.

'Ritual is the dramatic enactment of myth, designed to make a sufficiently deep impression on the individual to reach his unconsciousness' - The Dictionary of Symbols by T Chetwynd.

'There are plenty of guidelines in respect of ritual work, but anyone with any experience will quickly realise that ritual work is an extremely personal method of working magic and contacting the Gods. What works for one person need not necessarily work for another. Someone might feel right performing highly elaborate, ceremonial rites, whilst another person feels at home with something very simple and straightforward. The important thing is that whichever way we choose, we do not lose sight of our aim or confuse the issue. This may sound like something of a cliché, but when we realise that the main aim of a ritual is to create a two-way link between spiritual and earthly powers, it goes without saying that our intention should be as clear as crystal. Certainly for a beginner but also experienced people, this point cannot be stressed enough.' – An extract from Morgana - Ritual Works Vol 8 No 1.

All rituals must have intention, i.e., there must be a purpose for the ceremony, even if it is simple devotion. The purpose must be implicit before the working and not changed during the course of the work. And of course, there should be a method by which the work will be performed. It must not be performed haphazardly. This does not mean perfection of performance, but simply a high quality in execution. The ritual leader must know what they are doing and move steadily towards that purpose using whatever method has been agreed upon, not changing that method in the middle of the stream.

The mood is very important. One works on many levels in ritual, for we live on all planes simultaneously. It is the inner response to the outer action that affects the changes caused by what we term magic. The inner or subconscious change reflects directly upon our outer physical plane self and directly and indirectly upon the self that exists on the other planes. Therefore, emotional control is necessary so that concentration and meditation can effectively be worked.

There are many methods of working rituals, and the methods depend on the type of work to be done. However, here is a simple outline that you can follow in constructing your ritual.

The first and most important is establishing your intent. There must be a specific reason for any ritual work. Are you conducting an Esbat or performing a Sabbat celebration, or even casting your Circle to perform a meditation? Casting a Circle and going with the flow of what might happen is stupid and could be dangerous, so be very specific and focus your intention on what is to be done.

The intention must be precise with a beginning and an end. Once you decide on the purpose, you should establish a front door, a back door and a route through.

You then need to construct the ritual outline. You must decide how you are going to do the work and who plays what part by constructing a step-by-step script of the performance. There should be no ambiguity, with everyone concerned knowing their place and role within the ritual.

You must identify what Beings or Forces are to be invoked or evoked and develop the appropriate plans and contingencies to deal with any possible outcome, planned or unplanned. Note that an Invocation is an action designed to attract some being, spirit or force to ourselves whose nature is greater or superior to our own. Evocation is the emotion of impelling our actions or wishes upon other types of existence whose levels of development are less than our own. Knowing the difference can be crucial in the execution of the ritual.

You must also consult the Correspondences and determine what elements (colours, incense, tools, God forms, Spirits, etc.) and any other contributing factors or influences are to be used in the ritual.

Next comes the preparation of the Circle. The Coven and the area must both be properly prepared, and the Circle cast in an appropriate manner for the working. This means creating a standard Wiccan Circle, a generic Sacred Space or a full-blown Ceremonial Temple.

Only then are the Gods invoked and the rite performed, remembering to follow the agreed script.

After all is finished, give thanks, close the Circle, and return to the mundane world.

We were very lucky in our early days, having learned our lessons well during our course; we set about creating our Esbats and Sabbats in a constructive way, and very little went wrong. It wasn't until we started to perform a little bit of ceremonial ritual that we had problems. Ever heard the saying *'be careful what you wish for, you just might get it'*?

So, back to basics and following the rules, we were again on the right track to a successful evocation! Preparation is so important in any type of working.

I cannot stress that enough. Do your homework thoroughly before casting a Circle.

On the topic of Ceremonial and Wiccan Circles, here is a description of the differences and similarities:

Ceremonial Circles	**Wiccan Circle**
Necessary for all magical operations.	Normally used.
9' in diameter with a 6" annulus.	Mostly 9' in diameter
The boundary is physically delineated with masking tape, symbols, etc.	Usually, but not always delineated.
Divine names are inscribed in an annulus.	No inscription.
Divine Names at cardinal points.	Candles at Divine Points.
Candles at Cross Quarters.	No candles at Cross Quarters.
No exit/entry from the Circle once conjuration commences.	Entry/exit through doorway in NE corner.
The circle protects the magician	The circle contains and magnifies the power of the Witch
Protection from harm is ensured by Divine Names.	Protection from harm by own energies and powers of the Mighty Ones.
Altar usually East or Centre with Magician facing East.	Altar in the North or centre.
Power derived from the divine.	Power derived from the Witch.
Archangels sometimes worked at cardinal points.	A variety of thought forms worked at Watchtowers.
Archangels invoked starting East and Banishing starting in the North.	Watchtowers invoked in the East, banishing starts in the West.
Magical Circle is considered to be a flat plane.	Witches Circle is a sphere - an extension of the etheric body of the Witch.
Circle cast East, South, West, and North.	Cast North, East, South, and West.

Chapter Nineteen
The Goddess

According to Starhawk in her book *'The Spiral Dance'*, the resurgence of interest in Paganism and Wicca is related to feminism. For many women, finding paganism is the first time they become aware of a Goddess religion. However, it is a mistake to think of Paganism or Wicca as solely Goddess-inspired worship. The Goddess takes her place beside, not in front of, or behind, her consort, the God.

The Goddess has many aspects and thousands of names, and she is not separate from the world; she is the world. She is manifest in each of us and can be recognised internally. All Goddesses are one Goddess. Regardless of what aspect you choose to believe, the Goddess remains universally the mother of life, the ruler of birth, death, and love. She is always the Goddess of women and the feminine within men.

Now there is something to ponder, you guys, when someone tells you to bring out your feminine side!

Some of the most commonly known and used aspects of the Goddess are the Earth Mother, the Bright and Dark Mother, the Moon Goddess and the Triple Goddess.

The Earth Mother is probably the most widespread and vivid face that the Goddess presents. She is fertility itself, She is the source from which everything comes, the life of all plants and animals and the very planet itself. She is the body and the soul of the planet, and therefore, it is not surprising that ancient people saw her as voluptuous and firmly enthroned on and identified with the Earth.

This, together with the fact that the Heiros Gammos (the sacred marriage by which the King had ritual intercourse with a priestess representing the Goddess to affirm his sovereignty over the land) took place on a mountaintop, could explain why all mountains are sacred to the Goddess and referred to as 'she'. It is as good a reason as any to nurture and care for all life on Earth, and the Earth itself. It is in itself a form of worship.

The Bright and Dark Mother represents the polarity within the Goddess. This is not to deny the polarity between the God and the Goddess, but rather says that there is light and dark within all. This internal polarity of the Goddess is the very nature of life itself, a cycle of life, death, and rebirth.

At the heart of the Bright Mother is the Dark Mother, and at the heart of the Dark Mother is the Bright Mother. The Goddess is both the womb and the tomb; she gives birth, creates form, nourishes, and reabsorbs the outworn before its reshaping and rebirth. If she were not the destroyer, she could not be the renewer.

Another example of this internal polarity is the female menstrual cycle. I know this is one of those subjects most guys like to stay clear of, but you need to have a clear understanding of these energies. It is so important that if one day you become an HP and are sometimes required to use your feminine energies a little more than usual.

So, back on track once again. During ovulation, she is the Bright Mother, ready to conceive and give birth; at the time of menstruation, she is the Dark Mother, inward-looking and purging. The Bright Goddess represents consciousness or awareness of our environment, pleasure, comfort, and fulfilment. The Dark Goddess, on the other hand, is representative of the mysteries of the unconscious, intuition and an indirect awareness of fertility.

The Dark Mother aspect is not to be feared or reviled because she is in us all. Learn to use this aspect in balance with the Bright Mother to become whole and balanced. One way to get in touch with the Dark Mother aspect is through meditation and expanding and improving your intuition and divination skills, for it is she who controls them. She is the key to a greatly expanded awareness, including awareness of herself.

The theme of the Triple Goddess is found in the mythology of all lands; she is found in all cultures because she is archetypal. The concept of the Triple Goddess is as old as time; it crops up again and again in widely differing mythologies, and its most striking visual symbol is the Moon in her waxing, full and waning phases. The fact that the moon cycle is reflected in the menstrual cycle of women touches on deep and mysterious aspects of the feminine principle and of the Goddess herself.

All Goddesses are one Goddess - but she shows herself in many aspects, all of which relate to the three fundamental aspects of the Maid (enchantment, inception, and expansion), the

Mother (ripeness, fulfilment, and stability) and the Crone (wisdom, retrenchment, and repose).

Every woman and every Goddess-form contains all three - both cyclically and simultaneously. No woman who fails to grasp it can understand herself; and without grasping it, no one can understand the Goddess. That is why it is equally important for men to fully comprehend these energies and begin to know the Goddess within them.

In 1897, Charles Leland, an American expatriate journalist, folklorist, and author, received a manuscript from an Italian Witch named Maddelena. This manuscript became known as *'Aradia - Gospel of the Witches'* or *'The Vangelo delle Streghe'*. It has become one of the key sources of the witchcraft revival in modern times. It is said that Maddelena was a semi-literate peasant woman born of an Italian witch family and led a wandering life in Tuscany.

The Vangelo tells us that Diana was the first created before all creation; in her were all things; out of herself, the first darkness, she divided herself into darkness and light. Lucifer, her brother and son, herself and her other half, was the light.

Diana had a daughter by her brother Lucifer, whom they named Aradia. She was sent to Earth to instruct mortals in the art of witchcraft. Diana said to her daughter, *"Tis true indeed that thou a spirit art, but thou wert born to become again a mortal; thou must go to earth below to be a teacher unto women and men who fain would study witchcraft in thy schools. And thou shalt be the first of witches known, and thou shalt be the first of all in the world."*

When Aradia had been taught to work all witchcraft and had imparted it to her pupils, she said unto them:

"Whenever ye have need of anything, once in the month, and better it be when the moon is full. Then shall ye assemble in some secret place, and adore the spirit of me, who am Queen of all witcheries. There shall ye assemble, ye who are fain to learn all sorcery, yet have not won its deepest secrets: to these will I teach things that are as yet unknown.

"And ye shall be free from slavery. And as a sign that ye be really free, ye shall be naked in your rites. And ye shall dance, sing, feast, make music and love, all in my praise. For mine is the ecstasy of the spirit, and mine also is joy on earth; for my law is love unto all beings. Keep pure your highest ideal. Strive ever towards it: let nought stop you or turn you aside. For mine is the secret door which opens upon the land of youth: and mine is the cup of the wine of life: and the Cauldron of Cerridwen, which is the Holy Grail of Immortality.

"I am the Gracious Goddess, who gives the gift of joy unto the heart of man. Upon earth, I give the knowledge of the Spirit eternal: and beyond Death, I give Peace, and Freedom: and reunion with those who have gone before. Nor do I demand sacrifice: for Behold! I am Mother of all living, and my love is poured out upon the earth. I am the beauty of the green earth; and the White Moon amongst the Stars; and the mystery of the Waters; and the desire of the heart of man.

"Call unto thy soul. Arise, and come unto me. For I am the Soul of Nature, who giveth life to the Universe. From me all things proceed: and unto me, all things must return; and before my face,

beloved of Gods and Men: thine inmost divine self shall be enfolded in the rapture of the infinite.

"Let my worship be within the heart that rejoiceth; for behold, all acts of love and pleasure are my rituals. And therefore let there be beauty and strength, power and compassion, honour and humility, mirth and reverence within you.

"And those who thinketh to seek for me know thy seeking and yearning shall avail thee not: unless thou know the mystery; that if that which thou seekest thou findest not within thee, thou wilt never find it without thee. For behold, I have been with thee from the beginning; and I am that which is attained at the end of desire."

And so, we call our Goddess once a month in a ritual called the Moon Rite, otherwise known as an Esbat. In olden days, Christians believed our people were able to draw the Moon out of the sky with their heathen magic. However, on the night when She is at Her highest, the Goddess does seem greater and closer than normal. We understand Her cycles and use Her magic to give value to our workings. The Moon Rite is a means by which we can weave our magic, using the High Priestess as a Path through which the Goddess may manifest.

The Witch regards creation as a feminine development or parthenogenesis from which the masculine principle was born. Lucifer, or Light, lay hidden in ice, but the regeneration or messiah of witchcraft is a woman, Aradia.

Remember this: that all Goddesses are one Goddess, and if you want to see what the Goddess looks like, turn to the person next to you.

The Witch was once a real factor or great power in rebellious social life, and to this very day, it is recognised that there is something uncanny, mysterious, and incomprehensible in women, which neither she herself nor man can explain. For every woman is at heart a witch.

Now I suggest you turn back to Chapter 8, our first Esbat, and re-read the ritual. That particular Calling Down of the Moon is used quite widely today by most Alexandrians. Of course, there are ones that are more elaborate and some just as easy short callings, but the crucial thing to appreciate is your intention and that of the Coven, being all on the same page.

"We call to thee Lady, the Lady of Night. The Lady of power, the Lady of might." In so calling, men need to put their masculine energies forward and use a little subtlety to coax the Lady. Women need to use the connection they already have with their femininity to call the Lady.

The whole purpose of the calling is to send out a plea for the Goddess to be present, like sending out an invitation. This calling cannot ever be a demand like invoking elementals or other entities. That will never work and only land you in trouble! The whole idea is to be able to pay homage to the Lady and, if She presents Herself, ask her for a boon or help with work you intend to perform in your Circle.

The important thing to remember is to keep the rhythm going in a sing-song sort of way with the Coven focusing their energy on the HP during his calling and reinforcing his words with, *"Lady of beauty, Lady above. Come at our call and give us your love."*

Just to recap on what I said in the Esbat chapter, we believe, if performed with the right amount of intent and love, the Goddess will manifest Herself in the body of the HPS.

So after the Calling is completed, the HPS turns around to face the Coven wearing the face of the Goddess. And sometimes it can be quite scary when the first words you hear from the mouth of your HPS are, *"As you, my children, gather below"*, and it is definitely not the usual voice of your HPS. That's when you know the Goddess has arrived and Magic is afoot!

"Whenever ye have need of anything, once in the month, and better it be when the moon is full."

Chapter Twenty
The God

The God of the Wicca is worshipped in many forms, but his primary form is that of Cernunnos or Karnayna, the Horned God. This image of the God is the earliest that we know in human history, and it is an image of great power that has endured in the human psyche through centuries of repression. He is probably the modern Witches' favourite god-form, and the horned crown is the favourite headgear of the High Priest, as the lunar crown is of the High Priestess.

The God has two aspects corresponding to the sun: The Lord of Light, corresponding to the day, and the Lord of Death and Resurrection, corresponding to the night. As the balance of night and day alters throughout the year, so one or the other aspect of the God becomes dominant.

Modern Witches still worship the Horned God in the same way as did their ancestors. The four great Sabbats, *Imbolg, Beltane, Lammas,* and *Samhain*, are still celebrated in the same way as they were hundreds, even thousands of years ago, with dancing and feasting in honour of the God and turning of the seasons.

The God embodies the power of feeling. His animal horns represent the truth of undisguised emotion, which seeks to please no master. He is untamed, but untamed feelings are very different from enacted violence. The God is the life force, the life cycle. He remains within the orbit of the Goddess; his power is always directed towards the services of life.

Therefore, the God is the proud stag who haunts the hearts of the deepest forests, that of the Self.

He is the stallion, swift as thought, whose crescent hooves leave lunar marks even as they strike sparks of solar fire. He is the goat-Pan, lust and fear, the animal emotions that are also the fostering powers of human life; and He is the moon-bull, with its crescent horns, its strength, and its hooves that thunder over the earth. Yet He is untamed. He is all within us that will never be domesticated, that refuses to be compromised, diluted, made safe, moulded or tampered with. He is free.

The Descent

On some Esbats, we find it appropriate, depending on the mood, to narrate the following version of The Descent.

It is the time of the Long Night, and I have laid my thick mantle upon the ground. The branches are bare, the water hardens, and life slows to a crawl.

Those that could have long since fled South to the warmth of my brother, Fire, and the lands of the Sun, while I walk the Earth that lies submissive at my feet.

My breath runs hot, and my eyes are cold. Death is in the air, and the Moon reflects red off my horns.

Glistening like diamonds, the stars fill the night sky, the wind howls like a lonesome wolf, and I feel the pulse of her that fills my veins with heady wine. I lift my muzzle to the sky and bugle my challenge loud and far. Who will meet my challenge? Who will dance the dance of life with the Lord of Death? My hooves ring like steel against the stone beneath the snow, sparks lighting up the night, and the sounds of my movement shake the slumbering trees.

From the forest, a soft glow appears. A woman, old and wrapped warmly against the wind, approaches. Frail she seems, but there is fire in her eye. *"I will dance the dance,"* she says. Her legs begin to shuffle and sway, while I watch, intrigued by the woman, and I begin to answer her motion with movement of my own. And the dance unfolded.

Round the forest, we whirled, and the wrinkles slipped away from her. Younger she became, as veil after veil fell away, taking the years with them. The stars danced above in silent awe, while the Moon flooded us with cold light.

Faster and faster the dance went, and our eyes grew wild with the thunder of the pulse of the dance, and our feet drummed the dance, hooves and horn, laughter and the slapping of feet pounded out the beat. And the steam rose from our bodies.

The Earth herself split open from the dance. I led her down, down into the depths of the Earth, she shed her veils along the way, twirling and swirling, and the dance moved on. At last, I stood in the place of my power, and the Throne of Death stood silently waiting.

"Milady, will you stay here at the Throne of Death with me and dance the Eternal Dance, for I am struck by your beauty and would have you for my companion."

"No, for I love you not", was her reply.

Looking at the radiant woman who stood in front of me, I said, *"Milady, you have danced the dance of life with me as none has danced before. What boon may I grant you?"*

With stars in her eyes, she replied, *"I want the spirit of my son returned to Life. I want to know the secrets of Death."*

"None has asked such a boon; how dare you ask so much?" I asked.

"The Earth needs my son to live. They must have the light and joy of Spring, the heat of Summer, and the harvest of Fall to survive. They need my son. The dance must go on," she softly spoke.

"Then kneel, and learn the Secrets of Death," I answered.

And I taught her, with pain and scourge, with laughter and love, with youth and age and darkness, I taught her. I showed her the heights and the depths, and at last, I taught her the peace of the Slumber of the Dead.

Lying my Lady down in the Earth, she would sleep, and dream of Spring, and of the Dance, and the Seed in her belly would swell and bring life to a new world. And she and the child would dance, and sing, and grow old, and the child, lover, king, will die. Once again, as the Circle goes round, she will come to me in the woods, and we shall Dance the Dance of Life once more.

But for now, it is quiet and dark, and the Moon is bright, and the wind howls, and I walk the world alone.

A little further in this story, I talk about our first dark moon Esbat. It was a time when we were all still newbies and were experimenting. Look forward to reading this part of our adventure, but for now, keep in mind that Wicca is a fertility religion; we cannot have the Goddess alone, there must be a God, that polarity and balance always exist and must never be forgotten when celebrating life and the seasons.

The image of the Horned God, often associated with nature, fertility, and wildness in pre-Christian traditions was deliberately reimagined by early Christian authorities to represent Satan, especially as part of a broader campaign to suppress pagan rites and redirect spiritual allegiance.

By the middle ages, Satan was depicted with goatish features, shaggy fur, and horns, traits lifted directly from the Greek god Pan and similar horned nature gods. These became a prime visual template. It wasn't just aesthetic, it was a tactical move: by associating beloved deities with evil, Christian leaders could discourage participation in ancient rituals and frame them as dangerous or heretical.

Chapter Twenty One
Initiation

So far, within this story, we have hinted at different types of dedication rituals and initiations. When our group first formed, we had no choice back then but to 'initiate' ourselves. We did this by using the Circle Cross Ritual and a Coven Dedication ceremony.

I recommend that anyone in a similar situation today do the same. The Circle Cross is widely used within the pagan community, both in Australia and more so in Britain.

We knew then that sometime down the track we would eventually be accepted for Initiation to the First Degree within Simon's Covenant after we had shown we could survive on our own for a year and a day – or at least we believed that was the case at the time! As it turned out, during our second year, Evelyn approached Thomas and asked the big question; Initiation followed shortly after. We now had a 'real' Priestess with a real Book of Shadows. Suffice it to say, we all followed in her footsteps.

So let us have a closer look at what types of 'initiations' there are and the types of ritual surrounding each. The following is written basically from an Alexandrian perspective, bearing in mind that the 'standards' are specific to my Tradition; that is not to say other Covens and Traditions do not follow a similar set of standards.

Dion Fortune wrote so many years ago in her book, Esoteric Orders and their Work, *"The Path which leads to initiation is the way of life which enables a man to rise above the desires and limitations of his personality and live in his higher self, and the experience of initiation is the transference of consciousness from the personality to the individuality. Man sets foot upon the Path immediately he desires to do so. This is the first step and a very simple one. But it is only by the continuation of desire that he sets one foot before another, which is the treading of the Path. It is very few souls who maintain a sufficiently steadfast desire to enable them to make perceptible progress; but desire, steadily continued, will presently be found to have achieved the desired aim, and the candidate will be placed in possession of the necessary knowledge to enable him to make positive progress and to direct his efforts to a definite end."*

Alex also wrote, *"Why does anybody want to be a witch? It is a question that most people ask. Do they seek sensation or 'home away from home', or do they really want spiritual progression? The answer is that people come for all these reasons; neither does the reason matter, for one gets out of Wicca as much as one puts into it."*

During ancient Greek and Egyptian times, the mysteries of the Goddess were so powerful that the Priests would demand candidates sell all of their possessions and return money in exchange for initiation, which led to corruption. When the Christian Church appeared, the people were free to experience the new church's mysteries, which led to the demise of the old ways and worship of the old Gods. After establishing its power, the church was able to partially defeat the heathen culture. As a result, pagans were compelled into the Old Mysteries and bound to them by an oath upon their lives so that the teachings should survive.

Modern-day initiates are free to accept the teachings of the old ways and are told in their oaths: *'You are free to come and go as your conscience dictates.'*

'An initiation is a symbolic death and rebirth, a rite of passage that transforms each person who experiences it. It marks acceptance into a Coven and a deep personal commitment to the Goddess. It is a gift of power and love, which members of a Coven give each other: the experience of those inner secrets that cannot be told because they go beyond words. For the individual, it becomes a change that causes revelation and understanding and sparks further growth and change.' – an extract from Spiral Dance by Starhawk.

The timing of an initiation is important. Traditionally, neophytes were required to study for a *'year and a day'* before they could be initiated. This rule is not always followed in present-day Covens, but it is a good one. Magical training cannot take place overnight. It is a process of neurological repatterning, which requires time. Unless an Initiate can, at least to some extent, channel energy and move into altered states of awareness, he or she will not benefit deeply from the ritual.

There is another, more subtle aspect to timing. Initiation also means 'beginning', and what is begun is the process of confronting the Guardian of the Threshold. A new initiate may not yet have faced the Shadow, but he or she must be committed to doing so. The Guardian's injunction, *'Better to fall upon my blade and perish than to make the attempt with fear in thy heart,'* does not mean the Initiate must be fearless, but that they are willing, despite fear, to go on, not to run away, to face their defences even though the process may be painful. *'Are you willing to suffer to learn?'* They are asked because learning and growth always involve pain.

Death and rebirth are the themes of initiation. Death is the root of our deepest fears and the true face of the Shadow. It is the terror behind vulnerability, the horror of annihilation that we fear. We learn through the mysteries that the feared Shadow, the Guardian of the Threshold, is none other than the God, who is named Guardian of the Gates, in his aspect of Death.

We must strip ourselves of our defences, pretensions, masks, roles, and all that we assume and put on to cross that threshold and enter the inner kingdom. The door opens only to the naked body of truth, bound by the cords, our recognition of mortality.

'Initiation into the Craft is a magical awakening. The exact ritual procedure used to bring about this awakening varies from tradition to tradition and from Coven to Coven, but the outcome is the same - unfoldment of the magical self of the initiate.' - Initiation into Witchcraft by Selena Fox.

'An initiation is an event which marks, or causes, a change in the level of awareness. Ritual is the methodology by which this change is achieved.' Ritual and Initiation by A.K. Rush.

Every culture at every stage seems to have the phenomenon of these ceremonies, whose purpose is to facilitate and celebrate significant growth. Initiations vary in content according to what facts or states the initiate is supposed to realise, but the basic structure of the ritual seems to be universal: Separation of the individual from the rest of the community.

This symbolises a return to a primal state.

Physical and spiritual tests, such as fasting and meditation, that prove one's fitness. The psychological dismemberment of the person's normal mode of thought and behaviour leads to a symbolic 'death'.

- Education into the mysteries through tutelage.
- Vows of secrecy.
- Ending with ritual rebirth into the new community, by a new code of behaviour and often under a new name.

The purpose of initiation rituals is to teach several significant things: how to confront crisis and survive; how to contact deeper layers of awareness; and how to distinguish the sacred - in other words, how to implement a system of regeneration.

The Wiccan Initiation ceremony is similar to Qabalistic and Masonic initiations and, like them, owes its origins to the ancient mystery religions. A key difference with other forms of magical initiation, however, is that initiation is given to a man by a woman and to a woman by a man. The only exception is that a woman can initiate her daughter; she who gave the first birth can give the second. A man can also initiate his son because they are part of themselves.

Most traditions possess a system of degrees to denote the amount of training that the members of the Coven have undergone. There are usually three degrees. The First degree is the degree of the Initiate. The Second degree, you become an Elder in the Coven. The Third Degree is that of the High Priest or High Priestess.

Some traditions, like our own, have pre-initiation degrees that apply to what is called 'outer-court' teachings. We have two, the Paganing ritual and the Crafting ritual.

No matter what the degree structure is, the important thing to remember is that the material you are supposed to learn on your way up is the foundation on which you build your future understanding.

All too many people rush through the basics to collect as many degrees as possible, only to find that they have wasted their time pursuing the illusion of prestige that goes along with the degrees and never gained the knowledge and experience the degrees are supposed to represent.

Ritual nudity - in the First Degree Initiation, the Initiate is prepared by removing his or her clothes. Ritual nudity has a very ancient tradition. By the Celts, nudity was considered to offer supernatural protection, and although we have no record of how it was used in religious rites, we know that the Celts frequently went into battle naked, their bodies covered with war paint and tattoos.

In the mystery rites of Isis and Osiris, the Initiate also commenced the rite naked, although by the end of the rite, they had been reclothed in ritual garments. Other traditions prefer to use ritual robes, generally of a uniform design and colour, and these serve the same purpose as ritual nudity, which is the removal of the normal everyday persona of the individual.

In initiation, the removal of clothes also has another symbolic meaning, which is that naked, we are extremely vulnerable. By being willing to expose ourselves in a very literal sense, we have to make an act of love and trust, the two passwords which bring us into the Circle, and we also have to be willing to cast aside our persona and enter the Circle as we first entered the world, naked and vulnerable.

The two Outer Court 'initiations' are the Paganing and Crafting rituals; they are more of a dedication than an initiation. Let us firstly look at the Paganing ritual.

A Paganing is given to someone who has done no formal training. It is usually given to someone who has been accepted into a Coven as a trainee or neophyte. They then undergo 12 months of training before a First Degree. The ritual, known as the Circle Cross, is an introduction to the Elements and The Mighty Ones, where the Initiate gives their mind to the Goddess.

Before the ritual is undertaken, the pagan is required to have reached three standards. They have an understanding of the beliefs and practices of the religion in which they have been raised or an understanding of two mainstream religions (this gives them a benchmark on which to compare both paths); have investigated the beliefs and practices of paganism; and have a genuine desire to adopt the beliefs and practices of paganism. They must also be over 18 years old and of sound mind.

In preparation for the ritual, the Initiate is directed to refrain from stimulants (tea, coffee, chocolate, drugs, alcohol, etc.) for three days before the ritual;

to have no contact with other Crafters; to have no sex, and to not eat any protein for the last 24 hrs.

After their Paganing, they are advised that their training will be given by the HPS and HP and will last for a year and a day, during which time they will celebrate the Eight Sabbats with their designated Coven or Pagan Grove.

A Crafting is given to someone who has successfully completed a formal system training course. The Crafting Ritual is designed to enact an Oath of Secrecy from the Initiate and is a preparation for the First Degree, which is given 40 days after the Crafting ritual.

The standards expected of a Neophyte are that they must have successfully undertaken a formal System Course (equal to that of a fully trained Pagan); they must prove their dedication and enthusiasm to Coven leaders, and they must be over 18 years and of sound mind.

In preparation for the ritual, the Neophyte is directed: to refrain from stimulants (tea, coffee, chocolate, drugs, alcohol etc.) for three days before the ritual; to have no contact with other Crafters; to have no sex; not to undertake any craft or magical workings; and to not eat any protein for the last 24 hrs.

After the ritual, the Neophyte is told that a First Degree will be given after 40 days. During this time they will be banished from the Coven and have no contact with any other Crafters. They are not permitted to practice the Art and are advised to meditate on their future First Degree Initiation, and what it will mean to them.

In theory, a First Degree can be given in a normal year and a day. By the time the Initiate has undertaken the formal system training course (usually at least 4 months), being banished for a month after, then another month discussing their future and preparation for the Crafting, then the 40 days after the Crafting – that totals close to 8 months of pretty intensive training before the First is taken.

The First Degree Initiation is given to someone who has successfully completed the training given at the Pagan level or to have been Crafted. Their training must have included:

- A good understanding of the beliefs of the Wida.
- A good understanding of the development of paganism and matriarchal religions.
- Be capable of casting a Circle and holding the boundary of that Circle.
- An understanding of the eight Sabbats and being capable of fully participating in their observance.
- Knowledge and appreciation of the Esbat.
- A thorough understanding of the eight paths.
- A good understanding of at least three methods of divination.
- A good understanding of the principles of psychic healing.
- A good understanding of herbalism and proficient in making ointments, salves, tinctures, extraction of oils and herbal remedies.

- An understanding of the First Degree Initiation Rite.
- An understanding and use of the eight working tools.
- Capable of remaining silent.

In preparation for the ritual, the Initiate is directed that for one week before the ritual, they are: to have no stimulants (tea, coffee, chocolate, alcohol etc.); no sex; a cold shower in the evening and a hot shower in the morning; no contact with other Crafters; and for the last 24 hours, no protein.

The Second Degree initiation is usually given around 3 years after the First. Not all Initiates want a Second Degree; some are content being part of a working Coven and do not desire to teach or hive off to start their own group. Those who work towards a Second undergo further training that gives them:

- A thorough understanding of the First Degree Initiation rite.
- An understanding of the Second Degree Initiation and the meaning of Handing down of Power.
- A complete understanding of the principles of Apostolic Succession.
- A complete understanding of the Eight Paths.
- The capability to conduct the Rites of the Sabbats and Esbats.
- A thorough understanding of polarity.
- An advanced level of capability to conduct Pathworking and Guided meditations.
- Achieved a level of advanced Spells, Healing techniques, and Divination.
- An ability to write Rituals.
- Has the Eight Working Tools and has properly consecrated them.
- A complete understanding of the Legends of the Wida - the Legend of Atlantis, the Legend of Aradia, the Legend of The Descent, and the Legend of the Cauldron.
- A good understanding of the differing Craft traditions and a respect for them.
- A good working knowledge of mythology.
- Has memorised the Theban Script, and can translate short passages.
- Proficient in the use of the Middle Pillar Exercise and the Lesser Ritual of the Pentagram.
- Has a desire and proven ability to teach within the Craft.
- Has undertaken research into magical and pagan practices under direction.
- Has a love of the Mighty Ones, and their Children, and a desire to continue their worship.
- Has loyalty to the System and its Elders.
- Capable of teaching students on one level while knowing another.
- A complete understanding of the role of the HPS and HP in a Coven.

- A complete understanding of the First Book of Law.
- Has had a God/Goddess contact.
- Is capable of remaining silent.

The Third Degree is given to someone who must be prepared to form a working partnership and set up a Coven. Except in unusual circumstances, the Third Degree is a ritual for a working pair. As I intimated previously, the Third in Britain is usually given at the same time the Second is taken.

The standards of a Second Degree that are taken to the Third should include the following:

- Capable of performing the First and Second Degree Initiation rites and the Handing down of Power.
- Capable of teaching students on one level while knowing another.
- Has administrative and political ability and skills.
- Has a complete understanding and ability in the use of the Eight Paths.
- Has undertaken research into practices of ritual magic.
- Capable of forming a Ceremonial Circle with reference to a Grimoire.
- Capable of Magical Invocations/Evocations.
- Understand several methods of Ceremonial Scrying.
- A good understanding of Sexual Magic and The Great Rite.
- Understands the Female and Male Mysteries.
- Is capable of Advanced Healing and Spell work.
- Has worked on The Shadow.

As a Third Degree, a person is responsible for his/her own Path. Our System would expect the Initiate to research and develop specialities that he/she would use for the good of the Craft and the worship of the Old Gods.

I have hinted at several new topics in the previous few paragraphs that I haven't yet mentioned in this story. However, this is not a place to discuss such issues in further detail, for I believe it is best reserved for that time you find a teacher, and each is discussed in turn at the appropriate time.

Chapter Twenty Two
The Ordeal Revisited

Now you know the theory behind Initiation, the hows and the whys. Go back to the beginning and re-read my ordeal. In light of what you now know, I hope you understand my feelings back then and some of those reservations that played on my mind at the time.

At this point, some of you might say, What's the point? I don't like joining clubs. I've got everything I need from the internet to self-initiate, and maybe dozens of other reasons; fair enough, whatever suits you.

Wicca is a mystery religion, which means you have to experience a revelation during the initiation ritual and sometimes the handing down of power, which does not always occur, but at least your initiator shows you a doorway or path that leads to a revelation. This knowledge, magic, sensation, enlightenment, and the whole experience can never be acquired through self-initiation.

Let me tell you that initiation is like a marriage between you, the Gods and the Coven, or at least the Tradition you are joining and is supposed to last a lifetime. Someone once said that once you tread the Wiccan pathway, there is no going back. Once you have learnt a mystery, you cannot unlearn it. Therefore, think seriously before committing yourself to the Wiccan way.

Now might be a good time to talk about Craft names. During your Initiation, you get to choose a new name, your Craft name, or your Magical name. During your rebirth into the Craft, you shed the connections to your mundane former self and re-emerge as your new magical self.

Your Craft name is used when conducting Craft business, for instance, at an Esbat or Sabbat with your own Coven or other family Covens or even a conference or workshop run within a particular tradition or even in the public forum when you are representing your Craft. Your attendance at any of these events will not be as Joe Blow, but your chosen Craft name.

Your Craft name will eventually become a switch in your head. Every time someone calls you by your Craft name, that switch is activated, and you respond as your Craft persona, not your everyday self. If someone telephones me and says, "Hey Fred, how are you going?" I react as every day, Fred. If I pick the phone up and the caller says, "Good morning, Dylan." Instantly, that switch is thrown, and I respond accordingly. Just like if I call one of my Coven members. I would say, "Hello, Aaron, it's Dylan." Instantly, Aaron would shit himself and think, "What have I done?" Just joking, but you get the idea about using your Magical Name.

It does not happen in most traditional initiatory Wiccan systems, but in the general Pagan and witchy community, some people decide to name themselves Lady or Lord Whatever. Attend an open Pagan gathering and you will probably find half a dozen Lady Ravenclaws or something similar. Return the following year, and you will find she has changed her name to Moonstar! Many people use God or Goddess names or adopt character names taken from films or books. We think this is a wee bit ostentatious.

Let me offer some advice. The titles Lord and Lady are reserved for people who are Elders within an established tradition. A name taken from a Harry Potter book will not afford you credibility within a magical community, and the adoption of a deity name is seen as most pretentious.

People tend to use the internet a lot today to help them find their Craft name. They look up sites that offer the names of famous witches or a Book of pagan names. Some even have a computerised witch name generator! Whatever floats your boat.

My advice is to think long and hard and conduct some serious research. It is the same as getting a tattoo, once you get it, it is there for life and bloody hard and bloody painful to erase it! Why not try a meditation, even a pathworking, or another type of ritual or ceremony to find a name? Ask the Gods themselves. You never know, they may answer your call. Even divination works; use runes or the tarot. Whatever method you choose, your Craft name should reflect your new you when you emerge on the other side of that initiation door.

Someone is going to ask, "Why Dylan?" It's a Welsh name for starters, and Dylan was the son of... The answer is somewhere in this story.

Chapter Twenty Three
The Book of Shadows

Many books contain the key to the mysteries, but opening these books and discovering the key that will open the door to the mysteries is another thing.

Every tradition and every cult has had its books, its bibles. Those who have or will have read them will learn to understand the unity of all creeds, despite the differences existing in the rituals of various countries. The Sepher Bereshith of Moshe is the Jewish bible, the book of Zohar is the bible of modern magicians, the Apocalypse, and the Gospels form the Christian bible, the legends of Hiram are the bible of Freemasonry, the Odyssey is the bible of the so-called Polytheism in Greece, and the Hindu Vedas are the scriptures of India. The Witches also have their bible.

The Book of Shadows, the bible of the Witches, is one of the most controversial books in modern Witchcraft. Many present-day witches believe that a part of it has been adapted from the rituals of the Golden Dawn, which was formed in 1888 by MacGregor Mathers, Westcott and Woodman. Others say it was added to by Aleister Crowley and Dion Fortune.

'The leaders of the Alexandrians, teaching their wisdom and way of life, believe all these things to be true in part, just as the Holy Bible of the Christians is several books compiled over the ages by the great patriarchs and teachers of wisdom, added to and subtracted from over the centuries. We do not doubt that many of the origins of our rituals in the Book of Shadows are less than one hundred years old, but by tracing through the modern concept, one can find echoes of earlier traditions which mythical, classical, historical and theological research will prove beyond a shadow of a doubt to be true. Lines of Virgil, Solon, Plato,

the great teachers of Egypt from the Book of the Dead, echo across its pages' – an extract from The Book of Shadows, a part of the Alex Sanders Lectures.

The Book of Shadows is traditionally a hand-copied book of rituals, recipes, training techniques, guidelines, and other materials deemed important. Each tradition has its own standard version of the Book, and each Witch's book will be different as he or she adds to it with time from many different sources. Only another Witch can see your Book of Shadows. Also, traditionally, it may never leave your hands or possession until death, when it should be destroyed.

The foregoing is generally what has been in print and commonly known, but let us dispel the myth and cut to the chase.

A Book of Shadows is not just a hand-copied book of rituals, recipes, training techniques, guidelines, and other materials; it is a specific text. It does not contain recipes or spells added by the owner. It is an exact duplicate of the Initiates' Initiator's Book, complete with errors, blotches, and dirty marks. If you are Alexandrian, your Book is nearly an exact duplicate of Alex's. If you are Gardnerian, it is a near-perfect copy of Gerald's.

I say 'near perfect copy' because as each initiate copies their new book from their initiator's book, most tend to make some kind of mistake. So later in life then the initiate becomes the initiator, and the next initiate will copy their initiator's book, complete with mistakes. And so it goes. So my Book of Shadows is pretty close to Alex's copy, but with a couple of minor differences!

During a ritual, once when I was holding a candle and my Book for my HPS to narrate something from the Book, it caught alight. Before I could put it out, a couple of pages on the bottom, left-hand corner got a little scorched! All my Initiates from that day forward have had to burn the bottom left-hand corners of three pages from the Book! Just like the knots in a First Degree's Cord, anyone can identify themselves by their Book of Shadows; it is like a fingerprint.

The Book of Shadows itself is simple in construction, and First Degree Initiates tend to underestimate its utter simplicity. The Initiates' first experience of this book is during their Initiation ritual when the blindfold has been removed and he/she is presented with the tools of a Witch. The Initiate is then made aware of what his or her duties are regarding the keeping of a Book of Shadows.

The first task a new Initiate undertakes is to hand-copy their book from their Initiator's book. This task usually takes a few days, sitting down with your Initiator so that they can answer questions and, nearly always, decipher illegible handwriting! I remember being told the story of a new Initiate who lived in the Midlands of England, a half-day's ride on the train from her Initiator. She had a window of about two hours every Sunday afternoon that her Initiator was available, so she could write her Book of Shadows. It took her a couple of months to finally complete her work! I am sure someone is going to ask why they cannot obtain a photocopy of their Initiator's Book or have an electronic copy emailed to them. I am not even going to dignify that question with an answer.

The Warning written by Gerald Gardner in 1953 in his Book of Shadows, says:

"Keep this book in your own hand of write. Let brothers and Sisters copy what they will, but never let this book out of your hands, and never keep the writings of another, for if it be found in their hand of write, they may well be taken and tortured. Each should guard his own writings and destroy them whenever danger threatens. Learn as much as you may by heart, and when the danger is past, rewrite your book. For this reason, if any die, destroy their book if they have not been able to, for, if it be found, 'tis clear proof against them. 'Ye may not be a Witch alone'; so all their friends be in danger of the torture. So destroy everything not necessary.

"If your book be found on you, 'tis clear proof against you. You may be tortured. Keep all thought of the cult from your mind. Say you had bad dreams, that a Devil caused you to write this without your knowledge.

"Think to yourself, 'I Know Nothing. I remember nothing. I have forgotten all.' Drive this into your mind. If the torture be too great to bear, say, 'I will confess. I cannot bear this torment. What do you want me to say? Tell me and I will say it.'

"If they try to make you talk of the brotherhood, do not, but if they try to make you speak of impossibilities, such as flying through the air, consorting with the Devil, sacrificing children, or eating men's flesh, say, 'I had an evil dream. I was not myself. I was crazed.'

"Not all Magistrates are bad. If there be an excuse, they may show you mercy. If you have confessed aught, deny it afterwards. Say you babbled under the torture; you knew not what you did or said. If you be condemned, fear not. The Brotherhood is powerful. They may help you to escape if you are steadfast. If you betray aught, there is no hope for you, in this life, or in that which is to come. But, 'tis sure, that if steadfast you go to the pyre, drugs will reach you. You will feel naught, and you go but to Death and what lies beyond, the ecstasy of the Goddess.

"The same with the working Tools. Let them be as ordinary things that anyone may have in their homes. The Pentacles shall be of wax that they may be melted or broken at once. Have no sword unless your rank allows you one. Have no names or signs on anything. Write them on in ink before consecrating them and wash it off at once when finished.

"Never boast, never threaten, never say you wish ill to anyone. If any speak of the craft, say, 'Speak not to me of such, it frightens me, 'tis evil luck to speak of it.'

"For this reason: the Christians have spies everywhere. These speak as if they were well affected, as if they would come to Meetings, saying, 'My mother used to go to worship the Old Ones. I would that I could go myself.' To these ever deny all knowledge.

"But to others ever say, 'Tis foolish men talk of witches flying through the air; to do so they must be light as thistledown,' and 'Men say that witches all be bleary-eyed old crones, so what pleasure can there be in witch meetings such as folk talk on?'

"Say, 'Many wise men now say there be no such creatures.' Ever make it a jest, and in some future time, perhaps the persecution will die, and we may worship safely again. Let us all pray for that happy day."

The preceding is the text that was published on a bulletin board many years ago and made public, so I break no oath in re-printing it – of course, that is not to say it is what is actually written in Gardner's Book – you will never know until that day you make the assay.

So what did that all mean? Keep your mouth shut and do not show your Book to anyone who is not an Initiate! That is exactly why the Book of Shadows remains a secret, only to be viewed by Initiates. It was a tradition that was started many years ago, and I hope it remains for many years to come. For it is one of those little secrets you look forward to knowing as you get closer to your Initiation.

Most Initiates keep several Books. Their Book of Shadows, once created, is never changed in any way. Their working Book or Spell Book is a book they write all their recipes, their rituals and all other workings; a diary, if you like. This is what most non-initiates refer to as their Book of Shadows.

A Coven also keeps several special Books, each has a different name and all have a particular purpose that is specific to their group, Tradition or System, and of course, is always secret! I cannot tell you anymore – so let us move on.

"What of Witchcraft?"
"Speak not to me of such, it frightens me, 'tis evil luck to talk of it."

Part Three
Working the Craft

The Art, the Devotion, and the Discipline of Magic

If the first part of this book whispered 'open the gate', the second part is the firm step through it. No longer content to wonder at the moon, the seeker now learns to call down its light, to shape, to summon, to become. *Beyond a Year and a Day* continues, where the sacred becomes skilful, and the mystical becomes method.

Working the Craft is not just a manual of spells. It is a sanctum of practice, forged in ink and intention. These chapters illuminate the lived experience of magic: the trance that unlocks deeper knowing, the script that shapes unseen forces, the herbs and runes and sacred names that ripple outward to touch the world. This is where transformation becomes tactile, and power is not possession but presence.

Through *Morthwork* and *Magical Scripts*, through *Healing* and *Runecraft*, we meet the Craft in its daily devotion, as a rhythm of being, not a performance. The pentagram is more than a symbol; it is a compass. The altered mind becomes a doorway, not a distortion. And always, there is the quiet guidance of the elements, the watchtowers, the laws that shape what we dare to ask, and what we are willing to give.

This is not the path for the casually curious. It is the path of the committed, of those who would learn not only about magic, but with it, through it, as it.

Welcome to the crucible. The Circle has been cast. The work begins.

Chapter Twenty Four
Morthwork

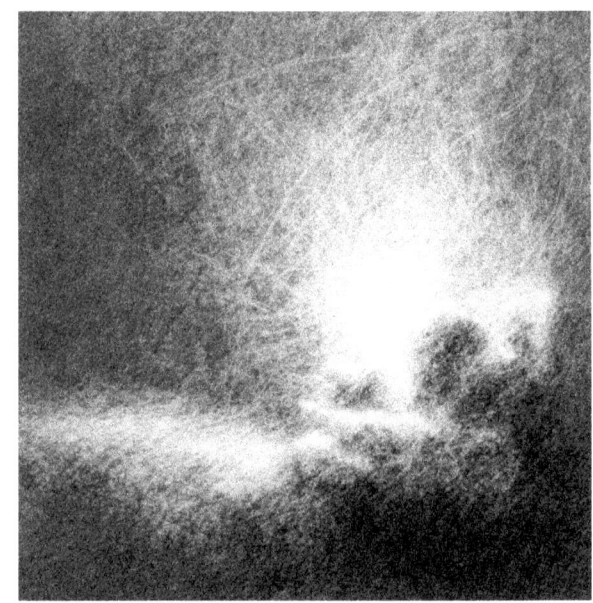

Morthwork is the creation of magic, achieved either tangibly or intangibly, without apparent cause. Aleister Crowley, in his book, *Magick in Theory and Practice*, defines magic as *'the science and art of causing change to occur in conformity with will'*. He further states that *'magic is the science of understanding oneself and one's conditions. It is the art of applying that understanding in action.'*

The word 'Morthwork' appears to be unique to the Sussex Tradition, and is only found in its Book of Shadows. When we refer to creating spells or other types of magic, we refer to that activity as Morthwork. However, it would also appear that the word 'morth' is an old Norman word meaning secret killings or murder. Believe what you may, but we certainly do not use magic for anything but good.

Most folks understand that magic is the act of creating a spell, a healing spell or a love spell using candles, incense, and chants, but it is a lot more and a large part of a Coven's work.

The words 'black' and 'white' seem to be used quite a bit today. Referring to a White Witch or Black Magic, etc. Believe me, there is no such thing. Nothing is black or white. Magic is magic, a Witch is just a witch, regardless of how and what they practice. Everything is in shades of grey, and it be on the practitioner's head how they conduct themselves; shades of bad or shades of good. Remembering that whatever you do will be returned threefold. If you want to be a bad arse and hex someone, fine, be prepared to suffer the consequences, just like someone who sends out healing energy in a magic spell to help someone, threefold return. On the other hand, karma is a bitch sometimes and has a wonderful bite.

We Wiccans believe that there are eight ways of creating magic. These separate paths can sometimes be combined or simply used alone. They are: *Ritual, Chants, Meditation, Cords, Drugs and Wine, Scourge, Dance, and The Great Rite.*

These are the Eight Paths to creating magic, but there are also Eight Festivals within the year - therein is another mystery! So let us break it down and look at each path.

A Ritual is probably the most customary method of working magic and is best performed in a Circle. It is a sequence of actions comprising movements, words, and objects, performed in an appropriate place and according to a prescribed structure. This is what we usually refer to as 'the script'. Think of it as 'theatre'.

There are three types of rituals: **Ceremonies, Rites and Spells.**

A Ceremony is an event of ritual significance performed on a special occasion. It can be a ritual of celebration or thanksgiving. It may mark a rite of passage, such as a birth or a marriage or a seasonal festival such as the Summer Solstice. For those involved in performing the ceremony, it requires a particular level of consciousness, which is intentional and focused. Those observing may not feel the same energies. Therefore, no specific outcome can be expected during the ritual. A ceremony is never altered during its performance.

A Rite is a ceremony performed to achieve a defined physical conclusion. It may be used in healing, to influence the earth's energies, some of the Major Sabbats, an Esbat, of course, or for many other reasons. A Rite differs from a Ceremony in that, as magic is affected by emotions, power does not necessarily flow as expected. A Rite is more flexible than a Ceremony insofar as it may change during its performance according to the wills of both Gods and men and other forces.

A Spell is a short ritual usually performed without any formal working area defined and at the whim of the operator. What better place than the witch's kitchen? A Spell relies heavily on a sudden burst of emotion. Passion is the key to creating an effective Spell. Spells may have traditional wording, so are ritualistic, or they may be created to serve a peculiar need. Ever cursed someone whilst driving your car? Most Spells are in rhyme, and they are the better for this, as the rhyming sequence ensures the exact same repetition each time, aiding their efficacy.

A Chant is the rhythmic speaking or singing of words or sounds and may range from a simple melody involving a limited set of notes to highly intricate musical arrangements. Generally, they should be simple and have heavily stressed beats, rising and falling with emotional tides. Their function is to impress upon the Old Ones your needs or to remind you of the reason for your actions (reinforcing your Will). Chants alter your breathing rate and rhythm, and so your heartbeat changes. Chants should be very carefully composed so that the vibrations are in harmony, thus drawing power. Chants will only be effective if you let yourself go and lose yourself in the vibrations.

Meditation is the result of constant thought on a single idea. You must first consider a facet of existence, then concentrate all your thoughts on that idea to the exclusion of all else, and after a period of practice, a state of meditation is achieved. This is called 'intent'. Prolonged periods of meditation combined with fasting can be very effective in putting you in touch with the realities behind existence, those that we call the Mighty Ones. Half-hearted meditation will achieve nothing. You must be prepared to spend several days in meditation if you are to achieve significant results without the use of other paths.

Our Cords are not only used to hold our pants up, hang our Athame on and identify our rank within our community; they are also used to perform some very special forms of magic, like immobilising certain parts of the body to aid in meditation. They are sometimes used to restrict blood flow, which is known as Warricking. It is an extremely dangerous practice and must never be attempted alone. A Worl Tutor (someone trained in the instruction and practice of the art) should always be present to assist with any warricking. Incorrect application of the cords will cause death.

The Cords are also used in knot magic and as a symbol for the magical link. Through the contemplation of certain knots, plaits, and other features of the Cord, a trance state can be achieved, much like in the use of a rosary or prayer beads.

Drugs used to gain the sight are either inhaled, swallowed or rubbed on the skin. Drugs can be used to alter the state of consciousness quickly, but only at the expense of losing control over the results; therein lies the danger. One of the better-known witch's drugs is Flying Ointment! This has many ingredients depending on your particular learning, including mandrake, opium, belladonna, hemp, and other illegal or noxious elements. Using any of these substances is a dangerous practice, and instruction in their safe preparation and use is given when an Initiate has shown a deeper understanding of the other methods of magic.

So, putting the illegal and insane use of hallucinogens aside, one of the best types of drugs is incense! This is a major tool for altering consciousness in either a physiological, psychological, or psychic way. Incense can be of either plant or animal origin, and care must be taken in selecting the appropriate incense for ritual, as the origin of the substance will determine its vibrational rate. Frankincense and patchouli are traditionally considered the best for opening the doors between the worlds, but many others are just as effective and equally as dangerous. Some incense commonly used in rituals are Sandalwood, which improves social gatherings; Pine for God festivals; Rosemary to improve concentration; and Rose for it calms thoughts.

Incense is a reminder to us of the smoke of the sacrificial fire, for the physical sacrifice is of too dense a vibration for its energies to be absorbed by the power that it attracts and to which it is offered. The incense smoke acts as an intermediary between the Witch and that which is invoked.

Wine is the blood of the grape, and, by Mystery, the blood of the earth and of the Gods. We can take the power of the Gods by drinking Their blood. Different wines have different effects. Wines are used for toasts, for example, Barley wine for toasting the grain God, White Chablis for the Moon Lady, Hock for Bridget, and Claret for Cerridwen. As a rule: white wine for the Lady; red wine for the Lord; light wine in Summer; and dark wine in Winter. Toasts should never be made with spirits. Use light wines to explore sky mysteries and heavy wines to explore earth mysteries.

Wine used magically should always be at, or slightly above, room temperature. Drink the wine slowly, and let it fully coat the mouth before swallowing. A period of fasting should precede the use of wine. Wine and dancing – maybe think about that.

Probably no other tool of the Craft is more controversial than **the Scourge**. As a Symbol of Power and Domination, it has led to accusations of sexual perversion by ignorant persons both within and without the Craft. Its prime importance is to cause purification and enlightenment, and not the 'gaining of sight' through flagellation, as most mistakenly believe. It remains in many of the older Covens as a most potent weapon.

The Scourge is seldom used alone; it is normally combined in use with Drugs and also the Cords. Gentle stroking with the Scourge thong tips will induce a light trance state. In our tradition, the Scourge is used and first seen by an Initiate on their initiation night. It is never shown, and only discussed with non-initiates in general terms and is saved to be a special surprise for only those who have the courage.

Magical Dance can be of three types: *Ring, Processional, and Chain dances.*

Ring dances, particularly when quick-moving and accompanied by chanting, cause an altered state of consciousness. It is important to keep your body relaxed and allow yourself to move in a very fluid manner, completely letting yourself go to the movements and chanting; this will allow your body to expand and merge with the other dancers.

Processional dances are used when you wish to establish rapport with powers of high vibrational rates. The dancing should comprise a series of highly stylised steps and gestures. These then become a form of dramatic meditation. They should always be stately in their performance.

Chain dances are used to re-enact some traditional legend that embodies the structure of a Craft mystery. They usually take the form of the leader performing some action, and the Coven following either mimicking the leader's actions or carrying out a complementary action.

Meeting dances are used merely to introduce members of an assembly to one another and are not magical. In all forms of dancing, the object of the dance must be fully understood by each of the participants before the dance is performed.

The last of the Paths is the **Great Rite**, also referred to as the Heiros Gammos, or Sacred Love Feast, for although no food is consumed during this ritual, it certainly nourishes for eternity. It truly is a great rite, for within it is magic worked by the Old Ones themselves. The greatest of all magic is the love of one for another. It is said that none may watch the marriage of heaven and earth, but let they who hath understanding look with the inner eye, for there is in love wrought so great a mystery that no morthwork may break it asunder.

This Path is seldom used today, except by older Covens who still stick to the ancient ways and tread the Wiccan pathway as they did in bygone days. Sadly, it has been replaced by the substitution of an Athame and a Chalice to represent the male and female principles.

The Book of Shadows recommends combining many of the Paths into one ritual, the more the better. However, the most important element in any of the Eight Paths is Intention. You must know that you can and will succeed. This is essential in every operation.

The Eight Paths cannot all be combined in one Rite. Meditation and Dancing do not combine well, but forming a mental image whilst dancing may well obtain results. Spells combined with the Scourge and Cords are good, with drugs and the Great Rite (only if you are advanced enough). Meditation following the Scourge is excellent.

These are the Eight Ways of Magic. There are many ways to perform and combine each Path. After suitable research and study, they should be practised sensibly with the right amount of caution, for they are the Witch's Heritage.

I have just touched on each of the Paths in this chapter. They deserve a book of their own to be fully understood, and that might be a task for another day, but for now, you might find elsewhere within my story hints on how to perform some of these rituals. So for now, good hunting.

Woody Guthrie, famously emblazoned his guitar with the phrase: "This machine kills fascists." The slogan was a declaration of purpose. Woody saw music as a weapon against oppression, inequality, and authoritarianism – a little bit like magic!

His music changed the course of American culture, and brought about the recognition of the folk tradition.

This is how we might view the true meaning behind Morthwork, a force that is invisible to the eye, but which has the power to shape a nation.

Chapter Twenty Five
Laws of Magic

Alistair Crowley said, *"Magic is the art and science of causing change to occur in conformity with will."* This change can occur in the mundane world; in the witch's consciousness; and most often in both, for changing one often changes the other.

Broadly speaking, magic can be defined as any event that disrupts a normal action and is, therefore, an expression of the mystical or supernatural rather than the natural. The Laws of Magic are the rules, beliefs, and attitudes that develop out of practical magic and have been classified in an occult tradition. They define the mechanism by which magic works.

The changes we make when we perform magic are mostly misunderstood by modern science because it works through subtle manipulations of the invisible. Our magic is performed on the Inner Plains, commonly referred to as the Astral, the same place our Circles are cast. However, the mechanisms of performing magic are subject to natural law, but the effects are sometimes evident in the mundane world and other times they are only manifest on a spiritual level. The workings of magic are not limited by the restrictions of time and space, for they do not exist on the inner planes.

The two primary laws of magic are 'belief' and 'mind over matter'. The mind controls the body, so it is imperative that you know yourself and your art, for without knowledge, there is no art and no control.

The most crucial law of magic is belief. You must believe in what you do, for without belief, there is hesitation and doubt, which leads to failure. That was the key to our success as a working Coven. We had up to a dozen witches sometimes working on a spell or a healing or some other form of morthwork. Our success rested in the fact that we all had the exact same intention and focus, and absolute knowledge of our subject matter.

Never attempt any magic or even a simple ritual without acknowledging the fact that you have one mind, one intent and a known outcome.

That focus and belief are what make a successful Coven stand out from those who just plod their way through without first doing their homework thoroughly.

Only belief will lead to success. With belief and knowledge, there is power. Therefore, here are the Laws. Study them well and absorb their meaning. Knowing and understanding these Laws will make the difference between success and failure. Luck has nothing to do with the outcome.

The Law of Knowledge says that to effect or affect a thing, you must know the thing. The more you know about yourself, the more you can know something else. With understanding comes control and power, and the more you know about a person or thing, the more control you have over it. Think about the spy world. The more intelligence that can be gathered, the better decisions that can be made. Without intelligence, you run blind. Knowledge is power.

The Law of Identification says that with your will, you can become anything - be one with anything by assuming the characteristics of the other thing. This is achieved by impersonating or mimicking something, similar to invoking the Goddess to enter the HPS or the God to enter the HP. The more you can know about the attributes, characteristics or qualities of the other identity, the better the imitation. You cannot use this law without first having a thorough understanding of the Law of Knowledge.

The Law of Contagion, also known as the *Law of Contact*, says that anything that has been in contact with something else maintains contact with that thing even after physical contact has been severed. The medium of that contact is the Aether. What an interesting Law this is. Think of the potential! For instance, imagine being asked to perform some absent healing magic on someone, and you do your usual witch's ladder or candle or cord magic. However, think about how it might be ultimately more efficient if you had physical contact with the person before conducting your magic! According to this Law, you have constant contact whilst performing the magic rite. The possibilities are endless.

The Law of Names states that knowing the True Name of something defines the action you take to focus a function on that thing. Simply stated, this means that knowing the true and complete name of a thing gives you complete control over it. There are two principles upon which this law is based. Firstly, a name is simply a representation of the meaning of a thing; a thing being defined as a phenomenon or an entity.

If the thing is water, one simply says 'water' instead of describing the construction of water. If the thing is an elephant, one just says 'elephant'. The names or terms water and elephant convey the definitions of water and elephant. Some choose to keep their Craft or magical name secret because they believe there is power in the name, which would be lost if known by someone else. This usually occurs after a Second or Third Degree initiation. His or her Second or Third Degree name is usually never told to anyone, except maybe his or her working partner. So, my Craft name of Dylan, which was taken at my First Degree Initiation, is not my real witch name, but the one I use to identify myself to the general public.

The Law of Cause and Effect states that under exactly the same conditions, using the same actions, you will always obtain the same results. I think I may have indicated this before, but to give you an idea, some members, especially newer members of a Coven, may have a whinge about doing certain rituals or celebrations the same way every time. Some might suggest, for instance, rewriting a Sabbat Round every year so that it does not get boring. Magic lingers, the effects linger, and the area retains a charge and becomes stronger as time goes by. So by performing rituals over and over again in exactly the same manner, you will always achieve the same results. So the trick is to get it right the first time, or keep doing it until you do get it right, then keep doing it the same way.

The Law of Infinite Data states there is more in the universe than we can sense or know. Learning never stops. There is always new information to learn. The sources of knowledge are limitless. You only need to be able to tap into them. This law can stimulate you to improve your capabilities. It can also serve as a warning that you cannot learn or know everything; therefore, it might be best to limit your dreams at times, as new dangers can always appear. Have you heard the term information overload? That is when the fuse trips and everything goes dark. Be careful, you never overstep the mark or push the envelope a little too far.

The Law of Association states that if a thing reminds you of something, it can, therefore, be used as a simulant for that something and consequently for magical purposes. This law is the most commonly and frequently used of all the laws of magic. It falls within the principle of sympathetic magic. Simply, this means things react upon each other under certain imposed or imaginary conditions. Our Book of Correspondences is a perfect example of this. Need I say more?

The Law of Infinite Universes states that if you change your perspective in one area, you change your universe. Everyone sees their universe or world differently; therefore, no two people have identical views of the world, thus making for an endless number of universes. This Law must be remembered when performing group magic because if one person's focus within the Circle is aimed at something slightly different to the others, the magic will be lost.

The Law of Invocation and Evocation tells us that we can use the power of the mind to tap into external and internal forces. Invocation is the act of contacting and asking for 'divine powers' to 'descend' on earth (similar to Drawing Down of the Moon). Evocation is the art of visualising and manifesting (calling forth) entities (spirits, angels or demons) to bring spiritual inspiration or to do the conjurer's bidding or provide information. Most ceremonial magicians use evocation regularly to elicit knowledge from the other side!

We Alexandrians are not averse to dabbling in a little evocative calling, sorry, I mean evocational calling, when a normal invocation just will not do!

The Law of Pragmatism states that if a thing works, it is true. This is a very useful law because it avoids moral arguments by analysing things with logic and practicality with a complete sense of objectivity. So, here is a question: Should morality be considered when invoking or evoking forces to do your bidding or when performing magic? Think of one particular Path that might be of relevance.

The Law of Predestination and Free Will states that events are predestined, and each person chooses whether and to what extent to participate in them. Some do not believe in fate, and that is fine because they each use their free will to change what has been predetermined. Others, who do believe, use that knowledge to make a change. Take the Tarot, for instance; it does not tell the querent what will happen tomorrow or next week. It simply shows a possible outcome if conditions do not alter. It therefore allows the querant to make an informed choice, free will!

Finally, **the Law of Polarity** states that everything contains and implies its opposite. This law suggests that anything can be separated into two opposite parts, with each part having its own essence, which is essential to many magical statements and arguments. Think of this argument in terms of Ying and Yang, good and bad, electric and magnetic, male and female. When you understand this law, you will realise the importance of polarity within the Craft and why nearly every action requires both sexes to obtain a result.

So, now we are moving closer to our understanding of how and why the Craft works and its rules. I've discussed the theory behind ritual and the Magic Circle, how and why we pray to our Gods and celebrate with them and use them to help in our magic. Now we know the laws and the ways of working, let us, in the next few chapters, look at the mechanics and tools we use.

"The universe is not only stranger than we imagine, it is stranger than we can imagine."
J.B.S. Haldane's 1927 essay collection titled Possible Worlds and Other Essays.

Chapter Twenty Six
Pentagrams and Watchtowers

The use of pentagrams within ritual developed from the Golden Dawn Tradition and eventually became part of the Wiccan ritual of casting a Circle and invoking the quarters. Calling the quarters, or sometimes termed Invoking the Watchtowers, involves ritual gestures using a magical weapon at the four cardinal compass points to summon elemental forces.

We will look at the actual operation of performing the Invoking and Banishing gestures of the Pentagram in a moment, but first, let us discuss the Watchtowers.

In Roman times, country dwellers built small altars or towers along the roadway and outside their villages in honour of their local deities or nature spirits. These later became known as Watchtowers, but later in the 16th century, Dr. John Dee and Edward Kelly's work involved the inclusion of Watchtowers as complex evocational designs within the Enochian magical system. Whether these ideas grew from the original Roman concept, we can only guess; however, this work was revived by MacGregor Mathers and expounded upon by the Hermetic Order of the Golden Dawn, whose magical system included the four Angelic Tablets that eventually became the four Watchtowers.

Each Watchtower was attributed to a direction and an element, East for air, South for fire, West for water and North for earth. In Christian-influenced magic traditions, they are understood to be the Archangels Raphael, Michael, Gabriel and Uriel, respectively.

When calling the Quarters or invoking the Watchtowers, Wiccan practitioners also include vibrating the elemental wind name. These names are: Eurus in the East, Notas in the South, Zephyrus in the West and Boreas in the North. It is interesting to note that all four are Wind Gods from Greek mythology!

I use the word 'summon' very deliberately, so as to the gestures involved in the action of invoking a pentagram. Usually, most Deities are politely invited into a Circle, whereas Elementals must be commanded. They are not rational entities and respond to language very literally. Commands must be made in a clear, concise and unemotional language, especially when banishing; otherwise, they may choose to hang around and possibly cause havoc.

The invoking of pentagrams and calling of Quarters is always performed after the Circle has been cast. This is an important point to remember because elemental forces are high-voltage energies. The Circle itself, once cast, acts as a buffer to these raw, wild energies.

When invoking the East Watchtower, for instance, the following words are used: *"Ye Lords of the Watchtower of the East, we summon, stir and call thee forth to witness these rites and guard this circle."* The Wind Elemental 'Eurus' is then vibrated, concentrating mainly on the vowels and not the consonants in the word.

Most usually, the invoking pentagram of earth is used at each quarter unless a special ritual is being undertaken using each elemental pentagram in their respective quarters. However, for the purpose of this exercise, let us use the invoking and banishing pentagrams of Earth.

Please refer to the diagrams below to see where the invoking earth pentagram starts. In this case, it commences at the uppermost point of the pentagram (5) and moves anti-clockwise, down to the left (1) and continues along each arm (2-3-4) until coming back to the start (5). This is the most important part of the pentagram – that is, sealing it.

Sealing a pentagram is that final deliberate act of tracing the last (extra) line of the symbol. So after you have cut five lines and come back to the start (in this case, the uppermost point of the

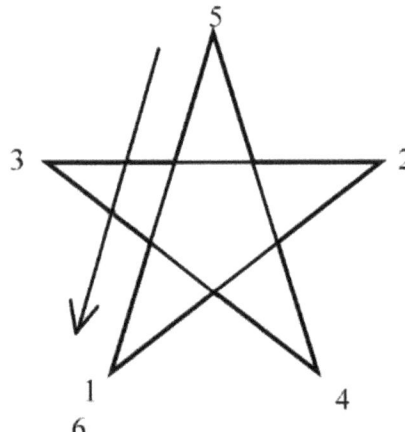

pentagram - 5), you must make one final cut (the sealing cut), that is, a downwards motion towards the left (6). This, in fact, makes six cuts, not just five.

An Athame is usually the preferred Tool used to invoke the quarters. This being held in your dominant hand. Stand at the respective quarter facing outwards from the Circle.

Start with the Athame pointing outwards about eye level and commence the first 'cut' that should finish in front of your left knee. Then continue up to your right and finish just outside the level of your right shoulder. Continue across to your left, finishing just outside level with your left shoulder. Continue downwards and to your right knee, then up to complete the five points in front of you at eye level. The final 'cut' or sixth stroke again downwards towards your left knee.

Each stroke should correspond to align with the words of the invocation like this: Ye Lords of the Watchtower of the East, we (commence the first stroke and finish on the word) summon (commence the second stroke and finish on the word), stir and (commence the third stroke and finish on the word) call thee forth to (commence the fourth stroke and finish on the word) witness these rites and (commence the fifth stroke and finish on the word) guard this circle. Then the final stroke.

Remember, each stroke must be very deliberate and precise, with the final sealing stroke used with as much force as possible.

Whilst performing these actions, you must visualise the pentagram forming at infinity, as a white light. The next and most important step is to vibrate the Elemental name (in this case, Eurus) and force the pentagram to move from infinity to the edge of the Circle. This is done by pointing your Athame outwards, vibrating the Elemental name as you pull the pentagram towards the edge of the Circle with your Athame. I do this with my eyes closed and finish vibrating the Elemental

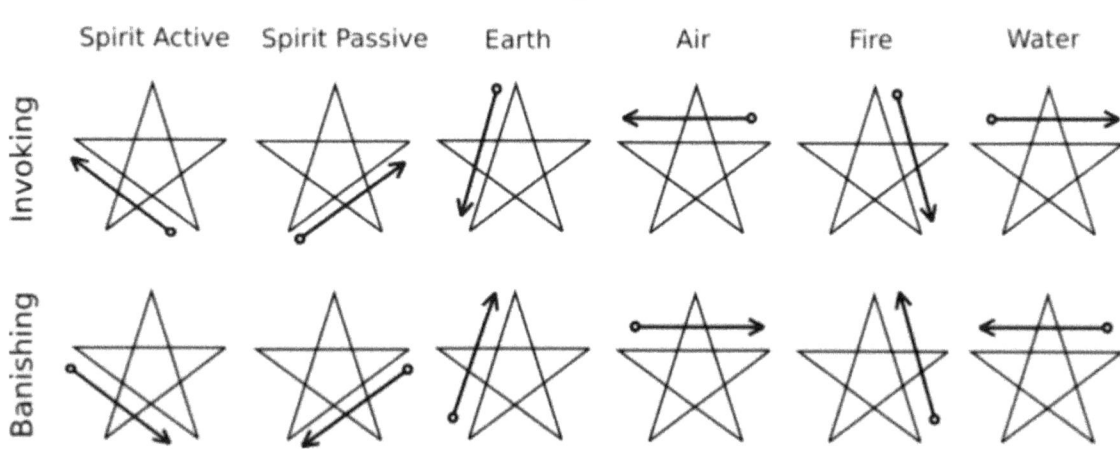

name as the tip of the Athame touches my nose, all the time doing the process in one breath.

Each elemental pentagram is performed in the same manner, sometimes including the wind name and sometimes without, depending on the circumstances.

Banishing is performed in the reverse order – again with that final sixth stroke using deliberate and strong actions, saying, *"Ye Lords of the Watchtower of the East, we thank thee for attending these rites now ere ye depart to thy lovely realms."* Once the pentagram has been cut, you should visualise the pentagram retreating to infinity and with your Athame touching your nose, thrust it outwards (do not let it go!) saying the words, *"Hail and Farewell."* Make sure you have banished the element because you do not want any residue hanging around that may cause disruption.

We will now look at the correspondences and descriptions of each Watchtower and a couple of different ways of calling the quarter.

First of all, EURUS rules the East and personifies your natural curiosity and desire to know about everything. This is the element of Air representing aspiration and faith. He is the healer of the Gods (Hermes or Thoth), the patron saint of travel. He belongs to the springtime and the dawn. The Angelic being of this quarter is Raphael, and the element of air is ruled by the Sylph.

The image of Eurus is a young man with brown hair, grey eyes, a lively voice and a friendly disposition. His colours are pale blues and greens, and his girdle is deep blue. As a healer, he bears a golden phial of healing balm.

Invoking Elemental, *"For the East, all wise eagle, great ruler of tempest storm and whirlwind, master of the heavenly vault, great prince of the powers of air, be present we pray thee and guard this Circle from all perils approaching from the East."*

Banishing Elemental, *"Powers of Air, I release you and bid you farewell."*

Invoking Watchtower, *"Ye Lords of the Watchtower of the East, I do summon, stir and call Thee forth to witness these rites and to guard the Circle."* Vibrate the elemental name "EURUS."

Banishing Watchtower, *"Ye Lords of the Watchtower of the East, we thank thee for attending these rites now ere ye depart to thy lovely realms, we say Hail and Farewell."*

NOTAS rules the South and is visualised as the personage of the sun at midday. Being god-like, he wears armour and is the champion of the light over darkness. He is the healer of insolence and disorder of natural forces. He belongs to the summer, for he is the grand master of the mysteries of light. He rules fire. This quarter is ruled by the Angelic spirit of Michael and the elemental beings, being Salamanders.

Notas has golden hair, brilliant blue eyes, and a commanding voice. His orders are obeyed without question. His robes or colours are deep greens, vivid blues, bright yellows, and the crimson of roses. His cord or girdle is golden yellow, and he wears the solar symbol on his breast.

Invoking Elemental, *"O thou lion, lord of lightning, master of the solar orb, great prince of the powers of fire, be present we pray thee and guard this Circle from all perils approaching from the South."*

Banishing Elemental, *"Powers of Fire, I release you and bid you farewell."*

Invoking Watchtower, *"Ye Lords of the Watchtower of the South, I do summon, stir and call thee forth to witness these rites and to guard the Circle."* Vibrate the elemental name *"NOTAS."*

Banishing Watchtower, *"Ye Lords of the Watchtower of the South, we thank thee for attending these rites now ere ye depart to thy lovely realms, we say Hail and Farewell."*

ZEPHYRUS rules over the West. His element is water. He is a fertility figure: the Lord of Resurrection who triumphs over death by the potency of love. He directs your attention to the moral as distinct from the intellectual side of the mysteries and presides over that companionship that should prevail in every circle. His cup is also the Cauldron of Regeneration. He is also the sunset. He belongs to the Autumn. This quarter belongs to the Angelic Spirit of Gabriel, and the elemental beings are the Undines.

Zephyrus has chestnut hair, amber eyes, and a friendly, sympathetic voice. His colours are red, russet, brown and russet yellows. His girdle or cord is red. His symbol is the horn.

Invoking Elemental, *"O thou serpent of old, ruler of the deeps, guardian of the bitter sea, prince of the powers of water, be present we pray thee and guard this Circle from all perils approaching from the West."*

Banishing Elemental, *"Powers of Water, I release you and bid you farewell."*

Invoking Watchtower, *"Ye Lords of the Watchtower of the West, I do summon, stir and call thee forth to witness these rites and to guard the Circle."* Vibrate the elemental name *"ZEPHYRUS."*

Banishing Watchtower, *"Ye Lords of the Watchtower of the West, we thank thee for attending these rites now ere ye depart to thy lovely realms, we say Hail and Farewell."*

BOREAS rules the North and is the Lord of the Earth. He is the light shining in the darkness. He is the light of experience or wisdom, shining brightly in the dark world on the eternal mother. He rules with tolerance and wisdom. He represents the development that will come to you in your circle with the sheer experience of life and death, until your soul has grown enough to take such matters in its spiritual stride, to seek better forms of being.

This quarter is the realm of the Angelic spirit of Auriel, and the elemental being is the Gnome.

Boreas is the kindly elder of the circle, with greying black hair and beard and dark eyes. His robes are sombre, belonging to the winter world and to midnight. They are black and dark brown, though they are decorated by the sparkle of moonlight. His girdle is black, entwined with silver; his symbol is the mirror.

Invoking Elemental, *"Black bull of the North, horned one, dark ruler of mountains and all that lies beneath them, prince of the powers of earth, be present we pray thee and guard this Circle from all perils approaching from the North."*

Banishing Elemental, *"Powers of Earth, I release you and bid you farewell."*

Invoking Watchtower, *"Ye Lords of the Watchtower of the North, I do summon, stir and call thee forth to witness these rites and to guard the Circle."*

Vibrate the elemental name *"BOREAS."*

Banishing Watchtower, *"Ye Lords of the Watchtower of the North, we thank thee for attending these rites now ere ye depart to thy lovely realms, we say Hail and Farewell."*

"Hail and Farewell."

Chapter Twenty Seven
Altered States of Consciousness

Before you can expect to benefit from any magical working or ritual and imagine them to actually work, it is essential for you to be able to adjust your consciousness level. Various methods of breathing, meditation, visualisation, pathworking or any altered state of consciousness are compulsory learning within your first year of training and study.

Within this chapter, I will offer several explanations and exercises that will help hone your ability to alter your consciousness level to adjust to a given environment or prepare for certain rituals.

Breathing techniques, meditation, pathworkings, etc., are grouped under the heading 'altered state of consciousness'. A friend of mine offered this explanation: *'An Altered State of Consciousness is any mental state recognised by the individual as different from his or her normal waking consciousness. As such, Altered States of Consciousness include sleep and relaxed states as well as more uncommon states such as meditative states, hypnosis, or drug-induced states.'* (An extract from Anna's workshop at the 1991 Wicca Conference.)

Altered States of Consciousness have some or all of the following general characteristics:

- Alteration in thinking, e.g., loss of judgement (or use of the rational mind), memory loss, changes in concentration;

- Changes in emotional expression, e.g., extreme detachment, ecstasy, the experience of godhead;
- Distortion in body image, e.g., feeling huge, numbness;
- Perceptual distortions, e.g., hallucinations, enhanced or reduced hearing, increased visual imagery;
- Changes in meaning or significance, such as feelings of profound insight and illumination;
- Hyper-suggestibility, i.e., more likely to accept what others say as fact;
- Inability or ineptness in communicating the nature of the experience to someone who has not undergone a similar experience.

Methods of inducing Altered States of Consciousness include relaxation and sleep; various breathing techniques, meditation, drugs, dance, chant, music, hypnotism, and invocation.

To work effective magic, you need to relax. In rituals, an altered state of consciousness is used to tap and focus energy. Using invocation to experience godhead and guided meditations and pathworkings to experience archetypes. The practised use of meditation will teach you to know yourself and increase your capabilities by removing the internal blocks that prevent you from working fully as a priest or priestess.

Another definition that may make a little more sense is this: *'Astral projection, pathworking, guided visualisation, and numerous other types of meditation and trance work are terms used by occultists when describing various techniques the psyche takes on its inner journeys. In a nutshell, a trance meditation is a pathway the consciousness takes into the visionary world of archetypes through an act of willed imagination.'* (Neville Drury - The Shaman and the Magician. P 49.)

'Astral projection, described by many occultists, involves the separation of the astral body from its physical housing, retaining only a cord of etheric energy as a connection. In other words, it is the creation of a complete, vivid, sensory metaphor state, through which all perceptions can be understood. The astral body may move through the physical universe, although with difficulty. Most often, it remains within the realm of energy and thought forms that is the astral.' (Starhawk - The Spiral Dance. p. 156.)

The idea of astral projection has been around for a long time. The word astral is from the Latin 'astrun' or star and is derived from Plato's doctrine of the existence of 'the souls of the stars'. Dante described the soul after death as being surrounded by 'its own creative power, like to its living form in shape and size'.

The great occultist and philosopher of the 16th century, Cornelius Agrippa, wrote of *'vacation of the body, when the spirit is enabled to transcend its bounds, and, as a light escaped from a lantern, to spread over space.'* (Cornelius Agrippa - De Occulta Philosophia. Antwerp, 1531.)

The practice of using drugs as an aid or shortcut to opening the astral doorway was probably the method used by witches in the Middle Ages and has become known as their 'flying ointment'. In the great occult revival in the late 19th century, occultists used a mixture of hallucinogenic drugs and smeared it onto their bodies to induce an altered state of consciousness. One such ointment contained: alcohol, cantharides, laudanum, betel nut, tinctures of cinquefoil, henbane, belladonna and cannabis. Talk about a euphoric high! No wonder they could ride broomsticks!

For nearly all methods of altering your consciousness, you must master various breathing techniques. The most useful breathing exercise for general use is called 4/2 breathing and is achieved by inhaling slowly through the nose, mentally counting one, two, three, four. Hold your breath and count one, two. Exhale at the same speed but through the mouth, again counting one, two, three, four. Hold and count one, two, then start again.

"Meditation is a passive form of relaxation that can help to calm and de-stress the body." Ian Aven - notes from his paper, Calming & Concentration, 1990. He adds, *"Its benefits include a reduction in the wear and tear of the bodily systems, reduction of anxiety levels, calming of mental activity and an increased ability to focus thoughts and discipline the will."*

The benefits of meditation can only be accomplished if it is regular. To achieve any results, you must give a firm commitment and set aside at least 15-20 minutes each day, preferably at the same time. Early in the morning is best, or in the evening, at least an hour after eating and well before going to bed and in a place where you will not be disturbed.

Sit or lie in a straight position that is only slightly uncomfortable, with eyes closed. You should wear loose-fitting and comfortable clothes. Relax and focus on your breathing. Allow your breathing to breathe naturally, and easily find its own rhythm. Let the air go deep into the lungs without forcing deep breathing. Breathe through your nose and out through your mouth.

Once unforced breathing has begun, on each breath out, let your muscular tension flow out with the breath. As you imagine this happening, you will start to feel deeper muscular relaxation. Now focus your attention inwards on a neutral thought. This might be difficult at first, but persevere. You should start to see results in a week or so if you are committed and regular.

Before any meditation or visualisation exercise, it is important to ground and centre your energy with that of the earth, thereby using the earth's energies rather than using your own. One method is the Qabalistic Cross; the other method is the Middle Pillar Exercise. The Middle Pillar transposes the Qabalistic Tree of Life onto the body and can be seen as an arousal of the Kundalini forces.

'The magical theory behind the middle pillar exercise is that by appropriate action upon the individual psychic machinery of the human personality, certain of its aspects may be aroused into activity, and this in its turn will cause external, objective energy to be drawn through into the 'sphere of sensation' or 'auric field' of the personality, thus charging it with the vitality of a very powerful kind'. (W E Butler - The Magician. 1959.)

The Qabalistic Cross is employed as a psychic energiser or as a preparatory formula to imbue the operator with the power necessary to establish a sealed and sanctified environment in which to conduct a ritual. Denning and Phillips write, *'It is a complete spiritual toner in its own right, and the student should use it frequently, whether to enhance the personal psychic energies in preparation for a further activity (ritual, meditative, or other), or as a mode of attunement to the great forces of life, or for the sheer joy of the work or bliss of being'.* (M Denning & O Phillips - Mysteria Magica. Vol 3. Bk 5. 1986.)

I have recorded detailed instructions further on in this story on how to perform the Qabalistic Cross and the Lesser Banishing Ritual of the Pentagram. These will provide a good working atmosphere for any practical work or as an opening or closing for the day. They can also be used to rid yourself of disturbing or obsessive ideas and as an aid to astral projection. They can effectively be used as a minor form of exorcism in dispelling an unwelcome atmosphere.

'Visualisation is the ability to see, hear, feel, touch and taste with the inner senses. Our physical eyes do not see; they merely transmit nerve impulses touched off by light stimuli to the brain. It is the brain that sees, and it can see inner images as clearly as those in the outer world.' (Starhawk - The Spiral Dance. P 63.)

Meditation is used to still the mind whilst relaxing the body. Visualisation uses that relaxed state for the creation of new states and increased awareness through controlled and conscious creation.

Here is a simple visualisation exercise developed by a close friend. (Stewart - unpublished notes, circa 1991.)

Sit (preferably) or lie in a straight position that is only slightly uncomfortable. Close your eyes and relax your body as much as possible. Your tongue should be on the floor of the mouth, jaw loose, shoulders and other joints and muscles relaxed.

Take a deep breath, fill your lungs with as much air as possible, hold (by stopping - not constricting or exerting the windpipe), release all used air, and exhale deeply. Repeat three times in a deep, slow, rhythmical way. On the third breath, feel the whole body as being completely relaxed and at ease, then commence 4/2 breathing.

Picture a large, ripe peach. It takes up your whole field of vision. Look at the peach; its orange/red skin is covered with soft, downy hairs. Now smell the peach - its sweet ripeness. Look at the shape of the peach, the ridges in it and any dents or lumps. Touch the peach and feel the skin, its softness. Can you still smell the peach? If not, bring the peach to your nose and smell it again; know the smell.

Now bite into the peach. Feel the skin break under your teeth. Feel the juices run over your tongue and drip from the sides of your mouth. Feel the texture and flavour of the peach in your mouth. Chew the peach. Swallow the piece of peach.

Now put the peach down. Be aware of all of the peach's sensory characteristics - know the nature of the peach.

Return to normal breathing. If you need to, take another two deep breaths, in and out and then open your eyes.

Some Eastern methods of meditation depend on directing the etheric currents in the physical body and concentrating on certain areas known as Chakras. These areas correspond with the endocrine glands. Changes in consciousness are brought about by producing changes in the chemical composition of the blood by checking or stimulating the different glands.

The Chakras are points of connection at which energy flows back and forth from the physical to the etheric body. Leadbeater writes, *'anyone who possesses a slight degree of clairvoyance may easily see them in the etheric double, where they show themselves as saucer-like depressions or vortices in its surface.'* (C W Leadbeater - The Chakras - A Monograph. 1979.)

The Root Chakra is the first centre and is located at the base of the spine.

The Splenic Chakra is found over the spleen.

The Umbilical Chakra is found at the navel, over the solar plexus.

The Cardiac Chakra is located over the heart.

The Laryngeal Chakra is in the front of the throat.

The Frontal Chakra is located on the brow between the eyebrows.

The Coronal or Crown Chakra is located at the top of the head.

In some texts, the head is compared to an inverted bowl and the base of the spine to a basin, the two being joined by a hollow tube. All power is promised to him who can syphon the lower energy towards the upper.

The Root Chakra is inhabited by the mysterious Kundalini, which is likened to a tiny snake, normally living curled up and asleep near the tailbone. When it is aroused, the serpent begins its ascent, piercing the gates of the Chakras one by one until it reaches the summit. (G R Parulski - The Philosophy of the Tantric Tradition.)

A very effective tool used to induce an altered state of consciousness is chanting and humming. The following is an extract from a workshop by Alan Moyse at the 1991 Wiccan Conference. It can be used to raise inner power or the divinity of Self.

Before starting, it is necessary to look at how we breathe. Most people breathe very shallowly, using only the top of their lungs. Trained singers and athletes, however, use the whole lung capacity.

First, sit up straight, with your spine in alignment. No slouching, but be comfortable. Place one hand on your breastbone and the other on your navel, and breathe in normally. Most people will find that it is only the upper hand that moves in time with the breath. Now try it, consciously inflating all of your lungs, and feel your lower hand move. This is the breathing style you need for effective humming or chanting.

The next step is to inflate the lungs fully and release the breath in a continuous flow. Keeping your hands in place, breathe deeply, making sure that you inflate the top and bottom of your lungs. Now, steadily breathe out, letting all the air out. Again, you should feel both hands move. Practice this breathing regularly - note that it is not hyperventilating (that is, a series of deep, rapid breaths to flood the lungs), but a steady, controlled form of deep breathing. It is also a good way to relax.

Different sounds can engender different 'states'. Most of us are familiar with the mantra 'Aum mani padme um'. The first sound - AUM - is a good, relaxing sound. Vowel sounds, intoned properly with full breath exhalation, make excellent chants. Some examples are:

AAH: as in the word 'father'. Good for joining a group.

EEE: as in 'feet'. A shriller sound, used for raising energy levels.

III: as in 'eye'. Softer than EEE, but still an energy raiser. Good for 'recharging the psychic batteries'.

OOO: as in 'more'. Useful for engendering 'healing' energy.

UUU: as in 'room'. Engenders a warm, comfortable feeling.

Other sounds which can be useful to experiment with:

NOR: as in the word 'gnaw'. I find this sound to be particularly useful as part of healing rituals.

UMM: similar to the AUM chant.

LLEU: This is almost the Gaelic 'clew' sound, produced by aspirating the C and L together, as in the name Llewellyn, pronounced 'Clewethlin' - the Gaels are a strange people! This sound, when intoned strongly and with force, produces a much heightened sense of self-awareness and the deity within.

Some people I know chant the runes, as Thorsson describes in his books, to good effect while meditating. Vibrating the runes while casting a Runic Circle is also very powerful. If you use names for your Watchtowers (e.g. Boreas) when casting a Wiccan Circle, try chanting or vibrating those names and see what effect it has on the circle.

Exercise 1

Be seated in a comfortable position.

Carry out 4/2 breathing for a cycle of 20 breaths (breathe in for the count of 4, hold for the count of 2, breathe out for the count of 4). Relax.

Remember any changes in perception or consciousness that may occur. Repeat this exercise every day for five days.

Exercise 2

Be seated in a comfortable position.

Carry out 4/4 breathing for a cycle of 20 breaths (breathe in for the count of 4, hold for the count of 4, breathe out for the count of 4). Relax.

Remember any changes in perception or consciousness that may occur. Repeat this exercise every day for five days.

Exercise 3

Use 4/4 breathing.

Hold your palms together in the 'prayer' gesture in front of the solar plexus. Look down at your hands. Gradually separate them to a distance of about 4 inches. Imagine a steel-blue glowing cloud growing between them and filling the space between your hands. Put your hands to your forehead.

Record any change in perception or consciousness that may occur. Repeat this exercise every day.

Exercise 4

Place a matchbox on the table in front of you, and sit so that you have a limited viewpoint of the matchbox's surface.

Relax. Without changing your viewpoint, examine the matchbox carefully, noting particular shades of colour. Close your eyes and try to visualise the matchbox as you have seen it. Open your eyes again and check the image. If it is not the same, continue to examine the matchbox and repeat the exercise.

When you are able to hold an accurate picture of the matchbox in your mind, imagine the matchbox from the other side, or from a slightly different viewpoint. When you can do this effectively, try to imagine the matchbox in one solid colour.

When the above exercises are mastered, imagine the matchbox, and then walk inside the image.

Keep a written record of the above exercise.

Exercise 5

Run a warm shower.

Commence 4/4 breathing. Hold your palms together in the 'prayer' gesture in front of the solar plexus. Look down at your hands. Gradually separate them to a distance of about 4 inches. Imagine a steel-blue glowing cloud growing between them and filling the space between your hands. Raise your hands towards the shower nozzle in the lotus gesture.

Step under the shower. Adopt 4/2 breathing. Relax.

Chapter Twenty Eight
Magical Scripts

Witches tend to use Magical Scripts or alternative alphabets as a substitute for the English language for many reasons. Primarily, to hide our secrets from the mundane world, but most usually, as a special medium to talk to the Gods.

The written word can be created in a physical format and transmitted across time and space. Our Egyptian ancestors understood the power of writing after the God Thoth created hieroglyphs and imparted this secret knowledge to the priests.

Although standard alphabets of Greek, Roman or Hebrew origin will suffice for many magical practices, it sometimes calls for a different kind of writing to address certain entities in an effort either to cloak the purpose of the writing or to allow specific spirits of a certain level to better understand the message.

Magicians and occultists trained in the Western esoteric traditions, as well as traditional Wiccans, consider writing as a magical practice in its own right. This resulted in the creation of Books of Shadows, Grimoires, and Spellbooks with their own inherent power.

People have created various methods of writing derived from the elements, the stars, the Angels and Gods to communicate with entities on the inner and outer planes. The scripts below are traditionally used in Wiccan magic and have very specific uses.

Passing of the River script or Passage du Fleuve alphabet is derived from the primitive form of the liturgical Hebrew alphabet and was created by Cornelius Agrippa during the 16th Century. It is also known as the Talismanic Script of Solomon the King. Its name is derived from the four rivers that flowed through the Garden of Eden.

Beyond a Year and a Day

Passing the River Script

This script is used to write letters to the Angels Samael, Sachiel, Cassiel, Archangels Haniel and Uriel, and for the addressing part of a letter addressed to the Archangel Michael. Hence, a very powerful script.

Theban script (over) is used for writing letters to Archangels Gabriel and Raphael, and for the message part for Archangel Michael. This script is named for Honorius of Thebes, and again, a version of it was developed by Cornelius Agrippa.

It is strongly related to the lunar energies, and this is why it is used for Gabriel, who rules the moon and for Raphael, who is related to Gabriel, because they both share the East/West energy. It follows a letter-for-letter replacement when writing, except that there is no J, U, or W. J becomes I. U becomes V. W is just U twice.

It is an alphabet most Wiccans use when they have something secret to write. It is also a requirement of the Second Degree to be able to translate and write short sentences using Theban.

The Celestial or Angelic script (over) was another magical alphabet used by Agrippa to write the names of angels and other celestial beings. It is based on the Hebrew script, with which it shares a one-to-one correlation except for the final forms of the letters kaph, mem, nun, peh, and tzaddi, which are not seen in this Angelic script. However, since Agrippa intended to use this script to communicate with angels and other celestial beings, he used forms of the letters that he derived from constellations in the sky, hence the angular nature of the letters with the little 'star points'.

a b c d e f g h i / j k l m
n o p q r s t u / v w x y z

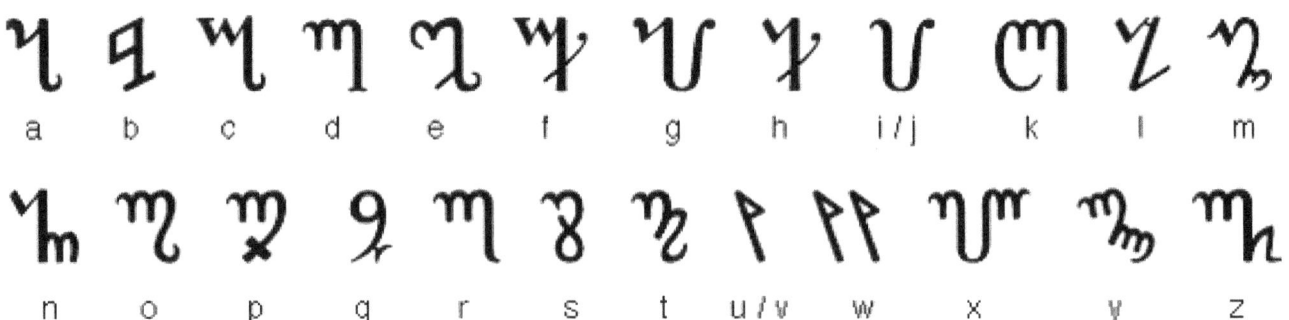

Theban Script

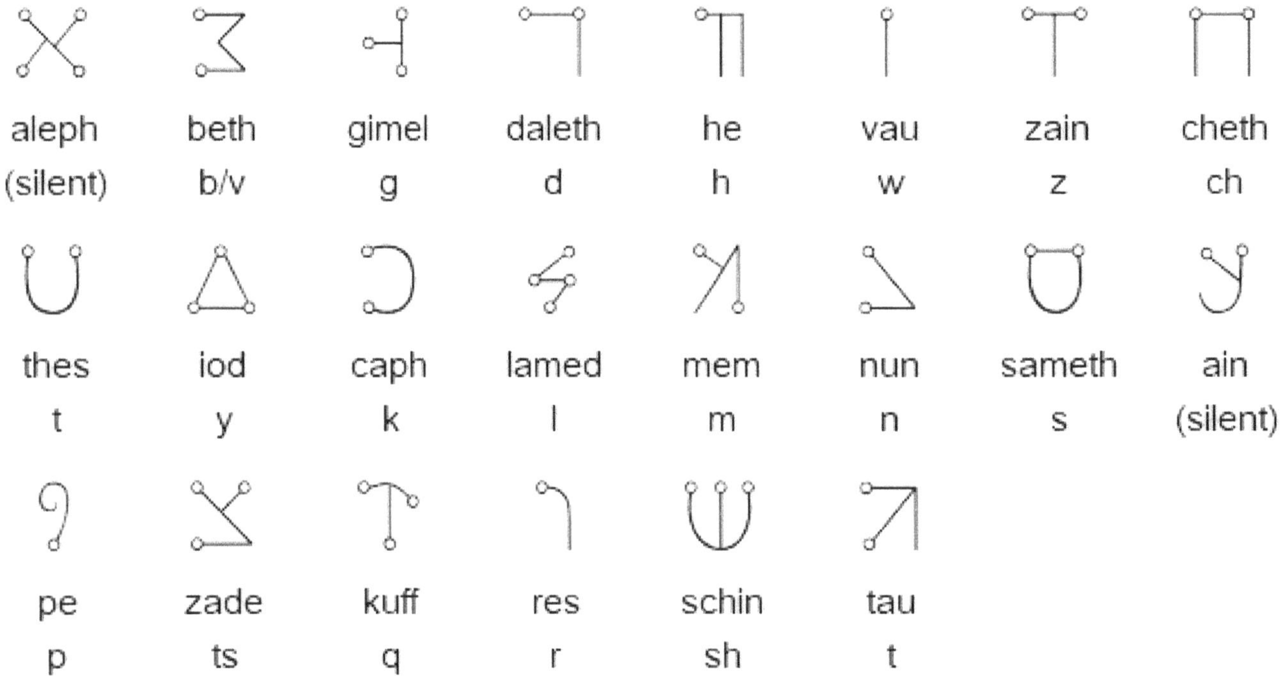
aleph (silent)
beth b/v
gimel g
daleth d
he h
vau w
zain z
cheth ch
thes t
iod y
caph k
lamed l
mem m
nun n
sameth s
ain (silent)
pe p
zade ts
kuff q
res r
schin sh
tau t

Angelic Script

Chapter Twenty Nine
Practical Magic

Talisman Creation
Book of Correspondences
Cord Magic
Writing to Angels

So far, in this story, we have discussed the theories behind ritual, the laws, and the practice of magic, altered states of consciousness, and we know how to cast a Circle and raise energy. So now let's put all that into practice, and I'll show you in detail how to create a Talisman, how to do Cord Magic and how to write letters to the Angels.

Every part of creating anything magical is based on 'Intent'. So let us just review what magic is again.

Magic is the science and art of causing change to occur in conformity with will. The science of understanding and the art of applying that understanding into action. The ritual is the process by which we create the magic. A ritual must have intention, a purpose, a method, and an ending.

The following three methods of practical magic are all prepared and conducted in a Circle and most usually involve more than just one person; however, if you are a solo, they will work just as well, you just need to have a little more energy and finely focus your will. The more people there are in creating things like a talisman, for instance, the more potent and effective the result will be.

Above all, you must remember that the moment the thought enters your mind, either on your own or from a friend asking a favour, the magic begins.

The creation and development of that energy begins on the astral, the second that thoughtform is produced and continues to grow as you travel down your path of creation. Never lose track of the fact that you are in the process of creation and your intent is foremost in your mind at all times.

Forgive me for harping on the issue of Intent, but you need to appreciate this is what magic is all about. If you can understand this concept, you are well on your way to creating something special.

I indicated earlier that years ago, one of our Covens became quite adept at **creating talismans** for a variety of needs, either for our own people or as favours for friends, for various reasons, including healing, business ventures, protection, and love, just to mention a few.

So, what is a talisman? A talisman is an object that contains certain magical properties and is charged with the force that it is intended to represent. Its careful construction will represent the universal forces in exact harmony with those of the intended purpose.

Its designer and creator must be familiar with all the symbolism connected to all the different planetary and elemental forces that represent the purpose. Elements like geomantic signs and symbols, planetary representations, alchemical implications, other magical associations, such as colours, scents, symbology, patterns, and Qabalistic correspondences. All of these elements must be in synchronisation with the elemental or planetary force associated with the talisman's purpose.

Some claim the power of talismans hinges entirely on the belief that their owner place in them. I do not agree. I believe our Coven has proved through experience and understanding that talismans work just as well when their owners are sceptical or even unaware of their magical purpose. It might be psychological and may work by influencing their owner's mind. But in my experience, they work not merely because of the confidence they inspire, but because they are created in harmony with the natural creative laws of the universe, given birth through ritual and endowed with the magic of creation. Even if a talisman is simply worn as an unusual item of jewellery, its owner is assured to receive the benefits endowed in it by its magical creation and purpose.

Ok, let us set up a scenario and follow the steps towards creating a talisman.

A friend of a Coven member will shortly go for a job interview as a financial manager in an accounting firm. This woman is qualified and experienced to perform the advertised job description; however, she is aware she has some serious competition from other applicants and wants to give herself the best advantage she can.

She is aware of our Coven capabilities and believes in our ways; however, does not follow any particular religious belief. She has asked for our help to make her a talisman she can wear or keep in her purse, not just for the interview but also for long-term use.

Before we start our research, we need to establish a few personal things about our friend, like her full name, birth date, the name of the company and the job title she intends to work for and maybe a copy of the job advertisement that may have been posted in the local newspaper. There could be more items we could obtain, but for now, we have enough to build a picture for us to work with.

Therefore, for the purpose of this exercise, her name is Lynda Harrison. She was born on 8 May

1976. The company name is Melbourne Accountants and Auditors Inc. The job title is Finance Manager.

The next step is to consult our **Book of Correspondences** and obtain information that will assist us in preparing various elements we will use to construct the talisman. This is going to be a painstaking and lengthy process, so follow me closely. Do not forget that this is the beginning of a magical process, so even in this early stage of research, focus your intentions.

My current Book of Correspondences is a folder containing photocopies of extracts from various books and other resources I have accumulated over the years. The primary sources I have used, separate from my own Coven and Tradition material from our own grimoires and Books of Shadows are; *777* by Aleister Crowley, *The Golden Dawn* by Israel Regardie, *Encyclopaedia of Magical Herbs and Incense and Oils and Brews* by Scott Cunningham, Linda Goodman's *Sun and Star Signs*, *Mysteria Magica* by Melita Denning, *Techniques of High Magic* by Francis King and *The Tree of Life: An Illustrated Study in Magic* by Israel Regardie.

I must say that *777* and the *Golden Dawn* material are instrumental in the original creation of our Book of Correspondences, as was our study of the *Qabalah*, the *Key of Solomon*, work by *Dr. John Dee* and other alchemists and magicians of the fifteenth century and beyond.

Being Alexandrian, we are by nature drawn towards Ceremonial Magic, so the process of making magic is in our blood, so to speak.

So, having our Book of Correspondences at hand, I grab a large piece of butcher's paper or a couple of A4 sheets and a pencil. My aim is to flip through my folder and notes and start jotting down keywords that correspond to the purpose of the task. Randomly over the paper, I write Lynda's details and the job information.

Then I focus on the primary attribute of the talisman, which is one of business and employment. I then discovered the following and wrote them on my paper:

Earth, Mercury, the Sun and Sunday. Stay with me because this is where it gets convoluted. Aries, Virgo, red, brown, gold, orange, the Goddess Demeter, the God Zeus, Laurelwood, frankincense and myrrh, the numbers 1, 4, 8 and 7. Also, nutmeg, cedar, high john the conqueror root, sage, St John's wort, oak leaves, waxing to full moon, honeysuckle, and vervain, third hour after sunset.

A secondary attribute is that of creative work and has the following links: Earth, Mercury, Sunday, waxing moon, gold, silver, violet, myrtle, valerian, the Triple Goddess, Thoth, cinnamon, apple blossom, pine oil, and clover.

On the third pass through my notes, I find the following: a lion and peacock, gold and yellow, cotton and gold lame, amber, grass, frankincense, bay laurel, yellow daisies and marigolds, almond tree, ash, and walnut. The archangel Michael, yellow, the numbers 1, 6 and 21. I also find the sigils of the Sun and Michael, and the magic square of the Sun.

I could go further and dig deeper into the various elements within the task and find things that correspond to Lynda in particular; for instance, she is a Taurus. I might write her name in a magical square, her favourite colour, and perfume. Also, looking at the company and specific links to find out about its operation and people and services.

At the end of the day, I end up with a large piece of paper with a whole lot of words scattered all over the shop! The next step is to grab a highlighter or coloured pen and start highlighting words that have a more significant meaning than others do, and start drawing lines between words. This is where your intuition comes in; do what feels natural.

At the end of the process, these are the words I have - Sunday, third hour after sunset on a waxing Moon, Earth, gold, red, silver, St John's Wort, oak leaves, patchouli oil, frankincense, the number six, vervain, valerian, the Triple Goddess and Archangel Michael.

The talisman itself will be made from a square piece of cloth with a combination of the various elements within and tied with a coloured piece of cotton or string to make a small bag.

I then start to collect the various elements I need to construct the talisman. They are: a 20cm square of red cotton fabric (20 = the sum of the magical numbers corresponding to business) and a 28cm length of gold cotton thread (the sum of the numbers corresponding to the Sephora Tiphareth).

A silver 20-cent piece (1+4+8+7=20) and a copy of the magical sigils for the Archangel Michael and the Sun. Patchouli oil, some grains of frankincense incense, a fresh sprig of vervain, valerian and lavender from my garden. An oak leaf, an image of the Triple Goddess and Thoth, and some dried High John the Conqueror root. A copy of the advertised job vacancy, and finally a piece of green coloured paper with Lynda's name, the company name and the job title written with a brown pencil, and all jumbled together.

Are you still with me? I told you it was a little complicated! Nevertheless, the whole process cements your intent firmly into the task, and when we eventually cast our Circle and start building the talisman, everything comes together as we chant the spell of making and finally give birth to our creation!

The next step is to write a rune or rhyming spell that we will chant whilst piecing together each element of our talisman within our Magic Circle. How about this: *'Goddess above, God below, give Lynda Harrison the job she knows.'* Yeah, I know, sounds a bit corny, but it does not really have to mean too much. Our Book of Shadows says, *'the words matter not'*; its purpose is to focus our will on raising the energy to channel into the talisman.

It is time now to put it all together. We have decided that our Coven will be meeting for our monthly Esbat, and it just so happens it falls on a Sunday. We decided to meet after sunset and aim to start working at 9.30 pm, the third hour after sunset.

We gather all the elements of the talisman together with a mortar and pestle and place them on our Altar. We cast our Circle as usual. We then sit in a circle on the floor, and my job is to explain (in detail) the purpose of our magic, who we are working for and to what end. I then arrange all the elements I will be using to make the talisman so that they are visible to everyone.

We then take the mortar and pestle and start to add each of the herbs and oils one by one. Each one of us, in turn, will add something as we start to chant the rune. As each element is added, I tell everyone its significance and correspondence.

The mortar and pestle are then handed to the next Coven member (passing it deosil, of course!). This will continue until all the plants, oils and herbs have been added and ground together. You should end up with a mixture of patchouli oil, frankincense, vervain, valerian, lavender, an oak leaf and some High John the Conqueror root.

The next step is to start putting the other elements together. I place the square of cloth in the middle, add the silver coin, then I fold up the sigils for the Archangel Michael and the Sun and place them on top. Then the images of the Triple Goddess and Thoth, and the copy of the newspaper advertisement. Then the piece of green coloured paper with Lynda's and the company details.

Finally, the contents of the mortar are poured on top of the paper. The cloth square is then pulled together, joining the four corners. With someone holding the cloth together, I then tie it together with the length of gold cotton thread, winding it around the talisman and tying it tightly, all the while repeating the rune, *'Goddess above, God below, give Lynda Harrison the job she knows.'*

If we are lucky enough to have both male and female members present, I will take advantage and use a female member to assist in consecrating and birthing the Talisman. If not, I do the consecration on my own.

We take it to the Altar and consecrate it by both holding it and sprinkling it with the salt/water used to create the Circle, saying, *'I consecrate thee in the element of water'*.

We then take it through the rising smoke from the Thurible, saying, *'I consecrate thee in the element of air.'*

Then over the Altar candle flame, saying, *'I consecrate thee in the element of fire.'*

Finally, placing the Talisman on the Pentacle, placing our hands over it and saying, *'I consecrate thee in the element of earth.'*

Nearly finished! We then hold the Talisman up and turn to the centre of the Circle and say, *'I call upon Earth to bond my spell. Air will speed its travel well. Fire will give it spirit from above; Water will quench my spell with love. Earth, Water, Air and Fire combine, give power to this spell of mine.'*

The Talisman is then placed between us on our chests, we embrace, kiss, and as we separate, we both catch the Talisman in our hands as it falls. Jobs done!

One final very important matter – when you banish the Circle, do not leave the Talisman on the Altar. Take it with you and keep it behind your back as the banishing pentagrams are performed. You do not want to undo all that hard work!

What do you do with the Talisman now? That is up to you; for Lynda, she hung it around her neck during the interview right next to her heart and later kept it in the top desk drawer in her new office at Melbourne Accountants and Auditors Inc.

Cord Magic

Cord Magic is an early form of folk magic and an easy alternative to candle magic. In most forms of cord magic, the spells are simply prepared ahead of time and then used as needed when each knot is untied, releasing the magic caught in the cord over several successive days. Cords can be a specific length and colour.

Many Covens use nine knots, but three is also a commonly used number, as are seven, ten, and thirteen. A spell or rune is often chanted as the knots are tied. Most folks are acquainted with this type of basic magic and have used the *'By knot of one my spell's begun'* chant, which should sound familiar, so I do not intend to cover this any further.

What I would like, is to show you is our method of Cord Magic that we use primarily for healing. This method comprises an even number of Coven members sharing one Cord between them, plus one other (usually the HPS). Her job is to focus and send the Magic out, either to its recipient or into the recipient if they are present in the Circle.

The method works by raising energy whilst stroking the cords and chanting a spell. When enough magic has been created, it is sent to the recipient by the HPS. Again, this is one of those occasions that this type of magic is created on the astral and is therefore very easily 'posted' to the recipient. If the recipient is physically present in the Circle, it can have a very dramatic and instant effect on the recipient.

For this example, let us say one of our Coven members has a bad lower back and needs some relief. After casting our Circle, as usual, the member lies in the centre of the Circle on her belly. Let us say we have six members (three male and three female – do not forget the balancing thing!) holding three cords. Male to female and intertwine cords to form a cartwheel. We tend to use a special set of cords in various colours for this purpose, for they never really lose all of their energy once they have been used in the same way a few times.

I also suggest you do not use your normal Cord, the one you received on your Initiation, because it usually has knots in it. The knots will hinder your stroking of the cord when you are raising energy and will distract you from the task. So use a plain cotton or wool cord of a colour of your choosing or appropriate to the task. For instance, using a blue cord when working on the Throat Chakra.

You can either sit or stand, whichever is more convenient, in a circle around the recipient with the centre of the cords directly over her lower back, or in other situations, over the affected part of the body. In this instance, maybe use an orange-coloured cord as it is close to the Spleen Chakra.

We have one special spell we use for healing and have never changed it in all the years we have performed this type of healing. It goes like this, *'This is the spell that we intone, flesh to flesh and bone to bone. Sinew to sinew and vein to vein, each one to its own again.'*

I think the origin of this spell lies with the Farrars and was created to heal the broken leg of a horse. Those Wiccans who have used it will confirm that it is a very powerful incantation and will nearly always work with most illnesses.

But of course, you must have the right people working under the right circumstances, all with the same focus, for it to work.

We start by putting a little tension on the cords, holding your end with one hand and commence to stroke the cord inwards; i.e. let the cord run through your clenched fist as you push from the end of the cord to the centre of the cartwheel. Everyone should do this rhythmically whilst chanting the spell.

As energy is raised, the Coven members do nothing other than focus their intent on the energy being raised through the stoking of their cords and chanting of the spell. This is continued, maybe for some minutes, even longer depending on the situation.

Now this is where the HPS comes in. It is her job to create a Cone of Power, a swirling mass of energy that circulates deosil around the Circle as more and more energy is created by the Coven members. At this point, the HPS should stand anywhere in the Circle so she can easily get to the centre of the cords.

As the Coven members work themselves into a frenzy, the words of the spell are intoned faster and faster, and they become jumbled and meaningless as their stroking of the cords becomes faster also to the point they become hot.

It is about this time that the HPS would realise that she has enough energy to be able to 'send' the magic to the recipient. This is done by either sending it out or down to the member lying on the floor. She does this by shouting *'Now'* at the same time putting her hand on the centre of the cartwheel, as each Coven member drops their end of the cord, and she pushes the cords and the energy and magic into the members' back below her.

If she were sending the energy out to the recipient, she would grab the cords from underneath and, as the Coven members drop their ends, she raised the bunch of cords upwards, forcing the energy and magic up and out, directed towards the recipient.

This ritual is very exhausting and creates a lot of heat. It depletes our members of quite a substantial amount of energy. It should, therefore, be performed at the very end of any gathering so that all that remains is to banish the Circle and eat! Because, believe me, everyone will be hungry.

Oh, I nearly forgot! Our injured Coven member is lying on the floor. She should have gotten up by now and is dancing, *'We've danced and sung our sacred ways'* with everyone else.

Practicing the Angelic Arts

The Angelic Art is an extremely powerful form of magic and should only be used in extreme circumstances and never for trivial matters that would best suit candle magic or the creation of an amulet or talisman, or any other form of lower magic.

In all the years I have been aware of the Angelic Letters, I have only had to use them a couple of times, and I have always been answered. However, I have known some folks who never heeded the advice and sought help for the most trivial of issues, only to find their asking resulted not in help but the exact opposite. Lesson learnt – do not think the Angelic Forces are trivial; you could get your arse severely kicked!

There are eight Angels: Auriel, Michael, Gabriel, Samael, Raphael, Sachiel, Anael and Cassiel. They should only be written to for help in the things that they rule. A letter written to the wrong Angel is considered lost to the magical post in a manner of speaking.

Letters should be written on the particular day of each and every Angel, but not necessarily in his hour on any one day, which gives a wider margin in which to work. It is not necessary to invoke or banish if this is not your particular wish. The magical letter will prove enough.

The technique of writing to the Angels and asking for help is very simple. Write a letter asking for help using a specific coloured ink on a specific coloured piece of paper using the prescribed method and script, and sign it.

What do you do with your letter afterwards? The fact that you have written it in the manner prescribed is enough. There is no need to 'post' it. Once written and signed, it is done. Your answer will follow. Once you have your answer, the letter can be destroyed (unless specifically instructed otherwise), or you can keep it for posterity if you choose; it matters not, the magic has been done.

A good idea is to pre-write the letter before casting a Circle. This gives you more time to concentrate on the wording and to transpose English into either Passing of the River or Theban scripts. Once inside your Circle, you only have to copy the script onto the coloured paper using the appropriate coloured pen. A normal Circle will suffice, and it is probably best not to confuse the issue with performing other magic; cast the Circle only for this one task, then banish.

The magic is governed by precisely how the letter is written. You will use either Passing of the River script, Theban or English to write the letter. These scripts can be found elsewhere in this story. The paper will be a certain colour, as will the ink used.

The paper for the letter must be exactly square. If you use a piece of A4, for instance, cut off the bottom 8.7cm to make it exactly 21cm square. Rule an inch line across the top and divide this into three or four equal spaces, depending on the Angel. Underneath, in the appropriate script, write: To (Angel name) (and his rank), e.g., *'To the Angel Michael, Archangel of the Sun and of Leo.'* Then write your plea and signature. You can write on both sides. Here is an example of a letter:

(See Facing Page)

How to Write to Angels

The following are details for each Angel with instructions on how to write each letter and the information on what to look for if your request has been granted. Do not forget to select the appropriate Angel for the task, and do not make your request trivial.

Auriel has a particular distinction because he is a throne Angel of God, to whom was given the power of transmitting magical ability to humanity through the planet Uranus. He governs learning and the development of soul and spirit. He can also

[Angelic script inscription]

Dylan Raventree

'To the Angel Michael, Archangel of the Sun and of Leo.'

Note: *The Angelic Letters we were given is not quite a complete version, but it was enough to work with. For a more complete version and detailed description of the Letters, David Goddard's book, 'The Sacred Magic of the Angels' is very much worth the read if you can find a copy.*

rule matters of trouble and nervous complaints. Therefore, you should ask his help in matters connected with these things, and these things only.

The result will come in quite a sudden and overwhelming manner, as symbolised by his sign - the lightning flash. He should never be invoked lightly unless he is one of your Guardian Angels. He can, and does, perform miracles. Never petition him unless you are prepared for sudden upheavals.

He rules the zodiac Aquarius, his planet is Uranus, and his private sign is the lightning flash. These you write first in green ink, crayon or pencil on white paper in your magical letter. You then write - *"To Auriel, Throne Angel of God and Magical Force"* then use Passing of the Rivers script throughout the letter.

Write his letter simply, write it on a Saturday, and keep it for fourteen days, including the day on which you wrote it. Never ask for help in matters you can take care of yourself.

Auriel rules all multi-coloured things; rainbows or pools of oil that glisten, anything that reflects multi-coloured light is a sign from Auriel. His animals are the chameleon, unicorn, and all lizards. His fruits are mangoes and bananas. His flowers are all multi-coloured ones (Dahlias, etc.). He has no particular tree but rules all freak trees, crosses of two types or ones that change the colour of their blossoms. He is said to rule Hydrangeas - they are magical flowers, they change like a chameleon.

If you unexpectedly see a rainbow, chameleon or unicorn ornament, glistening oil, any means of refracted light, mango chutney or fruit, his sacred insect, the dragonfly, then the spell is granted.

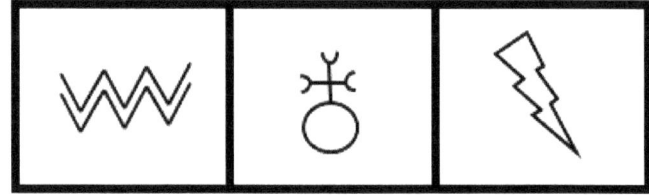

Sigil For Archangel Auriel

Michael is an Archangel and rules the Sun and Leo. His natural energy is that of the sunbeam. His animals are the lion and all the greater and lesser cats. He prefers oranges and pomegranates, and his tree is the laurel. Anything made of gold and orange blossom is sacred. Golden butterflies and daddy long-legs are his friends.

Ask his help in the matter of ambition, personal success, and attainment; anything of government affairs, Kings and Princes; and music playing or composition. He is present on your wedding day and your golden wedding day. Ask for his help in health matters concerning the spine and heart.

The sigil of Michael is represented by a lion's mane. The sun is shown by a circle with a dot. He has one other symbol, the crown. When writing to Michael, draw the three signs on the top of the letter as depicted below. You can use black ink on white paper.

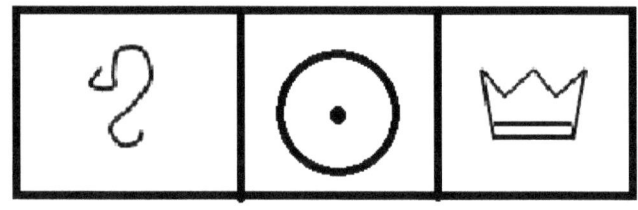

Sigil for Archangel Michael

Write in Passing of the River script, *'To the Angel Michael, Archangel of the Sun and of Leo'*. Continue writing with your request in Theban and sign your name in Passing of the River.

Write on a Sunday in any hour and keep the letter for seven days, Sunday to Sunday, then burn the letter. If a sign is not received, wait one month before writing another.

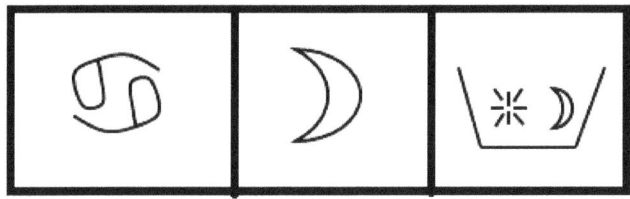

Sigil for Archangel Gabriel

Gabriel is an Archangel of the Moon. His natural sign is the moonbeam, and he rules only one sign, Cancer, the sign of the crab symbolised by two crab claws. His favourite animals are dogs (they bay at the moon), crabs and shellfish. He loves melons, lychees, pears, all flowers, white, and the night-scented stock, the weeping willow, spiders, moths - especially large night moths and large house and garden spiders (the small ones belong to Sachiel). His metal is silver.

Gabriel deals with matters concerning feminine functions, reproductive organs, ailments of breasts, likewise of or from childbirth, sterility, and warts (both sexes). He rules over domestic home matters, domestic equipment, and safeguards journeys by land or sea. He also guards against sea or airsickness, together with indigestion and stomach pain and complaints and all matters of women, but not love or money.

Letters can be written when doing New Moon Invocations, spells, or Full Moon Banishings. Requests for gain at New Moon, to dispel on Full Moon. Draw his three signs (above), address him; write your request and signature all in Theban. Write on any Monday or New or Full Moon. The letter should be kept for the full Lunar month, 28 days counting the day it was written on; on the 28th day, tear it up. Write on white paper, using blue ink or crayon.

Signs that your request has been granted include moonbeams illuminating you or your home, a gift of white flowers appearing suddenly and unexpectedly in your garden, and a strange dog making a fuss of you or barking under your window. Also, seeing a weeping willow where you had not thought there was one or hearing it rustle, receiving a gift in the form of shellfish or being invited to dinner where shellfish is served.

The same applies to melons, lychees or receiving pears or going somewhere where pear trees grow and are in fruit or blossoming. Receiving a gift of silver or going to a christening or hearing of a birth among friends or relations. The same applies to a baby entering your house for the first time or acquiring a new dog or puppy. To find your home infested with moths, or have a spider take up residence. Despite the spider and its appearance, if you cannot bear it, do not kill it; put it aside gently. If you see a spider spinning its web, it is a sure sign that the magic is being worked for you.

Samael is an Angel of Mars and rules two signs, Scorpio and Aries, shown by the upturned ram horns and the M symbol with the forked tail. The sign for Mars is the circle with an arrow, and his private sign is the sword, a symbol of his protection of humanity from enemies and evil when he is asked.

Here are the four symbols with which you begin the letter. They must be drawn in red ink or crayon on white paper, on a Tuesday. Keep the paper for 7 days and destroy it on the following Tuesday. By then, you should have received a sign from Samael.

Aries is the first or positive sign. Scorpio is the second or negative sign. They have equal value but different powers. Neither is it by any means a weak sign.

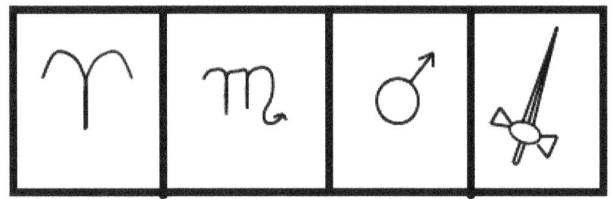

Sigil for Archangel Samael

Ask for his help in matters of recovering physical state after an illness, to overcome enemies and to help when the battles of life are generally too much. He assists physical courage, and works with people in the armed forces.

Call on him to help acquire the right kind of machinery and to secure a good bargain. In health matters, he can be invoked for ailments of the right arm, severe headaches, operations (he guides the surgeon's hands) and helps in the quick restoration of health. Rashes, infections, spots, accidents or risks with machinery.

Samael's animals are rams or sheep. He loves thistles, nettles, peonies, all except poppies. His animals are the scorpion and all stingers except bees. The horse chestnut, monkey puzzle, and pepper trees are his favourites, and his metals are iron and steel.

If your request has been successful, be alert to the following signs: the gift of a sharp knife or instrument, the falling of knives to the floor for no obvious reason, anything catching fire, sparks, coals popping from the grate, attacks of sneezes, or spilling pepper or spices. If you are stung by a wasp or feel a glow of heat in any part of the body for no apparent reason.

A sign of a cure is if you are asked about health, if someone suddenly gives you conkers or horse chestnuts, if you suddenly see a monkey puzzle or pepper tree, a mysterious red glow whose source cannot be traced, tingling or irritation in the right hand or arm for an unknown reason.

Raphael is an Archangel of Mercury and rules Gemini. He is of the water and the West. He is said to guard pilgrims on their journeys. He is a healer and associated with the sephirot of Tiphereth; also of divine love and balance, and harmony.

When you petition Raphael to heal, the cure manifests almost instantly, and sometimes a gentle buzzing energy is felt, or it can be very subtle. As a patron of travellers, Raphael makes your journey smooth. He is also able to combine healing with travel to guarantee that you stay well before and during your travels.

Letters should be written on a Wednesday in Theban script using black ink on yellow paper or yellow ink on white paper and kept for seven days.

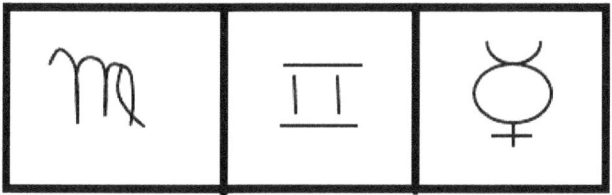

Sigil for Archangel Raphael

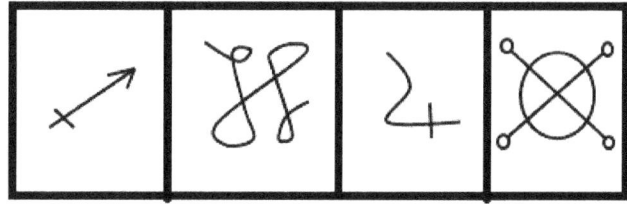

Sigil for Archangel Sachiel

The following are sacred to Raphael and are signs to show your request has been granted: all birds, non-stinging flies, especially bushies, yellow flowers, the aspen and silver birch trees, together with bracken and weeds. His metal is quicksilver. You can also expect to see darting lights and maybe experience an unusually great influx of letters and incidents or situations unexpectedly involving any of the above signs.

Sachiel is an Angel of Jupiter and rules Sagittarius and Pisces, shown by a feathered arrow and two fish symbolically linked. The fancy four representing Jupiter is actually the beard of Zeus or the Royal Swan. These are the symbols used to head your letter to Sachiel.

Write in purple ink on white paper or blue ink on lavender paper. Write throughout in Passing of the Rivers script and write the letter on a Thursday at any hour.

Ask for his help in these matters - law, judgment, money and an increase in wages, social life, securing the aid of people in power or position and better overall monetary conditions. In addition, health matters of blood or poor circulation, ailments of the right leg, trouble with the feet, ankles or varicose veins.

Sachiel is associated with elephants, whales, and all fish; his flowers are all purple flowers and lilacs. He favours grapes, and his tree is the Royal Oak. He is linked to all bees and the queen bee in particular. His metal is all coined money.

Signs that your petition has been granted include finding a foreign coin in your change, any coin found on the street, any gift in the shape of animals, or actually seeing such things. Tingling in the left leg or soles of the feet. Purplish haze or light or gold particles you see or think you see. An invitation or trip to or on the sea. Gift of any of the aforementioned signs and seeing any of the Royal Family in person.

Anael is the Angel of Venus and rules the zodiac signs of Taurus and Libra. Anael is the great Angel of love and affection; he rules love, creation, affection, marriage, peace and harmony and helps to create beautiful things.

Write your letter on a Friday at any hour and keep it for 28 days, including the day you wrote it. Write in Passing of the Rivers script with blue ink on white paper or red on any colour paper. Destroy the letter on the 4th Friday. These are the heading symbols:

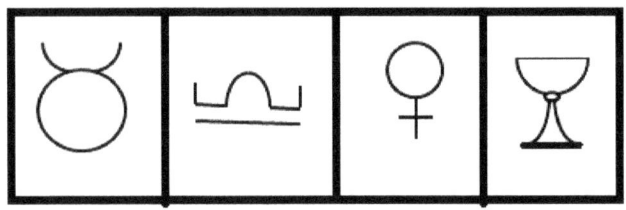

Sigil for Archangel Anael

The chalice represents the Cup of Happiness. Anael's favourite animals are the rabbit and all domestic pets, doves, lovebirds and bluetits. He prefers apples and persimmons together with roses, delphiniums, and the apple tree. He is familiar with caterpillars and butterflies, his metal is Copper.

Seeing or hearing doves are signs that your request has been granted, so are seeing or gaining lovebirds (blue budgerigars) and also seeing blue lights and receiving roses or delphiniums. If your pet plays with or stares at an invisible companion, if you suddenly see an apple tree, or receive a gift of apples, or receive as a gift any kind of ring, or find a ring in the street (any kind of ring).

Acquiring new clothes (pink, blue or luxury clothes). If these things happen within 28 days, it is a sign that your request has been granted.

Cassiel is the Angel of Saturn and rules the zodiac of Capricorn - the sign of the goat, written as a V with a hook. This is shorthand for the beard of the goat. He works slowly but surely; it may take time to receive a reply. Write in any hour on a Saturday on white paper with black ink or lead pencil; use Passing of the River script, including your signature. Keep the letter for three weeks.

His three heading signs are the sigil for Saturn (shorthand for the scythe - Cassiel is known as the Angel of Fate, the Reaper), Capricorn, Saturn and Cassiel's private sign (Jacob's Ladder).

Cassiel rules over old age legacies, the settlement of wills and other affairs of the deceased. Housing repairs, old folk, and pensioners. Stability in life matters that take time. Ailments of the left leg, complaints that come with age (rheumatism, cramps, cold and damp ills).

Cassiel's animals are the tortoise and the parrot. He loves all slow-moving insects and worms. His flower is the chincherinchee or everlastings, and his fruits include bitter aloes, all dried fruit, and all bitter herbs. He prefers slow-growing and evergreen trees, and his metal is lead.

Signs that your request will be granted include: a gift of or finding coal, suddenly biting something bitter, a present of the above flowers or white South African Violets. Having to attend a memorial or funeral service. An unexpected visit by an aged person, relief of the above ailments, and tingling in the left leg. Seeing dark green or blue mist in the room or around you. Receiving evergreen branches, seeing a worm, and finding a piece of lead. Seeing, unexpectedly, a tortoise or a parrot. Remember to listen to a parrot. A fall of soot down a chimney. If this happens, say, '*May the Angel Cassiel bless me by this sign he gives me*'.

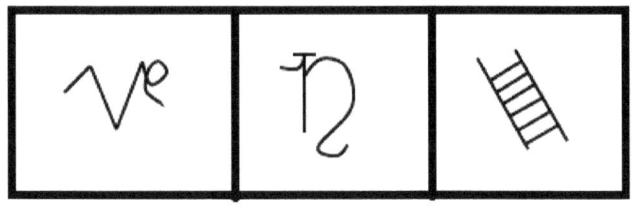

Sigil for Archangel Cassiel

Chapter Thirty
Herbcraft

A word of caution before proceeding further. When mixing and combining some herbs such as mugwort, wormwood and similar types; be extremely careful and do your research well. Some can be dangerous or toxic or generally not good to play with.

The use and preparation of herbs are traditionally a speciality of our people. Herbs can be used in medicine, in cooking, in cosmetics and as dyes. They are also used in creating amulets, talismans, and for other magical uses.

The green earth is an absolute magical food store of plants that possess incredible powers and have been used in magic and healing for centuries.

The basis of herb magic is knowing the power within the plant. As we know, magic is the practice of causing change to occur through the use of will. Herb magic is the use of herbs to cause needed change. To be successful, you must first know the powers of the plants; here lies the secret.

To work effective herb magic, as with any form of magic, you must remember three very important steps:

- There must be a reason for the work.
- A ritual and/or spell must be performed; and
- Once created, the spell must be forgotten.

In considering your preparation for conducting any magic using herbs, several elements must be considered: timing, tools, visualisation, and correspondences. Various procedures may be used, such as preparing sachets, poppets, infusions, baths, ointments, oils or incense. Your intentions may include spells for protection, love, healing, health, exorcism, luck or money.

So many different ways, so many elements, and so many reasons; the permutations are endless. Therefore, it is so important to take time, research, study and prepare the working in minute detail before executing the idea.

Let us start with preparing plants for medicinal use

by creating various concoctions.

Herbs are best when collected fresh. Use them immediately or dry them for future use by hanging them downwards, or on racks, and store them in a dark, airtight container.

Always collect the herbs in the hour when their power is greatest, e.g., herbs sacred to the Sun should be collected in the hour of the Sun, and preferably on a sunny day.

Take plants that are healthy and growing in their preferred climate; plants that are growing in an area that is not their usual habitat should be avoided. If in doubt, ask the plant!

Collect plants without dew or rain on them, if possible, for they will last longer. Ask the plant for permission to collect it, and cut the stem with a sharp knife or with a Boline, as this causes the least pain. Do not merely break the stem. Do not uproot the plant (unless, of course, you require the rootstock) as this will destroy the herb supply for future use.

The following are various methods of preparing herbs for medicinal and magical use:

Infusion – made into a tea using the green parts or flowers. Use 30 grams of the herb in 1 litre of boiling water and steep for about 10 minutes. Strain through three of four layers of muslin into a cup and add honey if necessary to improve the flavour. Infusions are normally taken lukewarm, from one to four cups per day.

Decoction - similar to infusion. Put plant material in cold water and bring to a boil. Green parts and flowers for 5 minutes, bark, roots, and seeds for 10 minutes. Steep for 3 minutes, strain and use as for an infusion.

Cold Extract - suitable for volatile ingredients destroyed by heat. Prepare as for an infusion except using cold water and steep for 8 to 12 hours. Use as an infusion.

Juice - suitable for oils, vitamins, and minerals. Chop up fresh plants or plant parts into small pieces and press to squeeze out the juices. Add water and press again. Use immediately.

Powder - grind dried plant parts with a mortar and pestle.

Syrup - useful for administering medicine to children, and for storing. Make a syrup by boiling 1 kilo of brown sugar in a ½ litre of fresh water. Add the plant material and simmer for 10 minutes. Strain through muslin and store in a cool, dark place. If only a small dose is required quickly, you can add the plant material to a little honey.

Tincture - for non-water-soluble substances and for storing. Combine 100 grams of powdered herb with 300 grams of 100% proof alcohol (vodka is most suitable. Do not use denatured alcohol or methylated spirits). Let it stand for two weeks, shaking the bottle daily, then strain the liquid into a dark bottle. Keep in a cool, dark place. The normal dosage is one spoonful.

Essence - extract the essential oil by first crushing the plant to extract the juice, then distilling the oil from the plant juice using a retort. Use 50 ml of the oil in half a litre of alcohol.

Ointment - make a decoction of the plant material. Add this decoction to olive oil and simmer until the water has completely evaporated. Add beeswax to get a firm consistency.

In determining the correct time to pick a particular herb, the following rules apply.

The Sun: rules plants resembling it in shape and or colour, and medicinal plants affect the heart.

The Moon: rules plants similar in shape and or colour, plants with a high water content (often with soft, juicy leaves) and trees and plants that live in or near water.

Mercury: rules plants with fine or highly divided leaves, and medicinal plants affecting the brain, nervous system, or speech.

Mars: rules plants with thorns or prickles and plants with a strong, acrid taste.

Jupiter: rules certain nutritious fruits and nuts, plants with a pleasant odour, the oak tree, and medicinal plants affecting the arterial system or liver.

Saturn: rules plants with cooling qualities, wood shrubs or trees that show annual rings and poisonous or narcotic plants.

Venus: rules plants with particularly pretty flowers, or with red fruits.

Here are some common herbs and their many uses, including medicinal, culinary, cosmetic, and magical.

Angelica - An ancient and highly aromatic plant, Angelica is praised in Northern European folklore as a panacea for all ills. In Livonia, Pomerania and Eastern Prussia, where this herb flourishes in the wild, there is an old custom among the peasants to march into the towns in early summer, carrying flower strips of Angelica and offering them for sale while orating an ancient Lettish chant, so old that its meaning seems to have been lost. Ruled by the Sun in Leo, Angelica should be collected during the daylight hours of either the Moon or Jupiter.

A biennial plant, the stem is round, grooved, hollow and branched near the top, tinged with blue and 3-7 feet high. It grows from a brown/red rootstock that has a spicy odour and a taste that is sweet at first, then bitter and sharp. The leaves from the sheaths that surround the stem are the lower ones, large and bi- or tri-pinnate; the upper ones are small and pinnate (leaves arranged in opposite rows along the leaf stem). Greenish white flowers with a honey-like odour are produced on long terminal stems in Spring and Summer.

Culinary: Mix seeds and stems to flavour drinks - Gin, Vermouth, and Chartreuse.

Cosmetic: Leaf - use for a relaxing bath. Also reputed to remove curses, hexes or any spells that may have been cast against you.

Aromatic: As an incense for protection, (using gum extracted from the root).

Medicinal: Leaf - make an infusion from fresh or dried leaves as a tonic for colds, to reduce flatulence and muscle spasms and to stimulate appetite. When crushed, it will freshen the air in cars and help prevent travel sickness.

Wormwood - Common Wormwood held a high reputation in old medicine. The plant was of some importance to the Mexicans, who celebrated their great festival of the Goddess of salt by a ceremonial dance of women, who wore garlands of Wormwood on their heads. Wormwood also reputedly counteracts the effect of poisoning by hemlock, toadstools, and the bite of the sea dragon.

There are three main types of Wormwood in use: Common Wormwood, Sea Wormwood (Artemisia maritima) and Roman Wormwood (Artemisia pontica). Culpepper tells us *'Each kind has its particular virtues .... the Common Wormwood is the strongest, the Sea Wormwood is the second in bitterness, and the Roman joins a great deal of aromatic flavour but little bitterness'*.

Aromatic: Burned as an incense to aid in developing psychic powers.

Medicinal: Above all, a stomach medicine for indigestion, gastric pain, lack of appetite, heartburn, and flatulence.

Caution: Pure Wormwood oil is a strong poison. Excessive use of the plant can cause poisoning, so be very careful.

Rosemary - Rosemary means 'dew of the sea'. Crusaders learned it from the Saracens, and hence its introduction into Britain, where it flourishes. Greek students were known to twine garlands of Rosemary in their hair to aid memory and stimulate their minds.

It is a good tonic, astringent, diaphoretic and nervine. It contains calcium, tannins, and volatile oils. It is good for weak digestion, wind, and nerve pains, stimulating circulation and increasing blood supply. It is a proven heart tonic that is not drastic. Externally, it can be used on wounds of all kinds, for bites or stings and as a wash for dandruff or insecticide.

Cosmetic: The tea may be used as a hair tonic or an after-shave.

Medicinal: One teaspoon in half a pint of water. The leaves can also be chewed.

Vervain - Considered as sacred as Mistletoe by the Druids, and was once called 'herba veneris' through its reputed aphrodisiacal properties, which more than likely meant no more than destroying 'first-night nerves' and allowing restfulness between assaults. Perhaps its use as a body and eyewash stems from here. The London Pharmacopoeia of 1937 recommended the hanging of Vervain around the neck to dispel dreams.

Medicinal: Nervine, tonic, emetic, produces copious perspiration. It can be used to good advantage in the early stages of colds, fevers, nervous disorders, certain types of fits and palsies. It is also good for sores and inflamed eyes. Vervain is best used as a nerve tonic. It is very good for insomnia and nervous exhaustion, and effective for headaches.

Dosage: One teaspoon of dried herb or two of fresh to half a pint of boiling water. Brew for 5 minutes, strain, and drink neat or with honey.

We cannot discuss herbs without mentioning the topic of aphrodisiacs! The word itself can send a tingle of anticipation down your spine. Throughout the ages, almost every culture has used various substances, usually herbal in origin, to put some zip into their love lives or in an attempt to cure the impotent. The types of preparation employed as aphrodisiacs ranged from the useless (except perhaps for their psychological effects) to the extremely dangerous, some being toxic enough to cause death!

However, leaving those dangers behind, there were four main types of herbal substances used as aphrodisiacs.

The first and most dangerous was the narcotic, used to intoxicate the user's object of desire, thereby rendering them incapable of responding to an unwanted sexual advance. These are not real aphrodisiacs, obviously, just a way of weakening another person's will. These substances are extremely dangerous in even slight doses and are now justifiably illegal in most parts of the world.

The second type was substances that would irritate the mucous membrane of the genitalia, hopefully producing a warm, itching feeling similar to sexual arousal. Unfortunately, what often happens is that the genitalia becomes inflamed, causing permanent damage. The prospect of kidney problems and other unpleasant side effects is also high. This type of so-called aphrodisiac is best left alone.

The next group of substances used as aphrodisiacs were herbs that alleviated medical disorders that interfered with normal sexual function.

Any herb that helped to alleviate the symptoms of a variety of genito-urinary tract infections or that supplied badly needed vitamins or minerals that were lacking in the diet could be considered an aphrodisiac, as they would allow a person with previous physical problems to function normally.

An example is *Ephedra nevadensis*, which has been used as a remedy for kidney, bladder, and urinary problems and as an aphrodisiac. In some parts of the world, Kelp (Macrocystis pyrifera) is considered to be an aphrodisiac. Kelp is rich in many vitamins and minerals, among them iodine, necessary for the proper function of the thyroid gland. Lack of iodine can result in excessive physical fatigue and a lowered sex drive.

The fourth type of herbal aphrodisiac is the one that seems to have the effect of directly increasing sexual desire and prowess, even increasing the intensity of the sensations felt during orgasm. After some extensive research and experimentation, the two herbs that seem to produce the best results in this regard are *Kava Kava root* and *Damiana leaves*.

Kava Kava is obtained from the shrub Piper methysticum, which is native to the Polynesian Islands. It has been used by the Islanders as a religious and visionary herb and aphrodisiac for most of their history. Since none of the active ingredients of Kava Kava is water soluble, the natives would pre-chew the roots and then blend this saliva/root mixture with coconut milk.

The resulting liquid was then fermented to produce a potent beverage that was used for important rituals. The effect of the drink is to relax spinal activity, producing a euphoric state of relaxation but without impairing mental activity. Some subjects also experience a tingling feeling in the genitalia, producing all the ingredients for an interesting sexual experience.

Overuse of Kava Kava will cause dangerous respiratory and skin problems.

Damiana is obtained from the shrub *Turnera diffusa*, which is native to the Southwest states of America and northern Mexico. The inhabitants of this region have used Damiana for many years as a remedy for nervous disorders and as a tonic and aphrodisiac.

Damiana seems to have a positive toning effect on both the nervous system and sexual organs, especially when combined in equal parts with *Saw Palmetto* berries. Some users of the combination tea (Damiana and Saw Palmetto) report that, taken an hour or so before sexual activity, it helps produce a more satisfactory experience.

The best results seem to be obtained when Damiana is taken in moderation over time. Using the tea, one cup per day for two weeks seems to have stimulating effects on sexual performance.

Use these herbs in a respectful manner and use them in moderation; over-indulgence or extended use may have harmful side effects.

Culpeper's Herbal

First published over 350 years ago during the reign of Elizabeth I, Culpeper's Herbal remains one of the most complete listings of herbs and their uses in existence. From Adder's Tongue to Yarrow, each of the 411 herbs is described in detail, along with its "government and virtues," remedies, and cautions.

Chapter Thirty One
Energy in Healing

We have previously covered our practices using Herbcraft and Morthwork. Combined, they figure prominently in any Coven's focus on undertaking any kind of healing work.

Fundamental to any type of healing is *energy*. So let us look at what energy, with regard to healing, is all about.

The total sum of matter and energy in the universe is constant. There is also a constant change from one to another. Matter is energy of a low vibrational rate. Levels of being are therefore merely expressions of energy, and there are many differing energy levels, e.g., gases, matter, light, sound, temperature, movement, and spirit. Energy that is of a high vibrational rate is called etheric energy. It permeates all and responds to magnetic and electrical fields.

Wow, a bit over the top? Simply, the human body consists of interactive energy patterns that give the appearance of several 'bodies'. The lowest of these bodies is the physical and is evident by the senses of touch, sight, smell, taste, and hearing. At a slightly high range is the emotional body, higher still the mental body, and the highest level is the etheric body.

The physical body is subject to the natural laws of this world, and it is through this body that irregularities in the other bodies are seen manifested.

Connecting the physical body with the higher bodies is the flow and ebb of the etheric or auric energies. Still with me? These energies move through the body in response to cosmic tides that are called electrical and magnetic fluxes, i.e., positive and negative, solar and lunar, male and female. These tides alternate, the electrical flux being greatest at noon and the magnetic flux at midnight. These fluxes are best seen as potentials, the electrical being that potential to increase the rate of vibrational energy, and the magnetic to decrease the rate of vibration.

As the etheric flow passes through the body, it does so generally in a flow from slightly above the crown to slightly below the soles of the feet, then upwards through the spinal area to the crown, and through the cycle again. Ring any bells? Middle Pillar exercise? Auras? Qabalah? Chakras?

Knowledge of these polarisations is important for two reasons. First, they determine which magnetic passes will produce the greatest response. Second, they determine the passage of the etheric force through the body, and so knowledge of the polarisation is necessary to determine and correct blockages in that flow.

As the etheric flow passes through the body, from electric to magnetic (positive to negative), competing electric and magnetic charges are channelled through meridians. When an energy imbalance occurs, a blockage results in one or more meridians, resulting in the energy flow being limited or stopped through that particular part of the body. Illness may manifest itself in anything from a mental condition to body dysfunction.

Methods of freeing the channels include acupuncture, moxibustion, massage, and psychic irradiation.

Methods of repairing body damage include spells, herbalism, Chromotherapy and magnetic healing.

So what we are basically talking about is our aura, that electromagnetic field which surrounds our body. The auric field is related to the radiating energy of the chakras. The colour and shape of auras are usually invisible to most of us, but with practice, you can develop the ability to see and sometimes feel an aura.

So let us first look at the Chakras. They help to regulate all the body's processes, from organ function to the immune system and emotions, and each chakra has its own vibrational frequency that corresponds to a specific colour. There are seven major chakras: the crown, the brow or third eye, the throat chakra, the heart, the solar plexus, the spleen or sacral chakra, and the root or base chakra.

Each chakra is responsible for controlling and relaying information to a different area of the body. Although they function from a central force and have a degree of interdependency, each is responsible for the actions and reactions of a different part of the mind, the emotions, or the body.

Because energy is transferred from one chakra to another in an ever-constant interchange, if there should be a blockage in an area of a single chakra, it can lead to inadequate functioning of the others, which in turn will cause an imbalance in bodily functions.

Blockages can be caused by negative thoughts that may not be on a conscious level but are purely subconscious. Those blockages can be cleared by deliberate application of positive thought by using a quartz crystal, which is capable of amplifying energy and intensifying the level of positive thought.

The quartz crystal you use should be a small one, not more than two or three inches long. The chakras are highly sensitive, and a large crystal would amplify energy to such an extent that it would be much too strong a force for you to cope with.

Each Chakra is associated with a particular colour. An alternative to using a quartz crystal is the method we call Chromotherapy, sometimes called colour therapy or colourology. A healing method which uses light in the form of colour to balance energy lacking from a person's body, whether it be on physical, emotional, spiritual, or mental levels.

According to science, chromotherapy is considered a pseudoscience and is not a medically accepted treatment, and therefore claims it to be ineffective. We of the Wicca tend to disagree. We don't just plonk some coloured light on a person's body; we use a little bit of magic, then plonk colour on the affected area.

All forms of healing techniques within the Craft use methods that are basically non-scientific and mostly esoteric in some form. That is why we are called Witches! Therefore, of course, science is always going to scoff at our methods. Using the right amount of Magic under precise conditions is always going to work for us, so why get into a squabble with academia? We will just keep our little secrets for the benefit of our own benefit.

Chromotherapy or colour healing utilises the vibrational rate of the differing colours of the light spectrum, and in conjunction with the Chakras, we find a very effective method of healing some conditions. Let us have a closer look at each Chakra and its corresponding colours and attributes.

First, the **Root Chakra** represents our foundation and feeling of being grounded. It is located at the base of the spine around the tailbone area. It relates to the material and physical world and corresponds to stability, security, and survival issues, including our basic needs of food and money. Its associated colour is red, but do not use red where nervous complaints are involved; it is too stimulating.

Imbalances in this Chakra manifest as anaemia, fatigue, lower back pain, sciatica, and depression. Frequent colds or cold hands and feet. Stimulants and motivating actions that may assist in clearing and/or cleansing the blockage or imbalance include physical exercise and restful sleep, gardening and pottery. Red food and drink. Red gemstones, red clothing, bathing in red water. Using red oils such as ylang ylang or sandalwood.

Next is the **Sacral Chakra**, which represents our connection and ability to accept others and new experiences and our sensing abilities and issues related to feelings. Ability to be social and intimacy issues. It is located in the lower abdomen, about two inches below the navel. It corresponds to our sense of abundance, well-being, pleasure and sexuality. Its associated colour is orange.

Imbalances in this Chakra manifest as eating disorders, alcohol and drug abuse, depression, lower back pain, asthma or allergies, urinary problems and sensuality issues, as well as impotency and frigidity. Stimulants and motivating actions that may assist in clearing and/or cleansing the blockage or imbalance include hot aromatic baths, water aerobics, massage, embracing sensation (such as different food tastes), orange food and drink, orange gemstones and orange clothing and using orange oils such as melissa or orange essential oil.

Next is the **Solar Plexus Chakra**, representing our ability to be confident and in control of our lives. It is located in the upper abdomen, above the navel, in the stomach area and controls self-worth, self-confidence, and self-esteem. It balances our intellect and ego. Its associated colour is yellow.

Imbalances in this Chakra manifest as digestive problems, ulcers, diabetes, hypoglycaemia, constipation, nervousness, toxicity, parasites, colitis, and poor memory. Stimulants and motivating actions that may assist in clearing and/or cleansing the blockage or imbalance include using your mind by reading informative books and doing puzzles. Sunshine. Detoxification programs. Yellow food and drink. Yellow gemstones and yellow clothing. Using yellow oils such as lemon or rosemary essential oils.

The **Heart Chakra** is next, representing our ability to love. It is found in the centre of the chest and controls love, joy and inner peace, forgiveness, compassion and the ability to have self-control and acceptance of oneself. Its associated colour is green.

Imbalances in this Chakra manifest as heart and breathing disorders, breast cancer, chest pain, high blood pressure, immune system problems and muscular tension. Stimulants and motivating actions that may assist in clearing and/or cleansing the blockage or imbalance include nature walks, time spent with family or friends, green food and drink, green gemstones and green clothing. Using green oils such as eucalyptus or pine essential oils.

Next, the **Throat Chakra** controls our ability to communicate and is located in the throat. It represents the self-expression of feelings and the truth, the right to speak and express oneself and one's beliefs and the ability to trust and loyalty. Its associated colour is blue.

Imbalances in this Chakra manifest as thyroid imbalances, swollen glands, fevers and flu, and infections. Mouth, jaw, tongue, neck and shoulder problems. Hyperactivity and hormonal disorders such as PMS, mood swings, bloating and menopause. Stimulants and motivating actions that may assist in clearing and/or cleansing the blockage or imbalance include singing (in the shower), poetry, stamp or art collecting, and meaningful conversations. Blue food and drink, blue gemstones and blue clothing and using blue oils such as chamomile or geranium essential oils.

The **Third Eye Chakra** is next, controlling our ability to focus on and see the big picture. It is located on the forehead between the eyes and rules intuition, imagination, wisdom and the ability to think and make decisions. Its associated colour is indigo.

Imbalances in this Chakra manifest as learning disabilities, coordination problems and sleep disorders. Stimulants and motivating actions that may assist in clearing and/or cleansing the blockage or imbalance include stargazing and meditation. Indigo food and drink, indigo gemstones and clothing. Using indigo oils such as patchouli or frankincense essential oils.

Lastly, the **Crown Chakra**, located at the top of the head, is the highest and represents our ability to be fully connected spiritually. It controls inner and outer beauty, our connection to spirituality, enlightenment and pure bliss. Its associated colour is violet.

Imbalances in this Chakra manifest as headaches, photosensitivity, mental illness, neuralgia, senility, right/left brain disorders, and coordination problems. Also, epilepsy, varicose veins, blood vessel problems, and skin rashes. Stimulants and motivating actions that may assist in clearing and/or cleansing the blockage or imbalance include focusing on dreams and documenting one's visions and inventions. Violet food and drink. Violet gemstones, clothing, and violet oils such as lavender or jasmine essential oils.

So, how do we actually work with the Chakras? A couple of methods and some simple examples, because this subject is worthy of a book alone. We suggested quartz crystals, and this is probably one of the easier methods, especially if working alone, because too many people tend to intensify the energy a little too much.

The same with coloured stones or particular gemstones. These, used together with essential oil rubbed on the Chakra area, work particularly well.

Finally, the use of chromotherapy. Using cellophane paper and a torch will work, or any similar method to focus the appropriate light colour on the Chakra.

Remember that whatever method you use, prepare the working as if it were a ritual and remember the rules of ritual and making magic. Prepare beforehand, build, and focus your energy to create your own magic, and remember you are not only working on the human plane but also the astral.

The primary method of healing that our Coven has used for many years involves Cord Magic and, in our opinion, is the most successful technique we have ever used.

So, having discussed 'energy', 'positives and negatives' and 'electric and magnetic', does it make a little more sense now when we prefer to work magic and create things like a Circle, and conduct initiations and teach male to female and female to male?

"Each chakra is a temple gate, carved with the glyphs of memory and desire. At midlife, the seeker walks barefoot through them, not to ascend, but to descend into the body's own mythos, where blood sings, bones remember, and the sacred is not above but within."

Chapter Thirty Two
Runecraft

Runecraft is one method of divination similar to tarot, astrology or scrying. It is the art of clairvoyance (the art and science of being aware of facts, objects, and situations by psychic means) using tools to 'divine' or 'ask of the Gods'.

Divination using the runes does not tell the future; rather, it makes you more aware of what is and allows you to change or take another path. The runes themselves are neutral, neither good nor evil, just like figures that can represent any quantity, suitable or unsuitable, true or false.

Our people believe that clairvoyance is a natural attribute, and like all natural attributes, it can be trained and expanded. Use of the runes is the best way to train your clairvoyance so that, with time, the tools can be done away with and your natural ability will shine through.

One of the main things to remember with any type of divination is responsibility. Divination should never be used to make money, to boast or to frighten or 'con' anyone. Runes do not foretell the future but are there to guide you through your problems by showing you what is likely to happen, giving you variables, and showing you how you should behave if an event comes to pass. The primary objective of runes is to help you take charge of your life.

The runes are said to have originated in the Nordic and Germanic tribes of Northern Europe around the second century BCE. They were used for both religious (divination) and secular (alphabet) purposes. Legend has it that the runes were obtained by Odin hanging himself on a tree for nine days, and the inspiration resulted in the runes. Unfortunately, the knowledge he obtained cost him an eye taken in payment by the Gods.

There were several different runic alphabets in use, but the most common was the FUTHARK, taken from the first six letters F U T H A R K. This alphabet contains 24 letters divided into three groups of eight - Freya's eight, Hagall's eight and Tyr's eight. There are 25 runes, the 25th being blank, and this represents fate; the will of the Gods, for this is beyond the knowledge of mortal beings. It shows that this is inevitable and has to be accepted. The meaning depends on the other surrounding runes drawn in the cast, but if it follows the Dag rune, it means death.

Runes should ideally be handcrafted, preferably from wood, but they can also be made from crystals or pebbles found on the shoreline. The important thing is that they are made of a naturally occurring substance. When choosing the shape and size of the runes, there are two important things to note - they should be uniform in shape and size, and all 25 of them need to fit in the palms of your cupped hands.

The rune symbols themselves should be either carved, painted or drawn. If they are painted, there are several traditional colours that can exert a magical influence on both you and the runes. Red is the traditional colour of rune magic and represents the active male symbol. Blue is the sacred colour of Odin and is, therefore, suitable; it is also the colour of healing. Green is the colour of prosperity, fertility, and growth; it is also the colour of the Goddess.

Your runes, once completed, should be kept in a fabric or leather pouch. The Runes should be laid out on a cloth when doing a reading. This cloth should be totally neutral visually, free from visual distractions and should not be patterned. A basic black or white cloth would be best.

There are two basic rules to follow when forming a question in Runecraft: keep the question simple, specific and unambiguous; and make sure there are four elements in a question - what do you want to know, who do you wish to know it about, in what time frame is the question set, and where is the question set.

Once the question has been asked and formed, concentrate, mix up the runes in the bag with your hand, select each rune from the bag and lay it out face down on the cloth in the sequence of the layout. When laid out, turn the runes face up in the order in which they were laid out and do the reading. Concentrate on the question while mixing, selecting, and laying out.

This is no right or wrong way of throwing the runes. There are many different methods, and you should try them - even developing your own method - until you find the way that works best for you. Here are a few you could try:

Draw a **single rune** and interpret the meaning.

Draw **two runes**; this gives more to work with for an interpretation. They can reinforce each other or be counter to each other.

Draw **three runes** that represent the three fates. The first represents the past; the second, the present and the third, the future. Some prefer to read as –the present state of affairs, the action which may be taken, the best possible outcome.

Another method is to use five runes that indicate the four basic directions around a centre. Using yourself as a reference, lay the runes deosil in the order, first – South, second – West, third – North, fourth –East, fifth - centre. Read as South, the basic influences underlying the question. West, problems and/or obstacles affecting the person asking the question. North, beneficial processes and/or influences. East, the immediate outcome. Centre, future influences and/or the influences acting on the reader.

A chant that can be used before doing any divination with runes: *'Stones of Lyr, Stones of Lyr, Tell me truly, show me clear, Let my eyes see sharp and bright, That I might get my future right, Show me what I need to do, This is the boon I ask of you.'*

Here follows the runes and their meanings according to our Tradition. We do not follow the rule of reverse meanings.

Rune Meaning

ᚠ Feu: cattle - Fortune and Fertility - means earned through effort, not inheritance. Possessions, investments, material vitality, good outcome, wealth, luck, creative energy. Love is fulfilled and happiness in romance.

ᚢ Ur: bison - Untamed unlimited strength - has a wild and martial quality. Good for situations with high risk and can indicate rapid change. New responsibility, success needs stamina and determination, the higher self, benefits from hard work, indicates health, a new relationship, or a career, a testing time.

ᚦ Thur: giant - This rune speaks of a decision which should be delayed, or it may mean some problems in the family. A protective rune, the 'helping hand', is used when faced with a situation beyond control. Gives strength to face a situation, protects against own folly, indicates luck, a warning of trouble ahead, possible conflict, and circumvents a problem before it is out of control.

ᚨ Ansur: God - A rune of communication. Asking and receiving answers from the Gods. Linked to the concept of Yggdrasil – travel through roots and branches for answers. It is the rune of the Elders and can indicate a blessing or gift from parents or older persons, or it may tell of visits with them. Associated with wisdom, occult power, revenge, healing, augers well for writing, poetry, public speaking, exams, learning, social skills, personal attraction, and controlled creative power.

ᚱ Rad: cartwheel - This rune tells of a pleasant journey to visit friends or to take part in some celebrations. Travel, possible change, decisions, and unexpected news of benefit to the receiver.

Ken: torch - Like the flame, this rune tells of the bursting forth of a new love, the getting for a girl and the giving for a boy. Very positive rune; imbues life with a protective and creative warmth, and symbolises gentle acts of creation such as writing music or creating talismans. It has spiritual connotations, enlightenment, and creativity from new ideas. It may mean warmth and comfort, the security of home, health, stability and a feeling of well-being.

Geofn: gift - The gift of the Old Ones is the harmony of a joining. This rune tells of a beneficial partnership. It has only a positive meaning. Strongly associated with gifts, both giving and receiving, giving creates harmony, exchange of energies, spiritual or material, necessary for balance, and can signify a lover, generosity, and harmony.

Wynn: comfort - This rune speaks of happiness, joy, or a fair-haired man who may travel in his work, or of a successful trip across water. Blessing, fertility, success, controlling will, likely romance, fulfilment in love or career, joy and happiness from success.

Hagall: hail - This rune speaks of the work of the Gods that could disrupt plans in the year ahead or of sickness, death, a wedding or a birth. Drastic change, disruptive forces, the unpredictable, and possible frustration indicate the need to understand the precise limits of a situation. This rune links directly to the primal forces of the universe. Being given its warning is itself a form of good luck.

Nied: necessity - This rune speaks of binding, a need for caution and constraint. Think carefully about your actions. A blocked situation, patience needed to resolve, indicates achievement of long-term aim or aims, an adverse indicator for love or sex, implies the need to build a bridge, can indicate delay, constraint, oppression or ill health.

Is: ice - This rune brings the cooling of ice to a relationship. Standstill, need to pause, a freeze is the wise choice of action whilst energy rebuilds, indicating a poor outcome for relationships or dynamic situations. In Norse cosmology, ice is regarded as an element in its own right. This is expressed as the combination of the elements earth and water. IS corresponds to winter resting of the Earth until spring arrives.

Jara: year - This rune tells of a waiting of

thirteen moons. Gentle gestation and change, reward for past effort, auspicious for legal matters, a start for relationships, birth, business, new enterprise, emphasis is on work as distinct from investment, associated with Yule and celebration. It is the rune of cyclic return and harvesting the reward for past work and effort.

Yr: yew - This rune speaks of a pleasant surprise. Outgoing, dynamic, go hunting, evolution. Yr is never evil but very protective; it will banish an obstacle to a just action, gives a defence, is associated with the dead, allows rest and has a role in rebirth. Yr is a mystical rune giving direct access to the other world.

Peorth: a dice cup - Secret, hidden, good for speculation, gambling, chance, finding things lost (goods or knowledge), indicates gain through high risk for a desirable result. Achievement through high risk.

Ilhs: elk - This rune speaks of a career change. Protection, shield, help, conductor, promote friendship, protect from own folly (like Thorn), both personally and financially, protection from enemies and evil thoughts of others, can indicate renouncing an opportunity for another with good results.

Sygil: sun - This rune speaks of your health and the need to rest. It could also indicate you are worrying too much. Healing, strength, centering, luck, bode well for physical health, clear thinking, self-confidence, aiding problem solution, success, achievement, and victory. Sygil, with its Sun association, is the most positive of the Runes.

Tyr: creator - This rune is another of love and romance. Justice, legal matters, dedication, bravery, good indications for a difficult or antagonistic situation, help to recover from illness or accident, achieve honour and victory through struggle, motivation, strength of willpower, bode well for business dealings.

Biarkan: birch - This is the rune of the family and speaks of happiness in the family, possibly through an impending birth. Women's mysteries, birth process, emotional stability, new start, household matters, growth, change, mothering, fertility, children, spouse, family, Gaia, initiation, new schemes. Biarkan is a protective and nurturing rune.

Eoh: horse - This rune speaks of moving, possibly a change of home. Shapeshifting, telepathic, linking, adjustment, change for the better, calls for planned change, not abrupt change, need to change circumstances, indicates flaws in a current situation, change through altered attitude, it may mean travel.

ᛗ Man: humanity - This rune indicates legal matters. Think carefully about them before committing yourself. Communication, co-operation, legal affairs, good for learning, inventiveness, serious mental application required; influences relationships, group enterprise, help which is objective and honest, possibly impersonal, co-operation despite ill feelings.

ᛚ Lagu: water - This is the rune of intuition and betokens a successful choice. It can also mean a woman or a birth. Occult, sex, influence, movement, creation, artistic endeavour, painting, music, writing, the mind beyond the rational, imagination, psychic powers, feminine intuition and awareness, our inner voice. Lagu is a feminine rune related to the Moon and the creative.

ᛜ Ing: the God Ing - This is the rune of completion and indicates a completed project. It may also mean fertility. Fertility, progression, grounded, astral, brings great power to any situation, excellent to bring matters to a successful conclusion, and has the power to retain success and freedom from worry. Ing is a male rune, the complement of Lagu.

ᛞ Dag: day - This is the rune of prosperity and speaks of a complete change of lifestyle for the better. Catalyst, made invisible, between the worlds, indicates the need to make a positive change, especially in personal values and attitude. Everything should be in the open, and no hidden dangers, security, particularly financial security, is good for an increase in financial position.

ᛟ Ogal: possession - This rune speaks of inherited possessions. Family values, centering, family responsibilities, family land, furniture, household goods, domestic activity, gardening, building, finances (in terms of investment in the future), family life, ancestry in general, care of the elderly, and any traditional family responsibility.

Part Four
Various Rituals

*The Myth, the Memory,
and the Mystery Made Flesh*

Ritual is where the Craft learns to speak in poetry. Here, in these woven rites and sacred enactments, magic is no longer theory or solitary spark; it becomes legacy, lived and passed from hand to hand like a flame.

In *Various Rituals*, we enter the heart of shared experience. The following chapters offer not only the choreography of the ceremony, but the soul beneath it. Each rite, whether joyous or solemn, unfolds as an echo of something older than the written word. *Wiccaning, Handfasting,* and *Dark Moon* workings do not simply mark time; they sanctify it. They are the ancient songs whispered through modern breath.

And yet, this is also where the practitioner learns the art of nuance: how to move with reverence in sacred space *Ritual Etiquette*, how to awaken ancient currents through names long spoken *The Fire of Azrael*, and how to journey not only across the circle, but within the self, *Pathworkings, The 29th Path, Pathway to the Sun*. These are the rites that shape the inner terrain.

The rituals described are not rote repetitions; they are myth in motion. They ask: *Who were you before the world told you? What will you become when you answer?*

Here, in the embers of tradition and the breath of invocation, the practitioner finds a mirror, not just of their past or future, but of the Mystery itself.

Welcome to the dance of shadow and sun, of body and breath and spell. The Circle is moving. Step in.

Chapter Thirty Three
Ritual Etiquette

I remember sometime during our initial course, we were told that we would be doing some practical work within a Circle. None of us had any idea at that time what to expect. We had never been to a public or even private Circle or ritual of any kind, and it was a little daunting, to say the least.

Once we knew the rules and understood them, we realised they were basic common sense, but sometimes people need to be reminded what common sense is! So here are some thoughts to keep in mind if you are ever invited to either an open public gathering, a Wiccan Conference or even the Mount Franklin Pagan Gathering, or a private one hosted by an established Coven.

Public Rituals are normally advertised in the common press or, more so today, in electronic media such as Facebook or other social media sites. The organisers usually plan to present the ritual to the lowest common denominator, which is usually someone who has little knowledge of Paganism or is interested in alternative beliefs. The ritual is nearly always scripted, and an explanation is given before the ritual.

Private Rituals are typically hosted by established groups or Covens, and your invitation is generally from a friend. Before you accept the invitation, it is prudent to ask a few pertinent questions like: what is the purpose of the ritual, who's going, what you should bring, are you the only new person going, what should you wear, and can you be expected to participate in any way.

As far as clothing is concerned, usually, you have a pretty wide latitude. At public rituals today, you might expect to find people wearing all sorts of clothing from jeans and casual wear to robes or medieval costumes. If you have no formal clothes to suit the occasion, you should probably wear something loose and comfortable and something that does not stand out.

As to what to expect at the ritual, if you have read most of this story and been around the Pagan scene for a while, you should have some ideas, so there is no need for further explanation, but if not, ask.

Final note - bear in mind that these are fairly standard rules and are presented to help you become comfortable with the fundamentals of attending rituals. However, bear in mind that rituals will vary considerably from one group to another. The best thing I can tell you is to keep an open mind and have a willingness to participate and learn.

So here are some points we give to those who attend our Circles:

- A Circle is a religious rite, and all participants should conduct themselves in a manner respectful to the Goddess. Your conduct is a reflection upon yourself and upon your people. Once the pre-rite grounding begins, the time for socialising and chit-chat is over. The time for silence and spiritual focus, and magical concentration begins.
- Individuals shall not be admitted to Circles while they are under the influence of any drugs, including alcohol.
- Be on time for all rituals/meetings - not early, not late, but ON TIME. There is no such thing as 'Pagan Time' in a Wiccan Circle.
- A ritual bath or shower should normally be taken before arriving at a Circle.
- No one shall partake of or use caffeine, cigarettes, food or drugs within 6 hours of a ritual (only if you are actually participating).
- All Initiates and Pagans attending a ritual will assist in preparing the ritual area under the direction of the HP. The Maiden and MIB will assist the HPS and HP if necessary.
- No one shall wear makeup or unconsecrated jewellery in a Circle.
- Notify the organisers as early as possible if you are too ill or incapacitated to attend a meeting or ritual.
- During a ritual, abide by any instruction given by HPS/HP.
- Do not sit, stand, eat or drink before the HPS – she is the representative of the Goddess and should be given the proper respect.
- The HPS and HP do not serve, prepare food or wash up during or after a ritual, except when they expressly wish to do so.
- Since traditional lore teaches that a consecrated object easily absorbs energy and becomes 'charged', therefore, do not touch such items without the owner's permission. This would apply especially, though not exclusively, to such items as Tarot cards, the Tools, ritual jewellery and other regalia.
- Once the Circle is cast, nobody leaves until the ritual ends. If you feel faint, simply let an Initiate know, and they will take care of you. In an extreme emergency, the HPS/HP may cut a door in the Circle and escort you out.
- A Circle is not for observers. A Circle is participatory. If you are not ready to focus and

contribute your attention and efforts to the ceremony, you do not belong in the Circle. If you do not wish to participate, you should excuse yourself before the pre-rite meditation and grounding begin.

- Once the rite begins, focus. Talking, joking, laughing, etc., are extremely rude and break the continuity and concentration of the ceremony. Such behaviour is cause for expulsion from the Circle, and offenders are unwelcome at subsequent Circles.

There will usually be an informal segment within a ritual, usually after Cakes and Wine. This is a time for relaxation and for discussion of magical topics, planning of festivals, group announcements, etc. It is not a time for disruption.

Wiccan Covens are not inviolably solemn, but they are serious. If you are not serious about spiritual development or expression, a Wiccan Coven is not for you.

Chapter Thirty Four
The Sussex Round

The Sussex Round is our way of celebrating the seasons, an excuse to get together with other witches and party! To drink too much mead, eat too much food, dance until you fall over, sing until you have no voice, make love like there is no tomorrow and enjoy and be thankful for life itself. To thank the Gods for their gifts and display our affection for the land and our friends.

As Witches, we have eight holidays a year, each one as magical as the next. But it is not just a celebration of the season, it is the story of our Gods, how they live, die and live again; we celebrate with Them and learn from Them. We celebrate the Cycle of Life of the Sky Father and the Earth Mother, and this is done through the Sun and the Soul of Nature. Sometimes the God is invoked in His Solar Aspect as the Sun, and sometimes in His Earth Aspect as Lord of Animals. *'But behind all is The Mother ...'*

The Festival of Yule

We start with the Festival of Yule celebrated at midnight on the 22 June; it is our Lady's Conception. It marks the Winter Solstice, the astronomical New Year, set at the point of the Sun's greatest travel to the North.

Our beliefs teach that on the Winter Solstice, our Lady, who journeyed below in search of the Lord, calls to our people for the Spirit of Him that we consumed at Lammas when she was made pregnant by Him, but the Body without Spirit cannot grow. We are the custodians of that Spirit from Lammas to Yule.

In the Yule rite, we try to draw back the Sun and give the Spirit to Him so that both He on High can fertilise the Earth Mother and He in His animal aspect can give His blessings unto the herds. The orientation of the rite is more towards the fertilisation of the Earth, and we work magic to try to catch the Sun in His journey by making a net to trap Him.

Before the ritual, we make a Solar Wheel, which is a circle of small thin sticks (like a crown of sorts) with four small candles set into the sticks. The wheel should be a little smaller than the Cauldron so that it can be placed inside the Cauldron and set alight.

The Altar is set to the North, covered in a black cloth and has only one light by which the Coven may see. In the centre of the temple is placed the Cauldron, containing sticks and dead leaves (which will be set alight later in the ritual).

The Coven is led into the temple from the West by the High Priestess, the Coven are carrying between them the Solar Wheel, and singing, *"Cold, cold, the Mother is cold, old, old, the winter is old, hold, hold, the wheel were told, for the sun we will call back tonight. Bear, bear, the wheel in the air, share, share the load without care to where the Altar lies bare, for the sun we will call back tonight. Clasp, clasp the cords in your grasp. Throw, throw, let the spell go. Here, here with song we will cheer, for the sun we will call back tonight."*

They Circle the Cauldron once and then lay the Wheel on the Altar, and the temple is created as normal.

Then the High Priestess turns to the North and invokes, *"Oh Lord of Light, held in the Mother, flee not from the Lady - Your Love She needs! Chase away darkness, allay our fears! Return to the land, and bring Her Your warmth!"*

The Coven form a ring around the Cauldron, facing outwards, and with threatening gestures, Athame in hand, shout, *"Yield, Oh Cold One, Yield! Yield! Yield to the Summer, free the field! Go! Oh, Dark One, Go! Go! The Sun is coming to melt Your snow! Leave, Oh Old One, Leave! Leave! Within the Womb we hear our Lord breathe!"*

They place their Athames on the ground, blades pointing outwards, and link their Cords in the centre over the Cauldron. Holding the ends of the Cords, they begin to circle, chanting, *"Father Sun, come down from the North. Dance with the Old Ones, Dance! Dance! Lady, Oh Lady, when is the Birth? Dance with the Old Ones! Dance! Dance!"*

The High Priestess lights the four candles in the Solar Wheel and carries it towards the Cauldron, saying, *"The Lord, He is coming to waken the land."*

The Coven replies, *"Dance with the Old Ones! Dance! Dance!"*

The High Priestess says, *"Open the Doors for Him, take knife in hand!"*

The Coven replies, *"Dance with the Old Ones! Dance! Dance!"*

The Coven picks up their Athames and circles the High Priestess. They follow her with their Athames as she lowers the Solar Wheel into the Cauldron, saying, *"Let the Light be born again."*

The sticks, leaves, and Solar Wheel are set alight, and as the Cauldron blazes, the Coven will leap over it.

The ritual is finished with a toast and the closing of the Temple in the usual manner.

The Festival of Oimelc

The great festival of Oimelc is next, which is celebrated at 3 am on the second of August. It marks the commencement of the birth season of animals when the ewes of our people's flocks begin to lactate in preparation to nurse the coming young.

The festival is also called Imbolg, which means in the belly. At this time, our God grows in our Mother's womb, and She goes into labour. Our Coven acts as midwife.

The ritual, the principle of our Earth Rite, for both endeavours to give Soul to the Mother. The Festival, in celebrating the start of the birth season and in raising the Cone of Power, is both a ceremony and a rite.

In performing the ritual, we wear hoods or scarves to disguise our personalities. The Altar is set to the North, displaying only one candle, a chalice of milk, and a Willow Wand.

The Coven enters the Temple from the West, slowly processionally, singing, *"The Lady and the Lord are one, birth will answer the warmth of the Sun, within the Wombs the young ones lie, reborn of the Old who in cruel winter die. Breasts fill, seed stir, all awakening, flax and fur. Life quickens, tame or wild, prepare now for the coming child. Sing now, dance now, ewe moan, seed grow, come we here in Sabbat hour, the Lady calls to us for Power."*

They circle the Temple once. The Coven goes to the South, the High Priest to the North.

The Temple is created in the usual manner, then the High Priestess says, *"Within the Womb all life awaits in slumber the coming of the Spirit to the Unborn. Let us give of ourselves that Spirit!"*

The High Priest goes to the Altar and takes up the Willow Wand, which he presents to the High Priestess, who rewards him with a kiss.

The High Priestess goes to each of the four points of the compass - East, South, West, then North, and strikes the ground four times with the Wand at each point, saying, *"Waken, Mother! Waken! Waken! As from us, the Power is taken! Teats give milk! New grass sprout! As we spin around about!"*

The Coven performs the Ring Dance, Besoms between their legs, with a high-stepping gait and loud stamping. They chant, *"We dance, we jump, around we go. As high as we leap, let the crops grow. Higher and higher and higher we bound; let all of the Mother be fruitful around."*

The Witches then twirl clockwise to deposit their Riding Poles outside of the circle of dancing and, on turning back inwards, join hands to form a complete circle. The Coven continues spinning, chanting, *"Grow, grow, crops thrive, show, show, mother alive! Green, green, fruitful ground, spin the circle, round and round."*

Gradually building up power. The call to Earth, the Power is made by the High Priest. When the Coven is sufficiently recovered, the High Priestess will say, *"The Mother thanks Her Children, and draws them to Her Breast. Take ye Her thanks."*

The High Priestess takes the chalice of milk to each of the Coven, who drink therefrom. When the chalice is drained, it is returned to the Altar. Toasting and feasting follow the usual closing of the Temple.

The Festival of the Spring Equinox

The festival of the Vernal or Spring Equinox is celebrated at 6 am on 21 September. It is a festival of birth, marking the end of the birth cycle of the animals, and giving praise for the new life. As a ceremony, it marks the cross-quarter between Oimelc and Beltane, and as a rite, it produces the Birth of the God. It is in the pain of the labour that we learn the Mystery of Rebirth, for it is only through suffering that we truly acquire knowledge.

The ritual mirrors the breaking forth of life from the dark grasp of winter. The festival starts in darkness and ends in light, and we know that this new life is only part of the eternal cycle. The light comes from the Mother, for what is not of Her?

The Altar is set to the centre, on which stands the Cauldron containing a single burning candle. Around the Cauldron lay unlit white tapers and a cloak of bright floral pattern, and a crown of flowers. The Coven is hooded or wrapped in dark robes or blankets to conceal their own brightly coloured robes underneath.

They enter the temple without speaking and sit around the Cauldron, meditating upon the significance of the festival. The High Priestess enters last and remains in the West.

The High Priest challenges, saying, *"Let all attend the Mother."*

The Coven stands around the Cauldron, placing their hands on the Altar. They tap the Altar top, chanting, *"Mother, Mother, Give! Give! Mother, Mother, Live! Live! Earth, Earth, Earth, Earth, Give birth! Give birth!"* The chant is being repeated twice.

The Coven covers the mouth of the Cauldron with their hands, palms down, fingers outstretched and touching the fingers of their neighbour.

The High Priest says, *"Guardians appointed, Keepers of Spirit, watchers in darkness, Lords of Beginning. The One is within you - the power you inherit, the praise you give in laughter and singing. Drawn was the spirit from depths within you, given to the Mother in Oimelc season. Assist now the Birth of Nature made pregnant; watch with Her heavings the fulfilled reason. Move now, the Mother, attend Her in labour, part now the curtain, let Him come hither. Deliver the New One, blessed with all favour, spread wide the Green Cloak of the birth season's weather. This is your work! See to the Mother on you rests the honour - it is won by none other!"*

The Coven takes up the tapers from around the Cauldron. Here follows the Sun Dance, to the chant, *"Spin now the circle, the work is done, let all behold the Sun! As we turn, the seasons change, we and time are one! In and out, around we go, let the circle spin. Let Gods on high and man below, toast the new-born King!"*

The last two lines are repeated until the Sun Dance is complete.

The Coven stops, and the High Priest says, *"Let us show that the work is done."*

The Coven carries the cloak to the High Priestess and adorns her with it. The High Priest crowns her with the flowers. All bow towards the High Priestess, who says, *"Let there be feasting in honour of the Mother."*

Toasts, feasts, and games are usually followed by the closing of the Temple.

The Great Festival of Beltane

The next is the Great Festival of Beltane, which is sometimes celebrated at 9.00 am on 31 October. At other times, the ritual is conducted late in the evening and continues until daylight. Beltane marks the Maturation. Beltane (need-fire) is the greatest of the Sabbats. It marks the end of winter and the beginning of summer and is one of the original celebrations.

The feast is dedicated to Bel, the God of Light and of the Underworld, and is referred to as the Feast of Mead. The festival is characterised by love trysts counterpointed by scourging to avert barrenness. Fertility is ensured for the coming summer by the anointing of the Maypole with Sacred Wine during the feast, and this power is shared by the Covenors during the revelries of the following day.

As can be expected of the Great Festival, the inner meanings are complex and deep. The rite embodies a tradition that would not be readily discerned by those outside of the Covenant.

Food of the feast should be of the berry type, and drink of mead, although any heavy, sweet white wine may be substituted.

The rite is to be performed upon a hilltop or other place exposed to the sky. A trench is cut to form a Circle large enough to contain a central balefire and Covenant, with the Altar being at the eastern edge of the Circle that is bare or covered with a plain cloth of green linen.

On the Altar is placed a bow and spindle with which the Magister will kindle the balefire. No lights are present, although unlit torches may be placed in a convenient spot to be lit from the balefire at a later time. The High Priestess stands at the Altar.

The Covenant is led into the circular area by the High Priest, all singing, *"Beltane Eve, for winter we don't grieve, for here we come long before the sun-oh, to welcome in the summers, to welcome in the day-oh. The summers come, the days grow long, and winters gone away-oh. What happened to the winter cloth, so white upon the ground-oh? It has flown like mother's milk to nurture the grassy furrow. Lad courts lass, and round they dance, a blushing all the way-oh! The winter's gone, the summer comes, and here we are tonight-oh!"*

The Coven all bow to the High Priestess and may present her with presents of flowers. They then arrange themselves to the West of the balefire.

The HP says, *"Let the Sabbat begin."*

The HPS says, *"Let the fire be kindled!"* Coven chant, *"Bel, Bel, give us fire! Fire! Fire! Fire! Bel,*

Bel, give us light! Light! Light! Light! Bel, Bel, give us hope. Let Light banish Night!"

The High Priest steps forward to the Altar, and there is silence. All others cover their faces with their hands, heads bent as if in mourning. The High Priest uses the bow and spindle to kindle the need-fire and then lights the balefire with this flame. When the fire is alight, the High Priest says, *"Let Sky and Earth show rejoicing!"*

Everyone jumps up and all couples kiss, and the High Priestess and High Priest, and in hand, leap over the bonfire. Couples follow. Where persons are uncoupled, they may leap the flames with the High Priestess or High Priest as appropriate.

The HPS says, *"Let there be feasting and games in honour of the Old Ones."*

Toast, feast, and games, then the Temple is closed in the usual manner.

The Festival of the Summer Solstice

The Festival of the Summer Solstice is celebrated at midday on 22 December. It marks the Wedding. The rite is performed upon a hilltop or other place exposed to the sky. The Altar is central and contains the Mother filled with straw or twigs. Four small balefires are at the four cardinal points (one at each), unlit. There is a torch next to each balefire.

All face in, standing around the Altar. Men say, *"The Sun!"* Women say, *"The Earth!"* Men say, *"Light!"* Women say, *"Birth!"*

All hands join. Coven says, *"A wedding! A wedding! There will be a bedding. The Lady and the Lord are here, come to feast in hearty cheer. Their mating will the new crops bring, new lambs for flocks in the coming Spring. Hope lies in their joyfulness. Sun to Earth brings fruitfulness. Let us to the marriage bed. Dance the Ring with merry tread."*

The Coven dances three times around the Altar chanting, *"We dance below, the Gods above, we dance with hope, we dance with love."*

They circle the Temple once. The Coven goes to the South, the HP to the North. The four Balefires are lit.

The HPS says, *"All is ready, all is waiting, see ye now the sacred mating."*

The HP says, *"Sky and Earth conjoined be, here in Mystery all may see."*

The High Priestess and the High Priest together light the Cauldron.

Coven sings, *"We shall dance and we shall sing, laughter to the Wedding bring. Between the Fires of Solstice Night, witness to the Sacred Rite."*

The HPS says, *"Let all enjoy the Feast with thanksgiving."*

Feast, dance, and games as appropriate. It is most appropriate on this night that all take part in the Sacred Marriage. Close the Temple in the usual manner.

The Great Festival of Lughnassad

The Great Festival of Lughnassad is celebrated at 3.00 pm on 2 February; this is the Harvest Festival, the Consummation, marking the start of the harvesting, and heralding the approach of Autumn.

It is sacred to our Sky Father, who as Lugh and Llew was cut down as His Power faded, to be reborn later to re-fertilise our Great Mother with the warmth of His Caress. The Festival is also called **Lammas,** for to the Saxon people, this was the time of the Llaf-masse (loaf mass) when the first-reaped grain would be made into a sacred cake and presented to their Gods in honour and thanks for a bountiful harvest. The Cake is symbolic of the body of the God, which we also eat.

The Festival should be an occasion to reflect upon our efforts over the previous moons to correct those parts of ourselves that are not in keeping with our attempts to unite with the Old Ones. Those weeds within our fields also take life from our Mother and warmth from our Father, but offer nothing in return to our people. They take and do not give, and in time will leach the Great Mother of Her Love-shew (Her ability to express love or offer nurturing gifts).

The Gule of August, as the Feast is called in the northern hemisphere, is the time to taste the first fruits of the harvest. Honey cakes and barley cakes should be eaten, as with any food that comes from the grain. Barley wine, if available, or otherwise beer is the drink with which to celebrate on this occasion. Have about you the fruits of your labours, for they are merely mirrors of what is within. Lugnassad is a ceremony because it celebrates the Harvest Home, and it is a rite for it fertilises the new harvest.

The Altar is set to the North with harvest fruits in abundance. To the centre of the Temple is the Cauldron, similarly bedecked and filled with water.

The Coven is led by the High Priestess and High Priest to the Temple, walking processionally, stately. The Witches hold aloft a sheaf of wheat that has been dressed in a cloak and shawl. They approach the area, singing, *"Corn Dolly, Kern Baby, Ivy Girl, Mare, Harvest Queen, cloak of green, earth grow hair. We hold thee high towards the sky; the grain has grown and now must die. All-gathering! Harvest Home! Hey! We bear thee to the Altar stone, Lady grown, standing lone. Happy people meeting here, stubble trampled fields clear. All-gathering! Harvest Home! Hey!"*

As the Coven enters the Temple, the High Priestess and the High Priest go to the Altar, stand together, and face South.

The Coven circles clockwise thrice with the song, and stops at the centre of the Circle, facing the High Priestess and the High Priest. They circle the Temple once. The Coven goes to the South, the HP to the North.

The HPS says, *"We are now sacred within the Holy Heart. Let the Sabbat begin."*

The High Priestess and the High Priest go to the centre of the Witches, and she says, *"Let us give thanks to the Old Ones."*

The Coven faces the North. The HPS says, *"We are blessed with an abundant harvest which we have earned by our efforts and through Your Will. Let the Three Seeds of Gold from the Crystal Cup give new life in time and place. Though all grow old, and the old pass away, the Lady ages not, but is ever renewed. Let Sky and Earth be joined!"*

The High Priest approaches the High Priestess. They embrace and perform the Great Rite. If it is time, the High Priest will be cut down, and his parts distributed amongst the Witches. If not, he will splash water from the Cauldron, first on the High Priestess, then on the Coven, as it circles chanting, *"Spin we now in Mystic Hour, Dance with the Old Ones! Dance! Dance! Age surrenders, bequeathing Power! Dance with the Old Ones! Dance! Dance! Dance with the Old Ones! Dance! Dance! Dance with the Old Ones!"*

The HPS says, *"The Lady is renewed, and the blush of Her maidenhood will flow in the rising Sun. Let us feast in Her honour!"*

Toast. Feast. Dancing, singing and games as suitable. Close the Temple in the usual manner.

The Festival of the Autumn Equinox

The Festival of the Autumn Equinox is celebrated at 6.00 pm on 21 March. It is the time of the Funeral. It marks the end of the harvest season, and is a thanksgiving ceremony to honour the Solar God and mark His passing. It is not meant that the God should be mourned at Lugnassad, for the magic that was worked to ensure the success of the harvest and to give power to the Mother for future crops would be made ineffective by our considerations.

The Festival is also called Michaelmas, for the Christians celebrate on this day in honour of their own aspect of the Solar God - Michael. As in the Autumn Equinox ritual, no magical working is undertaken; it is considered a ceremony and not a rite. The attitude in which the festival is celebrated should be one of quiet relaxation, as befitting the rest due after labour. The proper drink of the festival is cider, for it is made from apples, usually harvested after the grain is cut.

The Altar is set to the North, decorated with acorns, ears of wheat, and other symbols of Autumn. The Coven is led by the High Priestess to the Temple, walking processionally, with carefully measured tread. Except for the High Priestess and High Priest, they walk in pairs - male and female - with any unpaired persons in single file. The High Priestess heads the Coven, and the High Priest is at the rear. Each pair should have a wreath, made from evergreen boughs interspersed with dried leaves and grasses, which they bear between them.

The Coven enters the Temple, circumambulates it once, singing, *"The Sun, He is dead, our Lord He is gone, the night grows much longer, the daylight is wan, the harvest is stored up, the fields barren lie. The Lady Earth mourns Him, and all flowers die. We come here to toast Him, His eulogy hear, the cold Earth She took Him, he needs no king's bier. He is gone to the Mother - She has Him in care, the Lady laments Him, Her sorrow we share."*

As the Procession moves around the Circle, it drifts to the centre. After the second circumambulation, the High Priestess goes to the Altar and turns to the Coven, saying, *"We are now sacred within the Holy Heart. Let there be a leave-taking."*

The Coven pairs pick up the wreaths, and all stand

in a semi-circle around the Altar. The High Priestess stands between the Altar and the Coven, facing the Altar.

The HPS says, *"Farewell, oh Sun, Lord of the Sky. Your task is completed, the Lady now bears. Rest is Your reward, go now in peace. For the Sky Father and Earth Mother, will guard the time till Your Rebirth. Let all now mourn the Passing."*

The Coven will place upon the Altar the wreaths, and as the Witches step back from the Altar, they adopt the God position. The High Priestess, as the last Witch, will place her own private Sign of Mourning upon the Altar, and then adopt the God position facing the Altar. All will meditate on the significance of the Passing.

The HPS turns to the Coven and says, *"Let us now feast, for in death there is also joy, for we see the beginning of a Great Mystery - the Turning of Time."*

Toast. Feast. Close the Temple in the usual manner.

The Great Festival of Samhain

The Wheel turns to the Great Festival of Samhain, celebrated at 9.00 pm on 30 April. It is Summer's End, The Descent and the end of the year for our people. We celebrate with a feast and sacrifice in honour of those who have passed through the Veil to the Summerlands. As Our Lady journeyed to the Underworld in search of the Lord who entered the embrace of the Mother at Michaelmas, the Gates between the Worlds opened to permit Her entry. In the brief span from sunset to sunrise, the Veil is at its thinnest, and we may speak to those on the other side and learn those secrets of the past and future.

The Dumb Supper, if performed, should be a sharing in silence of the feast with those who have gone before. The food set aside should be left on the Altar or on the ground where the Altar has stood, and not consumed. For the Toasts, a still red wine should be used. *"Hey Ho for Halloween when all the Witches can be seen, some in black and some in green, hey Ho for Halloween!"*

The Altar is set to the North and covered with a black cloth. In the centre of the Temple is a fire on which sits the Cauldron. The Cauldron is filled with water in which is steeped mugwort, vervain, and wormwood. If the fire cannot be lit, the Cauldron should contain a Thurible instead of water, the same three herbs being compounded in the incense used.

The Coven enters the Temple from the West, singing, *"Ended the Year, the earth at rest lies, the morning sun slowly paints cloudy grey skies, we come to the Temple to see the year end, to seek a past loved one and greet an old friend. The Summer has passed now, the harvest is stored, the God is enthroned, Underworld Lord. Clothed in splendour, for Him our Queen seeks. Dark run the rivers, snow covers the peaks, light up the balefires, and be in good cheer. With singing and dancing, we start the New Year!"*

The High Priestess and High Priest go to the Altar, then circle the Temple singing, *"Thanks be to the Old, joy to the New, let our people sing. Loved ones join with us, old friends and true, hear our* chorus ring. *Warmth from our fire, food from our table, come and take your fill. The gates are opened, the Worlds are one; join us if you will."*

The Balefire is lit by the Devil (The MIB), if present, or another.

The High Priest goes to the East, the High Priestess to the West, and the Coven stands around the balefire. All reach outwards. HPS and HP say, *"Through the Gates our Lady passed in search of the Lord. The Summer has ended, sheltered the herd. Let spirits of ages past join with us here, as Summer doth end, so doth the Year!"*

The Coven takes offerings of food and drink to the Altar, where it is blessed by the High Priest. Bread and wine are shared by the Coven, during which the High Priest says, *"My body ye eat is the time that is gone, my blood ye drink is the time yet to come. Take ye my spirit in the bread and wine. Such is my soul wrapped in mystery divine."*

The Dumb Supper is celebrated. As midnight approaches, all sit around the coals of the fire (or kindle the Thurible) and stare into the steam of the cauldron (or rising incense smoke) as the High Priest invokes, *"Lord of Death and Life to come, open the gates, let friends share the cloak. Lady of Darkness, Great Queen enthroned. List to our wishes in spell intoned - Twixt worlds we wait in witching hour, hand joined to hand, calling ancient powers from Abred to Anwwn, this licence we give ye who have passed the veil, come to we who live!"*

When the communion has ended, the High Priest will say, *"Lord, heath earth, in darkness clothed, seated in splendour with She who is loved, keep well our people, let laughter and caring be outward signs of the love we are sharing. Thanks be for visions of souls gone to rest. We now make the parting at Sabbat-time blessed. Blessed Be the Old Ones!"*

It is customary for the Great Festival of Samhain to last until dawn, and the Coven to greet the rising sun. If this is not practicable, the temple is now closed in the usual manner.

*Answer us, O Ancient Horned One,
Provender and Power are Thine.
Hear and answer Gracious Goddess,
Grant us laughter, wit and wine.*

*Descend on us, O Thou of blessings,
Come among us, make us glad.
Since Thou art Chief of our Creation,
Why, O why should we be sad?*

*Beam on us, O Joyous Bacchus,
Banish heavy-hearted hate.
Accept our Craft, O Greatest Mother,
Let cheerful brightness be our fate.*

None Greater than the Triple Goddess.

Chapter Thirty Five
Wiccaning

A Wiccaning is a ceremony similar to the christening or baptism of an infant in the Christian religion. Its purpose is to formally name a child and present him or her to the world.

The infant is not necessarily expected to choose a Pagan or Wiccan path when they grow older. The ceremony is focused on the parents' beliefs and the family's communal commitment to look after the child and to ask the Gods for protection.

A normal Circle is usually cast, but it is not necessary. The ceremony should be done outside, preferably in a forest, park, near a river or on a hilltop. The Coven Elders or leaders officiate the ceremony. The child is usually held in the arms of the godparents, with the parents flanking the godparents.

The High Priest welcomes everyone, saying, *"We are met here to welcome and bless this new child. And to ask the blessing of the Goddess and God."*

High Priest and High Priestess lead the godparents with the child and parents deosil around the Circle.

The godparents are asked by the High Priestess, *"What do you name this child?"*

The godparents say, *"We ask the blessings of the Goddess and the God upon this child _____ (name), the son (or daughter) of _____ and _____ (parents' names), so that he (she) may grow in beauty and strength, in joy and wisdom. There are many paths, and each must find his or her own; therefore, we do not seek to bind _____ (child's name) to any one path while he (she) is still too young to choose. Rather do we ask the Goddess and the God, who know all paths and to whom all paths lead, to bless, protect and prepare him (her) through the years of childhood, so that when at last he (she) is fully grown, he (she) shall know without doubt or fear which path is his (hers) and shall tread it gladly."*

The High Priestess addresses the child, saying, *"May the Goddess ever smile upon you and with her love guide you through this life."* She anoints the child's head with water.

The High Priest also addresses the child, saying, *"May the God ever smile upon you and with his strength guide you through this life."* He anoints the child's head with water.

Godparents carry the child to the four Quarters, present the child to the Watchtowers and ask the blessings of the four elements.

The child is then presented to each person present, in turn, and each says, *"I ask the Goddess and God to bestow upon this child the gift of _____ (some blessing, i.e. health, wealth, beauty, etc.)."*

Cakes, wine, and festivities.

Chapter Thirty Six
Handfasting

To celebrate our tenth wedding anniversary, Evelyn and I reaffirmed our vows with a handfasting. Handfasting is an old Pagan custom that dates back to the time of the ancient Celts. Handfastings are literally the binding of a couple's hands together during the wedding ceremony to symbolise their connection and devotion to one another. Please feel free to use the following ritual if you like.

The Circle is cast by the HPS and HP before the guests arrive (not the bride and groom, but usually a pair of Elders that officiate the ceremony).

Those of the Craft and family, and friends, stand around the outside of the Circle. An introduction is given by the HPS and HP to all present, then the Bride and Groom are brought to the Circle by the MIB. Both are covered with capes. The Bride stands in the East. The groom stands in the West. The MIB stands between the Worlds. The Circle is cast (in token for the benefit of non-Craft members) by the HPS and HP, and the Quarters are called.

The HPS cuts a doorway in the East and West as she says, *"The Door is cut in the East; the place of beginnings. The Door is cut in the West, the place from whence our people came. There are those among us who seek the bond of handfasting. Let them be named and brought forward."*

The HPS and HP stand in the North.

The MIB brings the Bride into the Circle and says, *"I bring the Lady Evelyn from the House of the Oak."* The Bride removes her cape and hands it to the MIB, who escorts her to the HP.

The HP holds his Athame to the Bride's chest and says, *"Evelyn, do you come here of your own free will, to join with Dylan in this Sacred Bond?"*

The Bride says, *"I come with all love, honour, and*

sincerity, wishing only to become one with him whom I love. I have and always will strive for Dylan's happiness and welfare. His life would I defend before my own. May I incur the wrath of the Goddess should I not be sincere in all that I declare. All this I swear before the Lord and Lady. May they give me the strength to keep my vows." The HP says, *"So mote it be."*

The MIB bring the Groom into the Circle and says, *"I bring Lord Dylan from the House of Raventree."* The Groom removes his cape and hands it to the MIB, who escorts him to the HPS. The HPS holds her Athame to the Groom's chest and says, *"Dylan, do you come here of your own free will, to join with Evelyn in this Sacred Bond?"*

The Groom says, *"I come with all love, honour, and sincerity, wishing only to become one with she whom I love. I have and always will strive for Evelyn's happiness and welfare. Her life would I defend before my own. May I incur the wrath of the Goddess should I not be sincere in all that I declare. All this I swear before the Lord and Lady. May they give me the strength to keep my vows."* The HPS says, *"So mote it be."*

The HP invokes and anoints the Bride in the sign of the Third Degree (only if appropriate) and says, *"Lords of Power, of night and day, harken to these words I say! Earth and air and fire, and water be within your son and daughter. They who come to seek thy glory tread the path we know is holy."*

The HPS invokes and anoints the Groom in the sign of the Third Degree (only if appropriate), saying, *"Prepared are they this mystic hour, to cross the bridge to sacred tower. Earth beneath and sky above, they do come to join their love. Open now their inner sight; prepared are they for ancient rite."*

The HP says to the Groom, *"If you do truly desire, my Lord Dylan, to renew your marriage vows to this woman, I bid you pledge your service to her."*

The Groom draws his Sword and, kneeling, offers it to the Bride, saying, *"My Lady Evelyn, I pledge this sword, a symbol of my office, as I pledge my soul, ever to be in your service. Accept this blade as a token of my love for all which is mine shall also be yours."*

The Bride takes the sword silently in her hands and touches it to her forehead for the time of three heartbeats. Then she returns it to him and bids him rise, saying, *"My lord, I accept your pledge of love as I do accept the pledge of your blade. Thou knowest what is in my heart, as I know what is in thine. The magic of my will and of my love shall ever be yours."*

The HPS then says to the Bride, *"If thou dost truly desire, my Lady Evelyn, I bid you present this man, a symbol of your love."* The Bride takes her necklace and, kneeling before the Groom, holds it out to him, saying, *"Thou who art handsome and strong, accept my necklace of office, my treasure. I pledge that all which I am and all which I possess shall be yours. My love shall ever endure, and shall flourish like the vine and the tree."*

The Groom takes the necklace silently in his hands and touches it to his lips for the time of three heartbeats. Then he returns it to her and bids her rise, saying, *"My lady, I accept your pledge of love as I do accept the pledge of your necklace. Thou* knowest what is in my heart, as I know what is in thine. All which I have now, or shall have, shall ever be yours."

The HP then takes the Wand and holds it over the top of the Bride's head, saying, *"Thou shalt be the star that rises from the sea – the twilight sea. Thou shalt bring a man's dreams to rule his destiny. Thou shalt bring the moon-tides to the soul of a man, the tides that flow and ebb, and flow again, the magic that moves in the moon and the sea; these are thy secret, and they belong to thee. Thou art the Eternal Woman, thou art She. The tides of all men's souls belong unto thee. Isis in heaven, on earth, Persephone, Diana of the Moon and Hecate, Veiled Isis, Aphrodite from the sea, all these thou art, and they are seen in thee."*

The HPS then takes the Wand and holds it over the top of the Groom's head, saying, *"In thee may the Lord of the Forests return to earth again; hear the ancient call and show thyself to men. Shepherd of wild things, upon the wild hill's way, lead thy lost flock from darkness unto day. Forgotten are the ways of sleep and of night; men seek for them whose eyes have lost the light. Open the door, the door that hath no key. The door of dreams whereby men come unto thee. Shepherd of wild things, may you one with him be!"*

HPS and HP consecrate and charge the rings.

The HP picks up the rings on the Pentacle. The bride and Groom place their hands over the rings. The HPS says, *"Above you are the stars, below you are the stones. As time passes, remember, like a star should your love be constant, like the earth should your love be firm. Possess one another, yet be understanding. Have patience with each other, for storms will come, but they will go quickly. Be free in giving of affection and of warmth. Have no fear, and let not the ways or words of the unenlightened give you unease. For the Old Gods are with you. Be happy and you shall be wise now and always. For that is the Truth!"*

After a pause of five heartbeats, the HP asks, *"Is it your wish, Lady Evelyn, to be one with this man?"* The Bride says, *"Yes."* The Bride takes the ring, placing it first on the Groom's thumb, then on his index finger, then on the middle finger, and ring finger, finally on the little finger, saying, *"Of life, by form, by heart, by my troth and my plight. I take thee, Dylan, to my hand. At the setting of the Sun and the rising of the Stars."*

The HP says, *"Is it your wish, Lord Dylan, to be one with this woman?"* The Groom says, *"Yes."* The Groom takes the ring, placing it first on the Bride's thumb, then on her index finger, then on the middle finger, and ring finger, finally on the little finger, saying, *"Of life, by form, by heart, by my troth and my plight. I take thee, Evelyn, to my hand. At the setting of the Sun and the rising of the Stars."*

When this is complete, the HP then says, *"Then as the Goddess, the God, and the Old Ones are witness to this rite, I now proclaim you man and wife! Know that it is in the decrees of the fates that ye are to be united. Never more to be divided. What shall be shall be. Wherefore, take hope and joy, O children of time. And now as I join your hands, I betroth your souls."*

The Groom, using his Athame, pricks his finger.

The Bride does the same. They place their hands together. The HP binds their hands together with a cord made of two strands, two colours (black & red) and two fibres, saying, *"By the Power of the Goddess and in the names of these Her Children, you are bound together."*

With their hands bound, the lovers walk around the Circle while everyone chants, *"Earth and Air and Fire and Water, bond the Spirit of Son and Daughter."*

The HP says, *"Come now and be presented before the Guardians – the forces that bind all life together."*

The HPS guides Bride and Groom to the Eastern Quarter, traces an invoking Air Pentagram, then stands behind the couple saying, *"Guardian of the East, mighty powers of Air, guard and protect this bond between Evelyn and Dylan. May their love for each other burst forth as the petals of a flower on a spring morning."* All say, *"So mote it be!"*

The HP guides the Bride and Groom to the South, traces an invoking Fire Pentagram, then stands behind the couple and says, *"Guardian of the South, mighty powers of Fire, guard and protect this bond between Evelyn and Dylan. May the flame of their love burn bright as the sun."* All say, *"So mote it be!"*

HPS guides the Bride and Groom to the West, traces an invoking Water Pentagram, then stands behind the couple saying, *"Guardian of the West, mighty powers of Water, guard and protect this bond between Evelyn and Dylan, may they have the courage to accept each other fully in their love for each other."* All say, *"So mote it be!"*

The HP guides the Bride and Groom to the North, traces an invoking Earth Pentagram then stands behind the couple saying, *"Guardian of the North, mighty powers of Earth, guard and protect this bond between Evelyn and Dylan, may their love for each other take root in the earth and cause others to prosper because of their example."* All say, *"So mote it be!"*

The MIB lays the Besom in the centre of the Circle. The HPS says, *"Jump the Besom of renown, seal the union, wear the crown!"* The lovers jump the broom. All shout, *"Hurrayah!"*

The HPS and HP bless the wine (2 Chalices). Bride and Groom drink. Their hands are then untied. The second chalice is sent around the Circle.

The HP crowns the Bride with an herbal and floral wreath, saying, *"May the Goddess protect your destiny!"* The HPS crowns the Groom, saying, *"May the Goddess protect your unity!"*

The HPS scribes a Spirit Passive Pentagram over them.

Speeches by HP and HPS

The Circle is banished.

Chapter Thirty Seven
Funeral Rite

The following ritual was a Valedictory Ceremony held after the passing of one of our Priestesses. In all the years we have been in the Craft, we have only ever had to perform this ritual once. I can't remember who wrote this ritual. I think we all had an input, as sometimes we did, when it came to writing rituals.

The following items are required:

- A Cauldron with a candle in it, held in place at the base, which is then half filled with water and placed close to the Altar.

- Rosemary sprigs. Place a number of these on the Altar (one for each member present). They are later placed around the Cauldron by all during the ritual.

- Some personal item of the deceased, preferably their Athame. This is usually brought to the ritual by the partner, friend or nominated 'Custodian' of the deceased.

- A black cloth is used to wrap the personal item at the end of the ritual.

Ritual

The Circle is cast as normal.

The Coven then assembles in the South of the Circle.

HPS and HP at the North. (HPS at the West side, HP at the East side of the Altar.)

The Maiden moves to the Altar and picks up the Cauldron, moving deosil, places it at the centre of the Circle, then returns to the South.

The Custodian, partner, or friend moves to the Altar, picks up the personal item, and places it at the western side of the Cauldron, then returns to the South.

The MIB moves to the Altar, lights a taper from the Altar candle, goes to the centre and lights the candle in the Cauldron whilst facing West, then returns to the Altar, extinguishes the taper, then returns to the South.

The Maiden approaches the Altar and picks up the sprigs of rosemary. Walking deosil gives a rosemary sprig to each Coven member. The Maiden keeps three, one for herself and one each for the HPS and HP.

HPS faces the coven and says:

"Goddess of All Time, Mother of us all, we gather to commemorate the memory of our brother/sister (Name), *whose spirit has departed the life wherein we knew* (her/him) *and who is now at peace in the Realm of the Lord of Shadows.'*

In life, you cast your silent presence upon (Name) and guided their path into the practice of your Craft. Such was your wish.

In the wind within the trees and the roll of ocean waves, upon the land you whispered to (him/her), *'I am here.'*

Bathed in your protective silver light of night, (he/she) *heard you quietly call, 'Come unto me.'*

Beneath a golden Sun in verdant Spring, in warm and yellow Summer, the repose of Autumn time, and time of Winter grey, you gave the message to (him/her) *'You are one with this and all of this is Me."*

HP faces Coven and says:

"God of the Cycle of Life, Lord of the Seasons, Lord of Shadows, Giver of Life, and Guardian of the mystery of Death.

The harvest, which was the life of (Name), *is now gathered, and* (his/her) *shade is now within your care.*

Whilst in your Realm between the death and the rebirth, grant our loved one repose and guidance, rest, comfort and renewal.

As (he/she) *was your child in the life which now has gone, so may it be again in the cycle of rebirth."*

All join hands and form a circle, move widdershins in solemn procession.

When ready, the HPS moves towards the centre and kneels at the Cauldron facing West. All follow and kneel.

The Coven should form a North, East, South crescent, leaving the West open.

The Maiden gives a rosemary sprig each to the HPS and HP.

HPS says: "(Name), *our sorrow is that from us you are gone."*

(All repeat)

HPS says: "Our joy is that among us you once were."

(All repeat)

HPS says: "And will be so again."

(All repeat)

The HPS places a rosemary sprig at the side of the Cauldron. All follow to form a circle of rosemary.

A silent moment is taken for each Coven member to personally remember and farewell the deceased.

When all are finished, the Coven rises and all join hands to form a wider circle, then move deosil in solemn procession.

When ready, the HPS stops at the North, the rest of

the Coven completes another deosil circle, then the HP stops at the North alongside the HPS with the Coven moving to the South.

Cakes and Wine

The blessing of cakes and wine as per normal, then all sit around the Cauldron as the candle burns. The line between the Cauldron and the West should not be obstructed.

Coven should recount memories and anecdotes of the deceased with fondness and joy. When the discussion is at its natural conclusion, the HPS kneels, and all follow and kneel in a circle around the Cauldron.

The HPS says, *"Remember this. To fulfil love, you must return at the same time and at the same place as the loved ones; and you must meet, and know, and remember, and love them again."*

The Coven each place their fingers in the water and hold them above the candle flame until the water drops extinguish the candle flame.

The Rosemary sprigs are then placed in the Cauldron.

All stand. The Maiden moves the Cauldron to the West.

The Custodian of the deceased's personal items wraps it in black cloth and retains it.

Banishing the Circle

The Circle is banished as per usual, and all depart the area.

The Cauldron is left unattended in the West for a time deemed right by the HPS. (Until the following sunrise may be suitable).

The personal item is dealt with as previously arranged with the Custodian or at the discretion of the HPS.

Chapter Thirty Eight
Dark Moon Esbat

During our first year, we discussed the prospect of performing an Esbat on a new or dark moon. We thought about the energies at that time and what happened to the Goddess. Is She sleeping? Have Her energies waned? Could we possibly call her down? Maybe in another aspect? What about the God? After all, aren't the Esbats all about the Moon and the feminine? The God is the sun. But what if?

We had heard somewhere stories that it was dangerous or maybe at least inappropriate to call the Lady on a dark moon. So we thought about a balance. What if the God looked after things whilst the Goddess slept? Why not call the God, and draw Him down, whilst the Goddess and Moon recuperate? Don't laugh; remember, we were only newbies at that time, and only Pagans at that!

So, after many hours of research, discussion, and deliberation, we developed a very strong male-oriented ritual to honour our God. One where the Priest takes control of the Circle and the energies are raw and primal; not for the faint-hearted! We were really making headway in those days and were not afraid to try things once. I mean, what could really happen? Herne could come and bite us on the arse, or Pan could materialise and cause absolute chaos and pandemonium! The lesson here is, do not be afraid to give things a go. Follow the rules as best you can, and if you stuff up, you cop an arse kicking and learn not to do it again, at least not that way!

This ritual is best performed in a forest, dark and musty and far away from any ambient lights and civilisation as possible. You could do it in your lounge room or backyard, but believe me, you will not get the same effect.

A bell is rung around the circle area, or even better, a horn is blown to frighten away any lurking spirits and to let the Gods know you are ready to work. This should be done by the Man-in-Black.

The Altar candle is lit by the HP, and he says, *"From fire above to fire below. From fire within to fire without. May Michael's spear from there to here. Make the magic fire appear."*

An image of the God is placed on the altar, and all pay homage to Him by presenting their Athames to show their intention. All then anoint with anointing oil in order to take on their Magical Personality. The Coven then leave the Circle area except for the HPS and HP.

The HP then traces the Circle boundary deosil, starting in the North, pointing his Athame to the ground and finishing in the North. The HPS stands behind the HP and follows him whilst he draws the Circle, focusing her energy with his. If you have a partner, do not overlook this. It does make a difference.

Blessing of salt. The HP puts a small quantity of salt onto the Pentacle, raises the Pentacle and says, *"Blessings be upon this Creature of Salt. Let all malignancy and hindrance be cast forth hencefrom and let all good enter herein. Wherefore do I bless Thee and consecrate Thee in the names of Karnayna and Aradia."* All repeat, *"Karnayna and Aradia."*

Exorcising of water. The HPS puts the tip of her Athame into the bowl of water and says, *"I exorcize thee oh Creature of Water of all the impurities and uncleanliness of the Spirit of the World of Phantasm in the names of Karnayna and Aradia."* All repeat, *"Karnayna and Aradia."*

Mixing of salt and water. The HP pours salt into the bowl of water and says, *"But remember and ever mind, as water purifies the body, so the scourge purifies the soul. Wherefore do I bless thee that thou mayest aid me in the names of Karnayna and Aradia."* All repeat, *"Karnayna and Aradia."*

Asperging the Circle and boundary with salt water. The HP sprinkles the salt water around the perimeter, together with all Witches present and any other items around the Circle, starting in the North and says three times, *"Earth and water thou art cast, let no evil purpose last. If not in accord with me, then as I will, so mote it be."*

Sealing of the Circle with incense. The HP adds incense to the Thurible, then hands it to the HPS. The HPS elevates it and says, *"The four winds are the breath which doth purify our sacred land. Be far from us, forces foul and thoughts of evil."*

The HPS then carries the smoking Thurible around the perimeter, stopping at each Watchtower to present it to that Element.

Lighting the Watchtower candles. The HP lights a candle from the Altar Candle, carries it around the Circle boundary, lighting the Watchtower candles starting in the East.

Sealing the Circle. The HP then traces the Circle boundary with his Athame and seals the Circle. The HPS again follows the HP, focusing her energy on him.

Conjuring the Circle. The HP stands in the centre

of the Circle, arms outstretched; he allows his etheric body to expand to the delineated boundary of the Circle. Starting in the North, he turns around the Circle three times, as he conjures the Circle, saying, *"I conjure Thee, oh Circle, that Thou beist a boundary between the World of Men and the Realms of the Mighty Ones. A Guardian and a Protection that shalt preserve and contain the power which we will raise within Thee. Wherefore do I bless and consecrate Thee in the names of Karnayna and Aradia."* All repeat, *"Karnayna and Aradia."*

The HP and HPS then admit any Witch outside the Circle. The HPS will admit all male Witches, and the HP will admit all female Witches. They will kiss, take their hand and swing them deosil underarm.

Opening remarks. The HPS stands in front of the Altar and says, *"The place of this ritual is now consecrated to the honour of the Old Ones. This is a time that is not a time, in a place that is not a place, on a day that is not a day, between the worlds and beyond."*

The HP decrees, *"Let this World stand apart from time, for we now dance with the Old Ones."*

The Witches' Rune is sung and danced.

Invoking the Lords of the Watchtowers. Starting at the East, facing the Watchtower, the HP invokes an Earth Pentagram with his Athame and says, *"Ye Lords of the Watchtower of the East, I do summon, stir and call Thee forth to witness these rites and to guard the Circle."* He vibrates the name *EURUS*.

All move to the South, making an Invoking Earth Pentagram. The HP says, *"Ye Lords of the Watchtower of the South, I do summon, stir and call Thee forth to witness these rites and to guard the Circle."* He vibrates the name *NOTAS*.

All move to the West, making an Invoking Earth Pentagram. The HP says, *"Ye Lords of the Watchtower of the West, I do summon, stir and call Thee forth to witness these rites and to guard the Circle."* He vibrates the name *ZEPHYRUS*.

All move to the North, making an Invoking Earth Pentagram. The HP says, *"Ye Lords of the Watchtower of the North, I do summon, stir and call Thee forth to witness these rites and to guard the Circle."* He vibrates the name *BOREAS*.

Drawing Down the God. The HP will go to the North and face the South. He stands in God position. (Standing erect, left foot slightly forward of the right. Right arm folded across the left over the chest.)

The HPS kneels in front of the HP and gives him the Five-Fold Kiss, saying, *"Blessed be thy feet that have brought thee in these ways. Blessed be thy knees that shall kneel at the sacred altar. Blessed be thy phallus, without which we would not be. Blessed be thy chest formed in strength. Blessed be thy lips that shall utter the Sacred Names."*

The HPS invokes a Spirit Active Pentagram on HP, who then turns, faces North with his back to the Coven in Pentagram position. He visualises the Dark Moon. The HPS kneels and visualises a dark, starry night sky and calls, *"By the flame that burneth bright, we call thy name into the night. Witches all we seek thy throne, Your nameless* shore as yet unknown. In shadow and secret tide, reveal to us your hidden side. Ancient keeper of the dawn, Brother to whom we are sworn. Come to us this darksome night, show us all your hidden light. Bring your magic to us all, come in answer to our call. By the blood and by the sword, come to us and by your word. Open the door of mystery, open the door that hath no key. To the throne of the hidden sun, at dark, we call the come, O come."

The HP turns around in Stag Position (Standing erect with left foot slightly in front of the right. Hands in Solar Salute position on either side of the head next to the ears) and responds, *"I am the hunter - In the jagged edge of darkness. I am a sailor on the sea of consolation. I am a thief - In the tomb of the kings. I am a warrior in the battle against injustice. I am a rider - On the white horse of knowing death. I am a guide who leads them from ignorance. I am an explorer - On the frontier of the mind. I am the essence that activates consciousness. I have the juice - That is distilled into spirit. I am the beast that lurks in us all. I am a vagrant who teaches his children to seek the self. I am the brother of the moon - Born in sunlight. I am a priest - At the Altar of Life. I am the lover Who venerates the mother. I am he who worships she. I am I."* (Ian Aven circa 1990)

HPS gives the Fivefold Kiss to the HP, followed by all women. Horned salute (same as the Solar Salute) by all men.

Delivering the God Charge. All the Coven kneel. The HP says, *"Harken unto me for I am He who has existed throughout all time. I was there from the beginning, and it was my potency that charged the fertility of the Great Mother and created life from her empty womb. Myself it is in the Winds that sweep the worlds; myself it is in the Flames that give warmth and light to all beings. I am He who provides; the Green Man of field and forest fruitfulness; the lust of the bull that engenders life upon the cow; the strength of the boar that engenders life upon the sacred sow of Cerridwen; the speed of the stag running free in the forest, that no hunter can bring down save he who speaks the sacred words to call unto the spirit of the fleeing stag. I am Lord of the Dance; He who swirls through the starry universe with the world at his heels. I am He who dances on mountain and plain and hearth, and He who captures all things in his dance. And I am also Kerne the Dark Hunter; He with visage as dark as void and armour bright with flame. My name is Lord of the Hunt; my prey all those souls who must needs die and descend into the dark, chthonic depths of my bowel. For I bring life but death also; I am He at the gateway of the worlds, and to me shalt thou come in the end, thou who art my child and my prey."*

Whatever work there is to be done is now done.

Cheese/apple and Wine. The HP says, *"All is ready save the wine."* The HPS replies, *"Let the wine also be blessed."* The HP holds up the Chalice of wine and offers it to HPS. She holds her Athame between her palms, places the point in the cup and says, *"As the Athame is the male."* The HP says, *"So the cup is the female."* The HPS says, *"Conjoined they bring blessedness."* The HP says, *"And become one in truth."*

The HPS lays her Athame aside, takes the cup and drinks, then gives it to the HP with a kiss. HP drinks and hands it back with a kiss. The cup is passed around the Circle with a kiss.

The HP blesses the cheese/apple with his Athame and says, *"O Queen most secret, bless this food unto our bodies, bestowing health, wealth, strength, joy and peace, and that fulfilment of love that is perpetual happiness."*

After a period of feasting, the Circle is banished. All face West. The HP draws a Banishing Earth Pentagram in the air and says, *"Ye Lords of the Watchtower of the West, I do thank Thee for attending these rites and ere Ye depart for thy lovely Realms, I say Hail and farewell."* All copy his gesture with their own Athame and say, *"Hail and farewell."*

The Watchtower candle is extinguished. Do the same for the remaining Watchtowers in Widdershins direction. The Lord will then return to the Altar and extinguish the Altar candle.

"By the flame that burneth bright, we call thy name into the night."
"I am He at the gateway of the worlds, and to me shalt thou come in the end."

Chapter Thirty Nine
The Fire of Azrael

The Fire of Azrael is another ritual we developed in our first year. The inspiration came from Dion Fortune's book, *'The Sea Priestess'* - *'She took the poker in her hand and pushed the flaming driftwood to either side and in the hollow centre thus left, she piled the woods of the Fire of Azrael. Then we sat and watched them take the flame. And in those hours while the tide rose, there was delivered to me things whereof but few have dreamed and fewer still have known, and I learnt why Troy was burnt for a woman.'*

The Fire of Azrael is another form of divination and is best performed at the New Moon. The ritual should be conducted on a beach close to the water. The fire should be prepared using three kinds of wood: Sandalwood, Cedar and Juniper.

A Circle can be cast, but it is not necessary. At least four people are required: the HP and HPS, and two others. The HPS withdraws from the Coven a short distance. Two Covenors face each other across the unlit fire parallel to the sea, and the HP is seated facing the water.

First Covenor, *"Be far from us, O ye profane, for we are about to invoke the descent of the power of Isis. Enter her temple with clean hands and a pure heart, lest we defile the source of life."*

HP, *"Learn now the secret of the web that is woven between the light and the darkness; whose warp is life evolving in time and space, and whose weft is spun of the lives of men."*

Second Covenor, *"Behold we arise with the dawn of time from the grey and misty sea, and with the dusk we sink into the western ocean, and the lives of a man are strung like pearls on the thread of his spirit; and never in all his journey goes he alone,* for that which is solitary is barren."

First Covenor, *"Learn now the mystery of the ebbing and flowing tides. That which is dynamic in the outer is latent in the inner, for that which is above is as that which is below, but after another manner."*

HP, *"In the heavens, our Lady Isis is the Moon, and the moon-powers are hers. She is also the Priestess of the Silver Star that rises from the twilight sea. Hers are the magnetic moon-tides ruling the hearts of men."*

Second Covenor, *"In the inner, she is all potent. She is the queen of the kingdom of sleep. All the invisible workings are hers, and she rules all things ere they come to birth."*

First Covenor, *"Even as through Osiris her mate the earth grows green, so the mind of man conceives through her power."*

HP, *"Let us show forth in a rite the dynamic nature of the Goddess, that the minds of men may be as fertile as their fields."*

The HP rises, faces the land, raises his arms high and says, *"Be ye far from us, O ye profane, for the unveiling of the Goddess is at hand."*

The fire is lit. We found it best to prepare a small fire using hardwood and let it burn down until you have a nice, hot bed of glowing coals. Do this well before the ritual, and when it is time to 'light the fire', simply put a couple of pieces of the dried Sandalwood, Cedar and Juniper onto the hot coals.

The HP turns and faces the sea, says, *"O thou that was before the earth was formed, Rhea, Binah, Ge. O tideless, soundless, boundless, bitter sea, I am thy priest: O answer unto me. O arching sky above and earth beneath, giver of life and bringer of death. Persephone, Astarte, Ashtoreth, I am thy priest, O answer unto me. O golden Aphrodite, come to me, flower of the foam, rise from the bitter sea. The hour of the moon tide draws near, hear the invoking words, hear and appear - Isis Unveiled, and Rhea, Binah, Ge. I am thy priest, O answer unto me. O Isis, veiled on earth, but shining clear in the high heaven, now the moon draws near, hear the invoking words, hear and appear - Shaddai el Chai, and Rhea, Binah, Ge."*

The HPS appears from the darkness and walks to the edge of the water where the sea laps at her feet. She raises her arms high and wide, pauses, then lowers her arms and turns to face the Coven.

She slowly walks towards the Coven, stops and faces the HP over the fire, raises her arms in a curve like the Horns of Isis and says, *"I am she who, ere the earth was formed, was Rhea, Binah, Ge. I am the soundless, boundless, bitter sea, out of whose depths life dwells eternally. Astarte, Aphrodite, Ashtoreth, giver of life and bringer-in of death; Hera in heaven, on earth, Persephone; Levanah of the tides and Hecate, all these am I, and they are seen in me. I am that soundless, boundless, bitter sea. All tides are mine and answer unto me. Tides of the airs, tides of the inner earth, the secret, silent tides of death and birth. Tides of men's souls, and dreams, and destiny, Isis Unveiled, and Rhea, Binah, Ge. The hour of the moon draws near; I hear the invoking words, hear and appear - Isis Unveiled and Rhea, Binah, Ge. I come unto the priest that calleth me."*

The HP and Coven kneel. The HPS walks deosil and places both her hands on each person's head in turn. She returns and sits herself down facing the HP.

The HPS says, *"Let us now commune with the secrets of the fire."*

The Coven gaze into the fire and each, in turn, speaks of what they see.

Cakes and wine.

The fire is quenched, and the HPS says, *"Consummatum est. Those who have received the Touch of Isis have received the opening of the gates of the inner life. For them, the tides of the moon shall flow and ebb and flow and never cease in their cosmic rhythm."*

The HPS then throws a little food that has been left into the sea. She raises her arms for a moment and then lowers them. The HP and HPS lead the Coven away.

"Be ye far from us, O ye profane, for the unveiling of the Goddess is at hand."

Chapter Forty
Pathworking

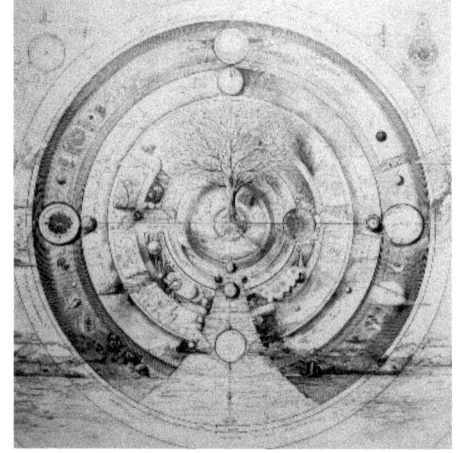

Throughout this story, I have mentioned the use of various methods of reflection, including the terms pathworking, meditation, the Qabalah, guided visualisations and other diverse methods of esoteric lore. All of these practices are tools used within our Craft, along with various breathing techniques and altered states of consciousness to advance or fine-tune our clairvoyance, just like divination or scrying. They are methods of discovering and understanding ourselves and finding and appreciating the creator and creation.

A Pathworking is a technique derived from the Qabalistic Tree of Life, a somewhat modern system developed from ancient beliefs through the Golden Dawn Tradition. The Qabalah seeks to define the nature of the universe and the human being, the nature and purpose of existence, and various other arcane theories concerning our existence. The use of the Qabalah presents a way to aid our understanding of these concepts and thereby attain spiritual awareness within and without.

The diagram (Next Page) represented by the Qabalistic Tree of Life is an arrangement of ten spheres or Sephiroth that represent objective states of consciousness and are associated with the Minor Arcana cards of the same number. Twenty-two connecting paths (labelled 11-32) join the Sephiroth.

Mundane human consciousness is conceptualised at the bottom sphere, Malkuth. The goal is to rise upon the tree of life until the mind is at one with the uppermost sphere, Kether, which is the presence of the Creator. This is achieved by travelling upon the twenty-two paths, each being a representation of one of the twenty-two Major Arcana. The imagery on a tarot trump relates to the corresponding aspects of the path it represents.

The idea of a pathworking is for the narrator to tell the story of a particular path, let us say, the 29th Path. This path connects Malkuth and Netzach and represents the tarot card, The Moon. During the journey, we become aware of our physical being and rise to the awareness of our emotional nature.

The symbolism associated with the sphere of Malkuth is the magical image of a young woman, crowned and throned together with the stone Onyx and red poppies. The symbols of the Path are the crayfish and the beetle, together with herbs like ash, elder, water iris, water lily and jasmine. Living beings are the dog and the wolf. The symbols of Netzach are the rose and the lamp. The colour is green. Living beings are the dove, the sparrow and the swan, and the magical image is a beautiful, naked woman.

All or some of these images are incorporated into the story being told by the narrator, and during the session, the narrator stops and engages in silence, thereby allowing the traveller to reflect and discover.

This topic is far too complex to fully discuss here, and I suggest you research your own systems of devising methods and visualisations using the correspondences to conduct your own journeys on the Tree of Life. There are a number of very good books available, so please refer to the suggested reading list at the rear of this book.

The following chapters are a sample of some of the pathworkings and guided visualisations we have used within our Coven.

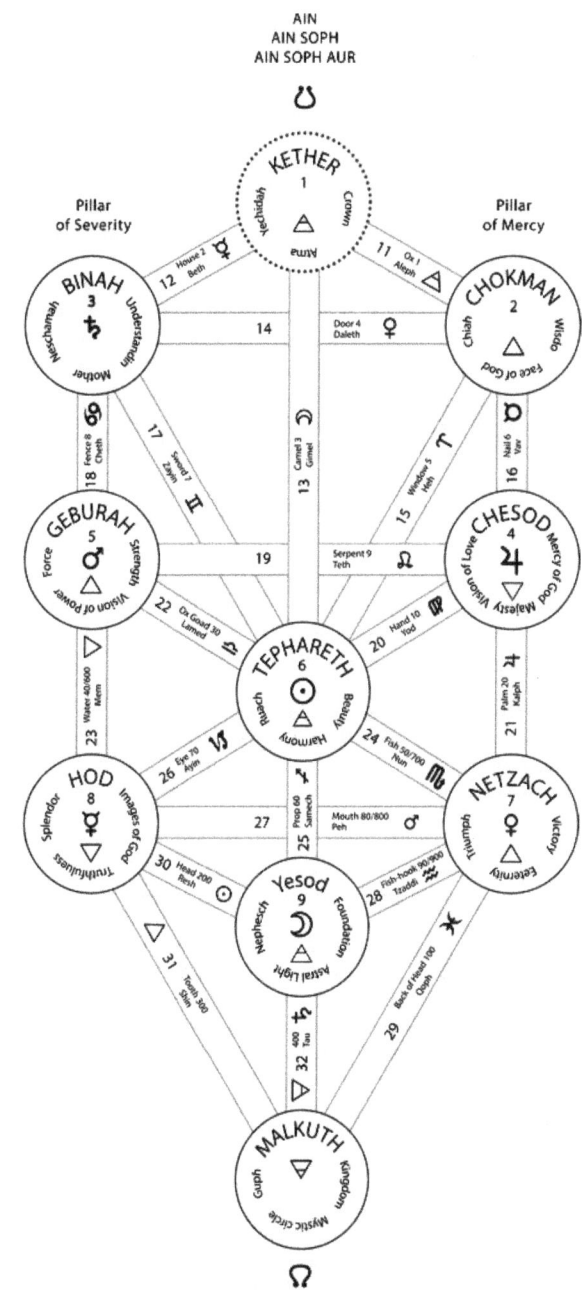

Chapter Forty One
The Twenty Ninth Path

This pathworking is the Twenty Ninth Path on the Qabalistic Tree of Life connecting Malkuth and Netzach, which is represented by the tarot card, The Moon. We normally undertake this pathworking within a Circle. One Coven member will act as the narrator as we sit or lie on the floor in a comfortable position. During the narration, the narrator will stop at various places to allow the travellers to experience their surroundings and discover.

One very important issue for the traveller to remember is that they must not anticipate what the narrator may say next. Do not start to travel ahead and start to imagine things that have not yet occurred. For doing so will send you off the path, and you will lose the intent of the working.

We centre and ground ourselves and start 4 x 2 breathing, then the narrator starts:

"Make yourself comfortable; allow your mind and body to relax. Now, close your eyes and allow these images to build in your imagination.

A beautiful young woman is seated on a throne of jet black. She wears a robe of browns, russets and green. On her head is a gold crown, which is pulsating with gold light rhythmically with your heartbeat. Behind her in a misty vagueness is a pool of water, and there, standing over the pool, are two huge double wooden doors.

Walk past the young woman and bow slightly in respect. Walk towards the doors. As you approach them, you see the image of the tarot card 'The Moon' on the front of the door.

The image depicts the Moon shining in the heavens, drops of dew falling, a wolf and a dog howling at the Moon, and halted at the foot of two towers, a path that loses itself in the horizon, a crayfish emblematic of the sign of Cancer, ruled over by the Moon, crawls through water in the foreground towards the land."

Wait for five seconds before continuing.

"Open the door and walk through. Turn around, close the door, and remember the door. See and feel its texture, the huge hinges holding it up and the handle."

Wait for five seconds before continuing.

"As you turn around and walk away from the door, you find yourself on a path on a hillside. Beautiful

rolling green meadows that disappear into the horizon. You can smell the sea air and look to your left down the hill to a beach. The gently rolling waves caress the golden sand in rhythmic dance, and beyond the breakers, you see dolphins at play."

Wait for five seconds before continuing.

"You now follow the path away from the hillside overlooking the beach and walk up into the rolling hills. In the distance, you see what looks like a cave in the side of a great mountain. As you walk towards it, you find yourself walking through a field of red poppies.

You approach the cave; it is dark and appears to reach far back into the heart of the mountain. It's about 9 feet in diameter, plenty large enough for you to walk into without stooping."

Wait for five seconds before continuing.

"As you walk into the cave and your eyes adjust to the light, you feel safe and warm. The ground is smooth, and you feel a well-worn path beneath your feet. As you walk on, you see a light at the end of the cave. Walk towards it."

Wait for five seconds before continuing.

"You eventually emerge from the cave on the other side of the mountain. You walk into a lovely green glade where there is a sacred well. To one side of the well, a green banner flies from a golden pole. What do you see on the green banner?"

Wait for five seconds before continuing.

"Within the water, two goldfish swim and above, a white dove circles. To the right of the well stands a beautiful naked woman with long amber hair. She holds a rose and stands on laurel leaves. About her feet are two coiled serpents, one black and the other white."

Wait for five seconds before continuing.

"She points into the well, and as she does, it fills with a brilliant white light. You gaze into the light, it's soft and soothing on your eyes. What do you see?"

Wait for thirty seconds before continuing.

"The light now slowly disappears, and you see the two goldfish playing in the well. You turn and thank the lady as she disappears into the forest.

Turn around and walk back towards the cave the way you came. Walk into the cave and through the mountain. You eventually emerge on the side of the hill in the poppy field.

In the distance on the adjoining hillside, you see the huge wooden doors through which you entered. Walk towards the doors, glancing to your right at the golden sands of the beach and the playing dolphins."

Wait for five seconds before continuing.

"Open the doors and walk through. Close them behind you and pass the lady on the black throne. Thank her as you walk by with a nod and a smile.

You continue to walk into the everyday world and become aware of the sound of my voice and of the room in which we sit. Spend a few moments quietly re-attuning yourself to your normal state and then open your eyes and stretch."

Chapter Forty Two
Pathway to the Sun

Another guided visualisation used by our tradition. I am unsure of its source, but over the years, it has become one of my favourite journeys, each time I discover something new and return reinvigorated and inspired to continue my path in life.

The narrator begins: *"You are standing just outside your own front door in the faint pre-dawn light of summer. You look down to find that you are wearing a loose and flowing linen robe in your favourite colour. It is belted with a strong cord upon which hangs your own knife. Upon your feet are stout and well-worn sandals, and a plain, solid staff is in your right hand. It feels smooth and familiar. Thus clad, you feel prepared for a journey that is old but still new.*

Taking several deep breaths to steady the feeling of anticipation, you walk down the steps into the street. Although the light is still very faint, the road is quite familiar. You leave the boundaries of the city quickly and find yourself walking down a country road that meanders over gently sloping hills. The grass smells sweet in the early morning air, and you can hear the songs of the birds. The dew from the grass makes your feet slightly damp and gives added zest to your journey."

Wait for five seconds before continuing.

"As the light intensifies, you see the huge stone monoliths atop a grassy hill on your left. The path that you are following meanders its way between the tussocks of ancient stunted grasses, and you follow it eagerly. Already the light grows stronger, and you hurry so that you will not be late. The stones loom majestically against the dark skies, and you realise as you near them that they form a ring of pillars reaching to the heavens.

Upon counting them, you discover that there are twelve, and this knowledge confirms that you are on the right path. Each stone has a zodiac symbol facing outwards to the world, and you walk quietly around the outer Circle until you find your own symbol."

Wait for five seconds before continuing.

"As you contemplate the ancient symbol etched deeply in the stone, the figure of an old man emerges from behind the stone. His white hair and faded robe proclaim his vast age, but his eyes are deep blue and seemingly ageless. He challenges your right to enter this sacred temple, of which he is the Keeper.

You stand firm and offer him the only password that you are able – 'I am a seeker of the Way of Wisdom.' He smiles, and his eyes seem to glow with pleasure at meeting another traveller. You feel very humble in the presence of such obvious wisdom and power. He conducts you around to the eastern quadrant of the temple and bids you to enter the Circle of stones. You turn to offer him your thanks for his guidance, but you are alone in the early morning."

Wait for five seconds before continuing.

"You enter the sacred stones with the light increasing in intensity at your back. You stand for a brief moment, gazing up at the Circle of stars framed by the immense stones as the stars begin to fade from the heavens. The dew upon your feet reminds you that you are still part of the Earthly Realm, and you go to the nearest stone and stand facing it. You rest your staff gently against its massive bulk and reach out until your palms rest, pointing upwards, upon the stone itself. A tingle, warm and vibrant, runs through both hands, filling your body with an inner glow.

Leaving your staff against this stone, you walk around the Circle of stones until you again find the one etched with your zodiac symbol. You rest your palms against this stone, palms upwards, and head bowed; silently ask it to impart some of its great store of knowledge to you."

Wait for five seconds before continuing.

"When it has done so, you silently give thanks. Returning to the first stone, you shed your sandals, leaving them at the base of your staff and walk over the soft, damp grass to the centre of the Circle, realising that dawn is about to break. Expectantly, you face the East where the light is brightening between two hills. You stand firmly, feet apart and hands raised in greeting to the rising Sun. Calmness and serenity envelop the stone Circle, and although you are expecting it, the first brilliant ray of light startles you with its sudden impact.

It streams across the damp grassland, forming a pathway of glistening golden drops that sparkle from the dew. You stand awed at the beginning of this road of living golden light that connects you to the Sun itself. As you accustom yourself to the light, you become aware of the indistinct figures that shimmer in the mist, lining each side of the path. They feel familiar to you, like old friends, and you are sure that you would know them all if only they would come into form a little more."

Wait for five seconds before continuing.

"The light strengthens as the Sun rises majestically from the valley until it sits poised on the hilltops. You take a step along the glowing pathway at your feet, feeling a slight vibration and surge of energy as your feet progress slowly down the road of light.

The vibration causes a glow to permeate throughout your body as you walk towards the golden light. You realise that all the people lining each side of the pathway are all yourself, incarnated down through a vast period of time. Each lifetime of growth and experience may be encountered upon this path, and they form a respectful guard of honour for the being that you have struggled to become. In each of them, you recognise your own expanding self, each contributing to the sum total of who you are right now. You do not need to speak or acknowledge them as they all still live within your own memory and can be contacted in the future if the need should arise."

Wait for five seconds before continuing.

"The light of the Sun streams forth from between what you now perceive to be two giant carved pillars of an ancient temple complex, and you mount the steps towards the great open doors of the temple. The roof of the temple is open to the clear skies, and the light shines forth from within the inner sanctum. To the left of the shimmering doorway stands the Lady, gentle and compassionate. You greet Her in your own manner. On the right of the doorway stands the Lord, strong and mighty. You greet Him according to your own tradition. Bathed in the radiance of the light streaming forth, you raise your right hand and draw a huge pentagram in blue-white light at the entrance to the inner court.

The symbol vibrates in the doorway, opening a gateway to the inner sanctuary. You enter, walking through a shallow pool of crystal clear water and then through an archway of living elemental fire.

Silently, you communicate with the great living light that resides within every true inner sanctum. This audience is yours alone, and words can never describe this meeting."

Wait for thirty seconds before continuing.

"Reluctantly, you turn, knowing that you must return once more to the outer world to learn and grow. Passing through the doorway, you seal it by raising your right hand, knowing that the way is now open for you to return to this sacred space as need and time permit. As you retrace your steps through the great temple, you notice that the pillars are all carved with the symbols of the great civilisations that have already passed their time on the earth plane. Their wisdom ever remains here in the universal Temple of Life. On your next visit, you may wish to stay and learn some of their wisdom, but today your path leads homeward.

Your footsteps make no sound on the well-worn flagstones, and you can hear music, clear and sweet, that seems to emanate from the building stones themselves. As you descend the steps, you feel the great doors swing closed behind you. A backwards glance confirms this, and two large, shaggy lions stand on guard. The pathway to the Circle of Stones now glistens with a softer silvery light as you thoughtfully tread its length. The misty figures are now gone, and you find yourself bathed *in the silvery glow as you step once more into the Circle of stones.*

The Sun is high in the sky, and your tread is stronger and firmer, strengthened by understanding and resolve. You walk across the Circle to collect your staff, only to discover that it is no longer plain and smooth. Its surface is carved and etched with strange symbols and designs that represent your own personal journey through the Halls of Time. Meditation upon its symbols and designs will open further paths to you when you are ready to tread them in this Otherworld. You sit on the warm, dry grass to put your sandals on as the Sun toasts your back."

Wait for five seconds before continuing.

"With a light heart, you follow the familiar path downhill from the ring of timeless stones. The fields are covered with a carpet of flowers waving gently in the breeze. The hum of the bees is mixed with the joyous songs of birds, and the Earth feels alive beneath your feet. Houses begin to appear as you near the world of civilisation once more, and you find yourself strolling down your own street to climb the familiar steps to your own front door. You open the door and enter, to discover that you are standing in your own room in comfortable, casual clothes. The Journey is ended."

'I am a seeker of the Way of Wisdom.'

Chapter Forty Three
Elemental Pathworking

The following is an Elemental Pathworking where you travel by boat to a secret shore where you are met by a man who will introduce you to the elements of the Other World.

To prepare for this pathworking, place the elemental tools in their respective quarters. Sword in the East, Rod in the South, Cauldron in the West and a Stone in the North. Candles should be lit at the four cross-quarters.

The narrator stands with the travellers around him in a circle. He says, *"Visualise yourself in a row boat travelling across a vast sea. Relax and breathe. You eventually arrive on an ancient beach where you are greeted by a man who says, 'I am pleased you have come. Welcome. Allow me to introduce you to the Sacred Elements of the Four Quarters and the Forces that control them and the places where they rule.'*

This is a journey of the mind. Open your senses and experience the Forces of Nature, and when you leave this place, take with you any knowledge that might be given, and use it wisely.

Before we begin, I must consecrate this land and invoke the Rulers of the Four Quarters. Pray silently and focus your energies on mine. For we are about to enter the realms of the Mighty Ones, to stand between the Worlds. Be ye now prepared, for we enter a time that is no time, in a place that is no place, on a day that is no day, for we now step between the Worlds!"

The narrator stands in the middle of the Circle with the travellers surrounding him, and he says, *"Lords of Power, of Night and Day, harken to these words I say! Earth and Air and Fire and Water be within your sons and daughters. Earth beneath and Sky above, join with us our rite to prove, banish evil, welcome calm, keep your children from all harm!"*

The narrator walks to the East, raises the Sword and says, *"All wise Eagle of the East, Great Ruler of tempest storm and whirlwind, Master of the heavenly vault, Great Prince of the Powers of Air, we await Thee."* He turns inwards, raises the Sword and says, *"I bring the Sword of Air. Come listen to its song."* Each traveller will approach the Sword and feel its energy.

He then replaces the Sword and walks to the South. He raises the Rod and says, *"O thou Lion, Lord of lightnings, Master of the solar orb, Great Prince of the powers of fire, we await Thee."* He turns inwards, raises the Rod and says, *"I bring the Spear of Victory. Come feel its heat."* Each traveller will approach the Spear and feel its energy.

The narrator replaces the Spear, then walks to the West, raises the Cauldron and says, *"O thou Serpent of old, Ruler of the deeps, Guardian of the bitter sea, Prince of the powers of water, we await Thee."* He turns inwards; raise the Cauldron and say, *"I bring the Cauldron of our Mother. Come taste her sweet waters."* Each traveller will approach the Cauldron and feel its energy.

The narrator replaces the Cauldron, then walks to the North, raises the Stone and says, *"Black bull of the North, horned one, Dark ruler of mountains and all that lies beneath them, Prince of the powers of earth, we await Thee."* The narrator turns inwards, raises the Stone and says, *"I bring the Stone of Destiny. Come know its strength."* Each traveller will approach the Stone and feel its energy.

The narrator placed the Stone on the ground and stepped on it, facing North, arms outstretched and said, *"The Stone is the Gate to the Old Ones, the Old Ones that are, the Old Ones that were, the Old Ones which always shall be. For we are of them and they are of us. Great Lady of Victory, Mother of our tribe, we honour Thee. Bull Horned Hunter, keeper of our herds, we honour Thee. The Gate is open. The Guardians of the Portals are present. Let us now visit their Realms. Follow me to the Portal of the East."*

The narrator takes the travellers to the East and traces an invoking air pentagram and says, *"You are standing high on a mountaintop while the winds swirl and whip around your body. Against the horizon, a yellow sun is rising, as flocks of birds soar and glide through the golden rays and cool breezes far above. A wonderful scent fills the air from the golden flowers, the Pipes of Lleu. The whole mountaintop is covered with them. Gliding on the windy gusts are small winged fairies with golden skin and glassy wings - the Wind Singers, or as you know them, 'Sylphs'. Listen to their song."* The narrator takes a few moments and allows the travellers to listen to the Sylphs.

He then takes the travellers to the South and traces an invoking fire pentagram and says, *"The mountain top drops away like a mist, and bubbling lava pits erupt all around us. Noxious orange fumes rise in long streams into the air. There are flames and billowing ash everywhere. In and out of the flowing lava swim serpentine creatures of gold and red, twisting and wreathing among the bubbles. High above us hangs the noontide sun of blood, scarlet flames spiralling from its searing* centre. These are the servants of Belinos, the dragon's breath, the Firedrakes, who are also known as Salamanders. Let us be gone and journey to the West."

The narrator takes the travellers to the West and traces an invoking water pentagram and says, *"We are now under the sea. Great beds of green seaweed float from the ocean floor, and fish and sea creatures swim amidst it. There is now a great churning of the water around us, and a giant being appears before you in thick clouds of sand that now settle to the bottom. This awesome creature is clad in shining silver scales and holds a long trident in its hand. Around his head is a crown of coral and shells set atop long dark hair that drifts out in all directions from his bearded face. Where his legs are supposed to be, you see a fish's tail. There are graceful mermaids wearing long strings of pearls wound around their scaled bodies, swimming around this awesome king. Hear his Majesty speak."* The narrator gives the travellers a short time to listen to His Majesty and then says, *"Thank his Lordship, for we now journey to the North."*

The narrator takes the travellers to the North and traces an invoking earth pentagram and says, *"We are now in a deep, dark and silent forest. Massive trees of untold age surround us, all gnarled and ancient. In between the roots of some of the eldest trees, move tiny men-like beings, clothed skilfully in leaf and bark. In their hands, they carry nuts, mushrooms, and other deep-wood foodstuffs. They do not see you in this dim midnight realm where dwarf and stone are one. The unmoving air hangs heavy with rich scents of woody decay. Do you see a cave? Herne the Hunter, Lord of the animals, needs to be summoned."*

The narrator throws a small sprig of mistletoe in the direction of the North and says, *"An offering."*

The narrator waits a few moments, then says, *"Stone glade in oak wood, ash branch into warrior head, smoke of hawthorn chokes the hags of air. Hear the flight of winter geese, the running of the wounded boar. Hear the clash of brave iron, in the name of the Lord of the Animals. Hear the breathing of the god, rampant and fertile. Hear the footfall of the antlered god. Hear Herne enter the stone glade in oak wood. Listen and watch."*

Again, the narrator gives the travellers a short time to commune with the Lord of the Forest. He then says, *"Thank the Mighty Antlered God in your own way, for we now journey home."*

The narrator again gives the travellers a short time and says, *"You have experienced the powers of nature. Take whatever knowledge has been given and use it for good, and know you may freely return here on other journeys."*

Standing in the centre of the Circle, the narrator says, *"I now give leave to our Guardians. Powers of Darkness, Powers of Light. Powers above and Powers below. Powers within, Powers without. Elements I have called, I now set you free. Go at your will and be ye now free."*

"Return now to your boat and sail away, taking with you the knowledge you have gained."

Chapter Forty Four
Lesser Banishing Ritual of the Pentagram

The Lesser Banishing Ritual of the Pentagram (LBRP) is one of the primary rituals of the Western Magical Tradition. Using visualisation, precise movement, and oral vibrations, the ritual dynamically creates a foundation for magical or meditative work; it balances, purifies, energises, and establishes the operator as the centre of the Universe inside a protected Circle.

This form of the LBRP differs from the original Golden Dawn version in that it banishes in a widdershins direction, not deosil. It also uses banishing elemental pentagrams in the corresponding directions as opposed to only a banishing earth pentagram. I believe this technique to be a more balanced and logical method than the original and tends to imbue the operator with more confidence and vitality.

A very important point for Australian practitioners – Do not change North and South with Fire and Earth, as most Australian Pagan practitioners tend to do – remember you are dealing with Elemental Forces that have nothing to do with the movement of the Sun! So, regardless of whether it 'feels right' to you to change the directions and elements, I strongly warn you not to!

The Ritual

Clean the area to be used and locate the four elemental quarters.

Perform the Qabalistic Cross

The Qabalistic Cross is a powerful invocation meant to create a condition of physical, mental, and emotional equilibrium, enhancing our ability to access non-physical energy.

Facing East, take your Athame in your right hand.

Touch the forehead and say, *Eheieh* (pronounced 'eh-heh-yeh').

Point the Athame to the ground and say, *Malkuth* ('mal-kooth').

Touch the right shoulder and say, *ve-Geburah* ('ve-geb-ura').

Touch the left shoulder and say, *ve-Gedulah* ('ve-ged-ula').

Clasp your Athame in both hands in front of your chest, pointing up and say, *le-Olahm IAO*. ('le-o-lam-ee-aa-oo').

Construct the Circle

At each quarter, perform an Elemental Banishing Pentagram – making sure to 'seal' each one. At the same time, visualise the appropriate colour. When vibrating the Deity Name, take a deep breath and slowly vibrate the Name, imagining your voice carried to infinity.

In the East, trace the banishing pentagram of Air, visualising the colour brilliant yellow. Bringing the point of the Athame to the centre of the Pentagram, vibrate the Deity Name, *Eheieh* (pronounced 'eh-heh-yeh*').

Holding the Athame out before you, turn to the North and trace the banishing pentagram of Earth, visualising the colour rusty red/brown. Bringing the point of the Athame to the centre of the Pentagram, vibrate the Deity Name, *Adonai* ('ah-do-nay').

Turn to the West and trace the banishing pentagram of Water, visualising the colour electric blue. Bringing the point of the Athame to the centre of the Pentagram, vibrate the Deity Name, *Eloah* ('ee-lo-ah').

Turn to the South and trace the banishing pentagram of Fire, visualising the colour of fire engine red. Bringing the point of the Athame to the centre of the Pentagram, vibrate the Deity Name, *Agla* ('ah-gi-le-ah).

Turn to the East to complete the circle.

The Invocation of the Archangels

After the Circle is constructed, face East, extend your arms in the form of a Tau Cross and invoke the Archangels of the Elements of the four directions. Say their Name with 'strength' and visualise them wearing robes coloured to that element.

Extend the arms in the form of a Tau Cross and say:

Before me, Raphael (pronounced 'Rah-fah-yell') - visualise the Archangel of Air wearing a yellow robe which rustles in the refreshing breeze blowing from the rear of the figure.

Behind me, Gabriel ('Gah-bree-ell') - visualise the Archangel of Water wearing a shimmering blue robe, standing in a giant column of water and holding aloft a Cup from which flows water.

At my right hand, Michael ('Mee-khah-ell') - visualise the Archangel of Fire clothed in robes of red holding aloft a flaming sword.

At my left hand, Auriel ('aw-ree-ell') - visualise the Archangel of Earth wearing robes of rusty red and brown, standing on a pentacle.

The Affirmation of the Circle

For about me, flames the pentagrams (focus on the ring of pentagrams surrounding you).

And within me shines the six-rayed star (visualise a hexagram centred on your solar plexus).

Repeat the Qabalistic Cross.

Facing East, touch the forehead and say, *Eheieh.*

Point the Athame to the ground and say, *Malkuth.*

Touch the right shoulder and say, *ve-Geburah.*

Touch the left shoulder and say, *ve-Gedulah.*

Clasp the Athame in both hands in front of the chest, pointing up and say, *le-Olahm IAO.*

"Those who regard this ritual as a mere device to invoke or banish spirits are unworthy to possess it.

Properly understood, it is the Medicine of Metals and the Stone of the Wise."

Aleister Crowley.

Chapter Forty Five
Elemental Balancing

A final Guided Visualisation for your contemplation. Again, it is one of those stories found under the dust of my notes taken so many years ago, its author lost in the mists of time – but if not, my appreciation and apologies to whoever you are if I have used this material inappropriately.

There is no need during this visualisation to take time to stop and start as previous visualisation. The narrator should use a steady voice, tone and rhythm as they say:

"About you all is impenetrable darkness; you float upon the waters of a black sea; you float endlessly, directionless; there is no direction, for there is nothing; but water; water stretches into the far corners of the universe.

Your body is light and floats upon the water; the water becomes warmer and warmer; you are floating upon the waters of the womb of the universe, and my voice is as the wind whispering in your ear.

You are becoming more and more sleepy; your past life is slipping away from you, floating away on the darkness of the waters; let it float away; be at peace; all is warm and dark, and still.

A great silence reigns over the universe; it awaits the moment of rebirth; your past life and thoughts are but a dream to you now; you are becoming sleepier and sleepier; you are at peace, at rest.

You are sinking; sinking into the deepest sleep, and as you fall into that sleep, you dream; you dream that you are sinking down, down below the waters; down, down to the great seabed; you lie there for a moment, your back resting on the sand.

The currents stir the sand against your trunk and limbs; the swirls of sand sink onto your body; softly the sand covers your eyes, face, and hands the sand envelops you layer by layer; gently and lovingly; slowly over a million years; the sand settles upon your body until you are buried deep beneath the sea; deep beneath the earth.

Deep beneath the earth, you lie; unmoving, waiting; whilst above you, time and change march on. Your limbs cannot move, but you hear within you the steady beating of your own living heart; buried deep, you lie in waiting. Far above you, muffled by earth, you hear the growing of seeds and the roots spreading struggle; far above you, the sea has receded, and a new world has come to birth. The earth is waking from a deep sleep, and all around you, you feel the quickening pulse of life; worms make their tunnels around you, and far above you hear the scraping and scurrying of rabbits.

A warmth steals through you; the sun is warming the ground above you, and you feel a stirring in your limbs; an urgency not felt for many a thousand years. The soil around you lightens and loosens; your hands move, and you thrust your hands upward; the soft soil falls about your fingers. The earth is crumbling, crumbling all around you; you struggle to your feet and climb upward. The soil falls in cascades all about you to your feet; you clamber upwards and so emerge, your eyes blinking and aching into the light.

The Wind blows against you; a wind not felt since long ago; the earth is blown away from your body. Your heart rejoices and your eyes see; all about you is the spring of a newborn world, green and fresh and in ecstasy.

Your spirit soars within you, and your whole body and being feels light, so light that gravity cannot hold you. You float into the air, higher and higher, leaving far behind the green and growing Earth.

You float higher and higher; about you, everything is blue. Blue sky stretches out all around you, as far as the eye can see. Your body is becoming lighter and lighter, and less and less dense; it is becoming a body of light. You are becoming transparent; more and more transparent; you are floating higher and higher, on and on.

You float and feel the air around you; you are floating like a gossamer sail in the blue. There is a great calm all around you; no wind can buffet you as you float in the silent blue.

Now the air is growing warmer and warmer; within you and without you, the air grows imperceptibly warmer, and looking upward, you see, hovering far above you, the fiery disc of the golden sun. Its rays reach out to caress you; its golden light beckons you; its warmth caresses your body, falling in cascades about you.

You are drawing nearer and nearer; closer to the sun; its light is becoming stronger and stronger, brighter and brighter, more and more intense; its orb is beginning to fill the whole expanse of your vision; you have no fear, and float, irresistibly drawn into the radiance of the Sun.

You are swallowed by the Sun's golden light, wrapped in a golden glow that becomes a golden flame. Journeying nearer and ever nearer to the centre, the source of its heat, the flame is becoming hotter and redder; your body is beginning to burn, but there is no pain; your whole being is aglow with flame.

Beyond a Year and a Day

Fire is within you, and fire is without you. Fire that does not burn because you are fire; you are the flame of life, and the flame of life is you. Flames run their flickering tongues along your golden, fiery limbs; flickering, licking tongues of fire; purging and cleansing in a golden glow. There is no pain, for you yourself are fire; only the flame of life around you and within you; a glowing oneness with fire.

Now you are beginning to move; your body is beginning to travel through the flames; you are moving away from the centre of the Sun, not back to Earth, but further and further away. The red flames are changing into many colours; the flames are becoming the colours of the sunset, amber, and orange, pink and gold; you are travelling through the Sun and emerging into night; the blackest night where no star shines.

Far below you, you see the flaming orb of the Sun, but leaving this behind, you turn and float away, leaving behind you all elements, and reaching nothing.

Be at peace now in the silence of the temple of the Gods; let all be still within you and without you; let all thoughts slip away from you, forget all cares and be at peace; lie still in the great darkness that is the womb of the Earth.

You are unborn; your former life is but a dream; it is no more; it is dead to you now; its achievements, its hopes, its fears, let all slip away from you.

You wait between the worlds, the past and the future; empty out all thoughts and feel a great breeze blow through you, cleansing and releasing you from the past.

Your body has dissolved into the darkness; you are finite no longer; you flow into the four corners of the universe."

"For what do you search?"

Part Five
The Future
The Path beyond the Threshold

Every rite ends. Every circle opens. And yet, something remains.

Beyond a Year and a Day, the journey no longer fits within the compass of lesson plans or seasonal rites. This final chapter is a lantern held aloft for those who have tasted mystery and hunger still. The seeker has become the practitioner, the initiate perhaps now the teacher, but the road does not end. It curves, deep and uncharted, into the future.

Here we ask: *What now?* What becomes of the Witch who has cast and conjured, invoked and healed? This part speaks not of certainty, but of readiness. It contemplates the quiet transformations, how the Craft infuses the ordinary, how the sacred becomes woven into washing dishes and tending gardens, how the Gods speak not only in wind and fire, but also in silence.

And so, *The Future* is not a destination. It is a devotion. A promise. A path that winds ever inward, ever outward.

My story, if you haven't already gathered by now, is a little different. We live in a different climate today. Things are much easier thanks to the Internet, or maybe not!

Feeling confused? Ok, let's recap in this final chapter of my story and give you a little advice, but remember, *'Don't believe a word that I say, go away and do your own research.'*

Chapter Forty Six
Beyond a Year and a Day

Looking back, our first year was a pretty traumatic experience, mainly the fact that we were tossed out into the dark, cold world of the occult and were forced to create our own home. Nevertheless, it was an experience and an adventure I would never change. Again, I sincerely thank Thomas for his tutelage and guiding us towards the light, and always, of course, the Lady Vivienne.

As you should now see, a seeker's first year studying the Craft under an experienced teacher is a life-changing experience; a journey of discovery, one of love, laughter, sweat, blood, and tears, where sometimes you might feel vulnerable, exposed and even threatened.

If you have chosen the right path, the one of magical enlightenment, you will know it is right, where somewhere along the way the proverbial light bulb is illuminated or that bell can be heard ringing, if not falling on your head! Believe me, it is not until that final assay does it all makes sense!

It was not until year two that everything started to fall into place. As a group, we each went through our Initiations and after we found a different way of looking at things. Opportunities arose that we did not expect, and our little group became part of a much larger family we never imagined.

Somewhere along the way, I think Evelyn and I must have proved our worth, and we were gently nudged towards taking a more leading role and ended up becoming Second Degrees.

Becoming Seconds presented us with much more information; new magical books we had no idea existed, an introduction to Elders within our own family, together with a pipeline to Britain and the source of our Craft. We now had access to untold new sources of rituals and other secrets.

Our group grew, and we took on a teaching role. We started to run courses and initiated our own, which eventually hived off and started their own Covens.

Sometime after receiving our Seconds, we had an opportunity to travel to Britain, which we made into a kind of pilgrimage. We visited Stonehenge, Chalice Well, Avebury, and dozens of other Craft sites within England, Scotland, Wales and Ireland.

We took with us our Book of Shadows because no one within our family had ever attempted to establish that our Book was legitimate. We had to make sure it was somewhere near an absolute copy of Alex's Book.

During the course of our adventures, we happened to be in London at the same time the British Pagan Federation was holding its annual meeting. We thought it would be a good idea to stick our heads in and introduce ourselves.

Having attended and assisted in organising similar conferences and meetings in Australia, we rather expected to see maybe a couple of hundred Pagans, Witches, and Druids having a friendly drink at the local. Not in our wildest dreams did we expect to be part of the thousands of people who walked through the doors of that conference hall over the weekend!

As a result, we made some extremely valuable contacts, made some everlasting friends, met some well-known identities, and were able to definitively establish that our Book of Shadows was a near-perfect copy of Alex's.

We returned to Australia as Third Degrees. How? Ask William Le Kat. In addition, we brought back more knowledge to distribute amongst our Australian Craft family. The next step in our journey was finding Sussex, and you have a fair idea of how that went.

So our journey continues, for once you take that first step, you never stop walking. For those who intend to follow this magical path and maybe attempt to find a group, organisation, or Coven to further their study, may I offer some guidance?

You have completed a course, read the books, and done your own research. So, where to now? How do you make contact with other like-minded people?

It is not always easy to find local Pagan or Occult contacts. There are two main reasons for this: first, many of us are secretive in order to avoid physical danger or verbal harassment; secondly, in the occult world, there is an extremely long tradition of secrecy deliberately practised to screen out the weak, the casual, and the merely curious. The maxim about tossing pearls before swine is fairly well heeded, especially by very dedicated practitioners who have no time to waste on the merely average. This is why the word 'occult' applies. It means hidden.

As a veteran High Priestess once phrased it, *'We don't go to them. They must come to us. The test of whether they are suited is the test of whether they can find us.'*

At the completion of any course, I usually offer the following comment: *"The fact that you all found us and have finished this course speaks for itself."*

Generally, I never advertise a course to the public. I select avenues by putting feelers out in an organisation like the local Pagan Alliance or similar groups. So, for most who eventually find us tells me it was meant to be.

In making contact with others, there are a few very important things to keep in mind. First, listen to the guidance of your inner self. Listen to your feelings in sensing whether or not to pursue your studies.

Beware of others who try to convince you that theirs is the only proper way of development. Such narrow-minded thinking reflects a lack of spiritual wisdom as well as an unhealthy perspective on reality. There are many traditions and many paths of Wicca, not all right for everyone. Groups and individuals vary in size, structure, methods of working, cultural roots, and other factors. You should try to connect with the path or paths that seem to harmonise most closely with your own vibrations, needs, and interests.

Finally, beware of those whose energies stem primarily from their own ego trips. Beware of teachers who constantly point out to you how wise and powerful they are, and how ignorant and weak you are. One who is truly wise does not have to proclaim it with pronouncements. Actions speak louder than words. Moreover, beware of those who try to control you with intimidation, guilt, and fear.

Lastly, I've said it before, and I'll say it for a final time: do not, ever, pay for the privilege of learning the Craft.

It is important for you to realise that magical bonds which form among those involved in magical study go much deeper than normal friendship bonds, and once formed, are very difficult to break. Therefore, always proceed carefully in forming new relationships with other magical people. This is especially true concerning involvement with a group. Joining a group is like joining a family and involves many of the same responsibilities and commitments.

If you feel like a coffee, I will be the guy in the black pointy hat sitting in the last cubicle with his back to the wall in that trendy coffee shop in your local town square!

"The Craft is not for Sale."

Final Reflection
Beyond the Veil, Into the Flame

The Thread That Binds, the Path That Beckons

What begins as learning becomes living. What begins as structure becomes soul.

This book does not seek to close a chapter, but to deepen it. Across the four parts, from the shaping of magical practice, to the artistry of shared ritual, to the quiet question of what comes next, it becomes clear: the Craft is not a ladder but a spiral. We do not ascend it once, but return to each point with new eyes and deeper hands.

My story is not one for the casual reader. It is for those who feel the thrum of power in their bones, who hear old names in dreams, who know that to work magic is to be worked by it in return. It is for the ones who will stir cauldrons and shadow, who will question, remember, and reforge the path in flame and silence.

Beyond the year. Beyond the day. Beyond even the words on this page. The fire still burns. The Circle endures.

Appendix One
Suggested Reading List

The following list serves as a roadmap, guiding seekers toward works that have shaped or deepened the teachings within this book. It extends the journey, offering portals into lore, magic, philosophy, and personal transformation.

You may notice that many of these texts hail from decades past, penned 20, 30, even 40 years ago or more. Their truths remain undiminished. Though newer books may echo familiar ideas, many are simply reinterpretations, revisions, or restatements of these foundational voices. Where you begin, and how far you wander, is yours to decide.

One title, however, stands apart.

What Witches Do by Stewart Farrar deserves pride of place as the first book every seeker should read. Few works distill the essence of the Craft with such clarity, integrity, and lived insight. For those standing at the threshold, it offers not just perspective, but a hand to hold.

Thank you, Stewart. Your words still walk beside us. You are missed.

Reference Material

777 Aleister Crowley
A Study in Witchcraft G.S. Roberts
A Witches Bible Compleat Janet & Stewart Farrar
ABC of Witchcraft Doreen Valiente
Aradia - Gospel of the Witches Charles Leland
Charge of the Goddess Doreen Valiente
Conversations with a Witch Lois Bourne
Dancing with Witches Lois Bourne
Diary of a Witch Sybil Leek
Drawing Down the Moon Margot Adler
Earth Sea Trilogy Ursula Le Guin
Eight Sabbats for Witches Janet & Stewart Farrar
Elements of Ritual Deborah Lipp
Encyclopaedia of Magical Herbs Scott Cunningham
Ethics and the Craft John J. Coughlin
Fifty Years of Wicca Frederic Lammond
Fire Child Maxine Sanders
High Magic's Aid Scire (Gerald Gardner)
Incense Oils and Brews Scott Cunningham
King of the Witches June Johns
Lid off the Cauldron Patricia Crowther
Linda Goodman's Sun Signs Linda Goodman
Magick in Theory & Practice Aleister Crowley
Malleus Maleficarum Montague Summers
Moon Magic Dion Fortune
Mysteria Magica Melita Denning
Real Magic Phillip Bonewits
Rebirth of Witchcraft Doreen Valiente
Religion without Beliefs Fred Lammond
Sea Priestess Dion Fortune
Spells and how they work Janet & Stewart Farrar
Spiral Dance Starhawk
Techniques of High Magic Francis King
The Alex Sanders Lectures Alex Sanders
The Complete Book of Saxon Witchcraft Raymond Buckland
The Dark is Rising Susan Cooper
The God of the Witches Margaret A Murray
The Golden Bough J G Frazer
The Golden Dawn Israel Regardie
The Kabbalah unveiled Mathers
The Meaning of Witchcraft Gerald Gardner
The Mists of Avalon Marion Zimmer Bradley
The Occult Experience Neville Drury
The Pagan Book of Rituals Herman Slater
The Paganism Reader Chas Clifton
The Pickingill Papers W.E. Liddell
The Sea Priestess Dion Fortune
The Training & Work of an Initiate Dion Fortune
The Tree of Life: *An Illustrated Study in Magic* Israel Regardie
The Way of the Goddess Ly Warren-Clarke
The White Goddess Robert Graves
The Witches' God Janet & Stewart Farrar
The Witches Goddess Janet & Stewart Farrar
What Witches Do Stewart Farrar
Wicca - The Old in the New Age Vivienne Crowley
Witchcraft for Tomorrow Doreen Valiente
Witchcraft Today Gerald Gardner

Author biography

Dylan Raventree, Priest of the Art Magical, Third Degree Alexandrian Witch, and ordained minister of the Fellowship of Isis, was born in the shadow of the mythical Isle of Arianrhod. As a tutor, advisor, and mentor within the Witch community, he is dedicated to guiding Initiates and Seekers alike in the Old Ways. With a steadfast devotion to the ancient Mystery Traditions, he leads others in honouring the Old Gods through sacred worship and celebratory rites.

Comment on Beyond a Year and a Day

"A must read for those who have ever wondered what happens within a traditional Wiccan Coven, or what it takes to begin one. In these pages Dylan shares a uniquely personal spiritual journey from Initiate to Elder within the Alexandrian and Sussex Wiccan traditions."

Jo Corvinus-Jones (Pagan and Spiritual Seeker)

"Beyond a Year and a Day is a candid and concise presentation of the beliefs, structure, processes, organisation, development and practices of a modern and eclectic Wiccan Coven. Written from the viewpoint of someone who has travelled the Path, seeking to be trained and, in turn, training others in the Way."   Stewart.

Copyright 2025 Dylan Raventree

This literary work is protected under the provisions of the Berne Convention for the Protection of Literary and Artistic Works. In accordance with international law, all rights are reserved to the author. Unauthorised reproduction, distribution, or adaptation of any part of this text is strictly prohibited and constitutes a violation of the author's intellectual property.

ISBN 978-1-7640447-1-4

Publisher: Ladder to the Moon
Contact for permission to use images or text:
Email: dylanraventree777 gmail.com

Disclaimer

This book is a work of creative expression, blending mythic narrative, ritual symbolism, and personal interpretation. While it draws upon historical, folkloric, and spiritual traditions, it is not intended as a substitute for professional advice, be this medical, psychological, legal, or otherwise.

All rituals, practices, and symbolic frameworks presented herein are offered for personal reflection and creative exploration. Readers are encouraged to adapt or interpret them in ways that align with their own beliefs, ethics, and discernment.

Names, characters, places, and events, though inspired by both myth and lived experience, are products of the author's life journey. Any resemblance to actual persons, living or dead, is sometimes coincidental and other times factual, where their names and identities have been changed or otherwise created and fictionalised.

The author and publisher disclaim any liability for outcomes resulting from the use or interpretation of the material in this book.

Beyond a Year and a Day

www.ingramcontent.com/pod-product-compliance
Lightning Source LLC
Chambersburg PA
CBHW042356280426
43661CB00096B/1136